**Seasoned *Authors* For A New Season:
The Search For Standards In Popular Writing**

Seasoned *Authors* For A New Season:
The Search For Standards In Popular Writing

Louis Filler

A Question Of Quality # 2

Bowling Green University Popular Press
Bowling Green, Ohio 43403

LC No.: 79-90128

ISBN: 0-87972-143-X Clothbound
       0-87972-144-8 Paperback

Acknowledgements

Grateful acknowledgement is made to the following for permission to reprint previously published material:

Journal of Popular Culture: John Reilly, "Chester Himes' Harlem Tough Guys," Vol. 9 (4), 1976.

Journal of Popular Culture: Andrew S. Horton, Ken Kesey, John Updike and the Lone Ranger, Vol. 8 (3), 1974.

Journal of Popular Culture: Thomas Doulis, "John D. MacDonald: The Liabilities of Professionalism," Vol. 10 (1), 1976.

Journal of Popular Culture: Louis Filler, "Review Essay," Vol. 11 (2), 1977.

CONTENTS

Introduction:

Still a Question of Quality

IT IS GRATIFYING to see how well our first collection of reevaluations has been received by active elements of the Modern Language Association, who have read the book, reviewed it and used it in their work. The book's purpose was not to foist some single method of approach on students of popular literature, but to provide them with stimulus, ideas and information helpful to their own judgments of values in the field, and by a variety of talents. Popular writing is by its very definition shoreless in its possibilities. Therefore, not for us to be lost in its mere quantity requires an outgoing attitude, a receptivity to the resources of others, their experience, their viewpoints.

The abilities displayed in the first collection of *A Question of Quality* were many. Several critics employed explication intensively and to good ends. Several preferred an appeal to the readers' sensibilities. Edgar A. Branch not only emphasized James T. Farrell's philosophic stance in explaining his method, but, considering Farrell's lower prestige in later years, and the blunted awareness of his technique, quoted an actual piece of his narrative as evidence of the points he made. Indeed, quotations were a staple of the essays—quotations from partisan and other critics as well as from passages of the writers' tales and poems intended to give substance to critic-allegations.

Biography is not literature, and good intentions do not necessarily make for art, but everything helps, especially in such uncertain times as our own when the continuity in our literary traditions has been harmed, and one impression can sound as reasonable as another. But the goal has been to create legitimate interest, valid inquiries. The essays emphasized the many-mansioned nature of our literary heritage, and the fact that no one was committed to swallowing authors or categories of writing whole in order to get sustenance from them. Jeffrey Hart, for instance, is a sensitive critic in many respects. But he is partial to a body of work and prejudiced against other bodies. Moreover, he admires some writings and despises others for political rather than esthetic reasons.

Frederick Eckman, in *Question of Quality* did not endorse Edna St. Vincent Millay entirely in his essay, but, in reviewing her poems. found variations of quality and surprises which he was able to impart. Robert Olafson unveiled an entire corpus of sophisticated reference and inspiration in B. Traven's "proletarian" fiction, and showed that it seized interest not for "popular" reasons alone, or ideological sympathies, but

1

because it was artfully arranged by a master storyteller.

Mark Spilka was all but dazzling in his unfolding of hidden meanings in Eric Segal's *Love Story*—meanings of which Segal himself and his large and dreamy readership had less than a hint. It is well-known that it is often more difficult to explain the badness of bad fiction than the quality of good, and Spilka not only displayed much which explained *Love Story*'s failure, as well as success, but indicated a method by which such explorations could be further pursued, as in Segal's *Oliver's Story*.

A word is due about Ross Lockridge's *Raintree County,* unique in that, despite its national circulation and movie, it attracted no canon of criticism of aid to students or professors. In this case, *Question of Quality 1* accorded the novel two essays, one substantially antipathetic to Lockridge, the other partial to his work. This far from completes the story of *Raintree County,* but, at least, it breaks ground for further inquiry.

A Question of Quality was and is less concerned for praising or debunking than for clarifying: for adding insights into our stores of literary achievement, too little savored and experienced in recent times. Art at its best is not an adjunct of life, but part of life itself: a fact which has been confused by our more recent emphases on sensation at the expense of intellect. Cliches take over. What did John Steinbeck accomplish besides *The Grapes of Wrath*? Why read Erskine Caldwell? Are mystery stories worth reading at all? The several authors in the first *Question of Quality* did not answer such questions categorically, and in several cases provided only partial responses. But they put them on display, and so enabled readers to activate themselves, matching responses with their own memories of past reading and attitudes.

A revelation of the work done was how often professionals harbored prejudices and assumptions which they themselves did not know they had. One well-esteemed academic critic said that he had not read anything by John O'Hara and had no idea of his place in letters. Informed that O'Hara had thought well of himself, and had been seen as a successor of—possibly a superior to—F. Scott Fitzgerald, he answered: "Of course, he isn't." He hastily corrected himself, recalling that he had admitted having no contact with O'Hara's prose. But this anecdote, told to a good number of other cultural academics brought out the candid fact that many of them operated similarly, carrying about notions for which they had no evidence.

It is likely that this is an impulse in human nature which will survive any and all methods and explications to the contrary. But criticism, if it is to justify its existence today, and to serve new readers must do more than satisfy prejudices, especially in a time which downgrades reading in practice and even theory. A picture is worth a thousand words, say audio-visual instructors. Marshall McLuhan stirred the literary market-place several years ago with the idea that books had been rendered obsolete by television. Since he set down such thoughts in a book, he did not help his argument. But there is enough evidence that imagination—the imagination of the tale-spinner and poet—has been impugned by circumstances to make their urgency and use a matter of first consideration for those to whom some words are important and even irreplaceable.

The problem of assessment is really the problem of continuity. *Lying Prophets,* by Eden Phillpotts is probably a great book, but who reads it? Phillpotts, having established his position in the English letters of his time, went on to an acknowledged and satisfying career which did not include significant assessment of its weight by critics. Who reads Stephen Phillips's *Paolo and Francesca,* if only to understand its amazing vogue at the beginning of the century? And, in America, who outside the Twayne Series copes with Robert Herrick, whom Perry Miller merely hated, Ernest Lacy, William Ellery Leonard, Ludwig Lewisohn, Ben Hecht, T.S. Stribling, and as many more as insight and conscientious recollection will suggest? It is easy enough to say that time has told the tale respecting such worthies; but criticism has not. And the mind which slurs over their careers will slur over vital aspects of even the most "in" names, ranging from Willa Cather to Edwin Arlington Robinson, the latter's name once fused with Frost's but strangely, in past decades, not at all. It is probable that we have not only lost striking perceptions of use to students, and even to talented instructors. In some cases we have actually lost acquaintanceship sufficient to enable us to judge the values in careers for our own individual use.

The old *Bookman* had faults, and ended as an outlet for dogmatists and partisans. But in its heyday it was rich—well, overrich—with literary discussion of books, personalities, surveys of literary production. Our own production has actually decreased, despite electronics. We are in tightened intellectual and related economic circumstances (Marx was not wholly wrong), but these facts have raised even more serious questions of the quality of whatever we are printing and having printed, as compared to our production in the days of affluence. Our resources are more limited. All the more reason for seeing to it that those we have are rationally used. We have had seasons which have all but solicited the production of random and irresponsible tales, "poems" (justified as self-expression), and everything but essays embodying personal experience, human understanding and philosophy. But those seasons are gone. No one need any longer listen to anyone; nor need one be abashed by preferring trash. So the challenge to human reasonableness, to drawing lines between quality from other excrescences becomes more urgent all the time.

This second collection of essays continues to probe the values in a variety of authors who have had in common the fact of popularity and erstwhile reputation. Why were they esteemed? Who esteemed them? And what has become of their reputations, to readers, to the critic himself? No writer here has been asked to justify the work of his subject, and reports and conclusions about this wide variety of creative writers vary, sometimes emphasizing what the critic believes to be enduring qualities in the subject, in several cases finding limitations in what that writer has to offer us today.

In all cases, however, the essays throw light on conditions, impulses, attitudes which impelled the author to writing, and the popular audience which gave patronage. Most literature in time becomes literary history, but in great measure much of it leaves a residue from which new readers can profit.

Louis Filler

The Eye and the Nerve: A Psychological Reading of James Dickey's *Deliverance*

Harold Schechter

> Put on the river
> Like a fleeting coat,
> A garment of motion,
> Tremendous, immortal.
> Find a still root
>
> To hold you in it.
> Let flowing create
> A new, inner being.
>
> James Dickey, "Inside the River"

Explore thyself. Herein are demanded the eye and the nerve.
Henry David Thoreau, Walden

IN A BOOK about the relationship between literary value and popular appeal, the case of James Dickey is an interesting and particularly apt one, since he is a writer who has not only enjoyed both critical and commercial success, but also seems to have pursued both art and media celebrity with equal gusto. A poet who rose to literary prominence within a few years of the publication of his first collection, *Into the Stone* (1957), a National Book Award winner in 1966 (for *Buckdancer's Choice*) and former poetry consultant to the Library of Congress, he seems, at the same time, to be totally captivated by Hollywood glitter. Not even Norman Mailer has played opposite Burt Reynolds in a movie (as Dickey did in the film version of his bestselling book *Deliverance*) or squired Cher Bono Allman to a presidential ball.

When I first saw the full-color photograph of Dickey and Cher which *Newsweek* printed as part of its coverage of Carter's inauguration and which fairly resonated with allegorical significance—suggesting any number of morals about the seduction of the American artist by glamor and fame—I was reminded, not so much of Mailer as of Mailer's hero, Hemingway, who, with a fine Emersonian scorn for foolish consistency, wrote savagely about selling-out (in "The Snows of Kilimajaro") while feeling no aversion to picking up a few extra dollars by doing endorsements for Ballantine Beer ("You have to work hard to deserve to drink it. But I

4

would rather have a bottle of Ballantine Ale than any other drink after fighting a really big fish").[1] The resemblances between Dickey and Hemingway, of course, run far deeper than their common taste for stardom; indeed these similarities go right to the heart of the issue with which this essay is concerned: namely, determining the artistic value of *Deliverance,* a book which has been a big commercial success and has also generated a fair amount of critical controversy over the question of its merits. (Though there is some divergence of opinion about Dickey's poetic achievement, the problem which the present volume addresses—that of the connection between "popularity and value in modern creative writing"—does not arise in relation to his poetry, simply because, like almost all the serious poetry written in this country, its appeal is limited to a small, "elite" audience. I intend, therefore, to devote this essay to *Deliverance,* taking his poems into account only insofar as they bear on the themes of the novel.) The qualities which critics and readers alike have found increasingly off-putting in Hemingway's work are the very ones which unsympathetic reviewers denounced in *Deliverance:* the obsessive *machismo,* the preoccupation with proving one's manhood (a preoccupation which may or may not conceal a strain of latent homosexuality) by pitting oneself against nature and other men in situations of great stress, danger and violence. Writing in *Saturday Review,* Benjamin DeMott took Dickey's novel to task on precisely these counts, deploring its "shoot-'em-up mindlessness" and dismissing it as an "emptily rhetorical horse-opera played in canoes"—an opinion echoed by several other reviewers, one of whom, discussing Dickey's literary antecedents, claimed that the main influence on the novel was not the writing of Hemingway but "that of Edgar Rice Burroughs, who is much more fun."[2] In a sense, Dickey himself must be held at least partly accountable for judgments like these, not only because of his own pronouncements about the book—his insistence that it be regarded primarily as a simple "adventure yarn," "an exciting story"[3]—but also because of the he-man image he has always been at pains to project, the hunter-soldier-athlete-poet persona played up in his dust-jacket biography: "James Dickey is a former star college athlete, night fighter pilot with more than 100 missions in World War II and the Korean conflict, hunter and woodsman..." etc., etc. This kind of thing encourages us to respond less to the art than to the anamolie, as we might, paraphrasing Samuel Johnson, to the sight of a dog walking on its hind legs: what's really impressive is not the poetry but that a former fighter pilot and college jock should write poetry at all.[4]

In any event, even Dickey's detractors tended to concede that the novel was entertaining, if trivial and wildly improbable. His admirers, on the other hand, regarded *Deliverance* as a brilliantly done thriller—a masterpiece of suspense, ranking, as L.E. Sissman wrote in his *New Yorker* review, "up among such classics of the form as 'The Thirty-Nine Steps,' 'The Wages of Fear,' and 'Rogue Male'."[5] Various critics and reviewers attested to the book's powerful, visceral impact. "It will curl your toes," declared Evan S. Connell on the front page of *The New York Times Book Review.*[6] It will "make your hands cold," said Donald W. Markos in the *Southern*

Review.[7] "I felt every cut, groped up every cliff, swallowed water with every spill of the canoe, sweated with every draw of the deadly bowstring," Nelson Algren wrote in *Harper's.*[8] Even those people who praised the novel, however, saw little in it besides a compelling plot and some fine descriptive prose. L.E. Sissman, for example, though he called *Deliverance* "a suspense story that transcends its genre," read it basically as a commentary on the crazy, random violence which, more and more, is coming to characterize life in America; whereas other critics tended to interpret the book's concerns strictly in terms of the recurrent themes of Dickey's poetry: the call of the wild, the dangers of cutting oneself off from the primal energies of nature (from the "moiling of secret forces" beneath the surface of things which Dickey evokes in his poem "The Shark's Parlor"), and so forth. Moreover, many of the people who liked the book shared with those who didn't some serious reservations. One recurrent complaint had to do with the quality of the characterizations, which reviewers in general found to be two-dimensional. Lucy Rosenthal, for instance, though basically enthusiastic about the book, nevertheless thought that the characters were "almost interchangeable with one another," while Algren commented that "the characterization is thin-running to types.[9]

My own response to *Deliverance* was similar to the one described by Connell, Markos and Sissman. I too found it extremely gripping—and not just while I was reading it. Dickey's novel has possessed my imagination for a long time now, and in a way which cannot be wholly or even primarily accounted for by its effectiveness as a "page-turner." In fact, over the course of several rereadings, the construction of its plot has come to seem just a little *too* slick to me, the work of a man out to write a very calculated bestseller, who not only has all the formulas down pat but also the artistry to conceal the contrivance. And yet, despite my growing awareness of the book's more mechanical qualities, its power has remained essentially undiminished for me. That *Deliverance* does indeed have a strange compelling effect on readers can be seen in some of the extreme reactions it has produced. Leslie Fiedler put his finger on this feature of the novel when he remarked once that *Deliverance* is a book which has killed people. (Dickey himself was obliged to make a public announcement urging readers not to attempt to duplicate the canoe trip described in the novel, after several people had already died trying.) Needless to say, not many books have the power to move people so deeply. The question, then, is: what is the source of this power?

Paradoxically, it is one of the book's weaknesses which supplies us with a clue to the mystery of its strength. For to say that *Deliverance* is long on action and short on fully developed characters is really to say nothing more than that it possesses one of the typical traits of what Richard Chase describes as the classic American romance. The romance, writes Chase, "following distantly the medieval example, feels free to render reality in less volume and detail" than the novel does. "It tends to prefer action to character, and action will be freer in a romance than in a novel, encountering, as it were, less resistance from reality....The romance can flourish without providing much intricacy of relation. The characters, probably rather two-dimensional types, will not be complexly related to each other or to society or to the past." Another characteristic of this form, as Chase defines it, also corresponds to one of the "flaws" of Dickey's book—its supposedly "impossible" plot. According to Chase, we may expect the plot of the romance "to be highly colored. Astonishing events may occur, and these are likely to have a symbolic or ideological, rather than a realistic, plausibility. Being less committed to the immediate rendition of reality than the novel, the romance will more freely veer toward mythic, allegorical and symbolic forms."[10]

Chase's definition provides us, I believe, with a yardstick for measuring Dickey's achievement in *Deliverance*. It is my contention that Dickey's bestseller is a work very much in the tradition of the "American prose romance"—a tradition whose development Chase traces from its beginnings in the "haunted, nocturnal" melodramas of Charles Brockden Brown, through the symbolic classics of Hawthorne and Melville, and up to the Gothic masterpieces of Faulkner. Like the work of these authors, *Deliverance* derives its special power, I believe, less from the excitement and suspense of its plot than from the richness of its mythic or archetypal imagery. Though the novel begins in a very realistic and precisely evoked social setting, it quickly turns into one of those "projective fictions" (to use a phrase Leslie Fiedler applies to Charles Brockden Brown's *Edgar Huntly*)[11] which seem "not so much written as dreamed." This type of fiction, writes Fiedler, deals "with the exaggerated and grotesque, not as they are verifiable in any external landscape or sociological observation of manners and men, but as they correspond in quality to our deepest fears and guilts as projected in our dreams or lived through in 'extreme situations.' Realistic milieu and consistent character alike are dissolved in such projective fictions, giving way to the symbolic landscape and the symbolic action, which are the hallmarks of the mythopoeic novel."[12]

What Chase calls the "dark romance" and Fiedler the "mythopoeic novel," Carl Jung labels "visionary literature." The visionary novel, he observes, usually consists of "an exciting narrative that is apparently quite devoid of psychological exposition." It portrays events which "astonish" us, "evokes a superhuman world of contrasting light and darkness," reminds us of "nothing in everyday life, but rather of dreams, night-times fears, and the dark recesses of the mind that we sometimes sense with misgiving." "Mythological themes clothed in modern dress," he writes, "also frequently appear."[13] What distinguishes Chase's "dark romance," Fiedler's "mythopoeic novel," and Jung's "visionary literature, " then, is a dreamlike—or more properly, nightmarish—atmosphere, plus a wealth of primordial imagery: a mythic dimension which resonates with that deeply impressive force which Jung calls "numinosity." And these, I believe, are precisely the features which distinguish *Deliverance* and give the book its "curiously compulsive power."

The mythic substructure underlying *Deliverance* is easy enough to sketch, since the story corresponds in every respect to the archetypal pattern commonly known as the "night sea journey" (Leo Frobenius), the "monomyth" (Joseph Campbell) or the hero's quest. Responding to a "call for adventure"—a summons of some sort which rouses him from the comfortable, if stifling, routines of his life—the hero leaves the workaday world behind and crosses a threshold into a region of darkness and danger (the Descent into Hades or *Nekyia*).[14] Within this alien realm, he passes through a series of initiatory ordeals ("The Road of Trials"), achieves the boon of spiritual illumination ("The Treasure Hard to Attain"), and returns, transfigured, to the daylight (Rebirth). Ed Gentry, the hero, undergoes just such an archetypal adventure. But in addition to the mythic imagery in *Deliverance,* there is the psychological meaning of the myth. Dickey himself, in the interview in which he declares that his purpose in writing the novel was "to tell an exciting story as simply as I could," also remarks, "I think it's important, as you get older, to discover...different parts of yourself."[15] My psychological reading of *Deliverance*, therefore, relies primarily on the insights of Carl Jung, not only because he is the person who dealt most extensively with the psychological significance of myth but also because, in his own practice, he concentrated on the treatment of patients very much like Ed Gentry, a middle-aged businessman, successful in his career but increasingly dissatisfied with his life and conscious of encroaching old age, who must, if he is to survive the "mid-life crisis" he is passing through, undertake the perilous journey of self-exploration to "discover the different parts" of his own inner world.

In *Deliverance* the story proper is preceded by a pair of epigraphs, one describing the narrator's problem, the second suggesting a solution. The first, from Georges Bataille, says, *"Il existe a base de la vie humaine un principe d'insuffisance"*—"There exists at the base of human life an element of incompleteness." That Gentry is indeed feeling that his life lacks something essential is made very clear in the opening section of the book. This prologue, entitled "Before,"[16] introduces us to a character suffering from that malaise which, according to Jungian psychologists, commonly afflicts men and women during the second half of life—that depression which descends upon "middle-aged people who, having been successful in their chosen career, suddenly awake to a feeling of emptiness and lack of meaning in their lives."[17] "We had grooved as a studio" (16), he thinks, referring to the thriving advertising agency he runs with his partner, Thad Emerson. "We had made it as it was; we had made it" (23). But as he walks back to his office from a lunch date with some friends, this "middle-aged responsible" man—"Vice-President Gentry" (18)—is suddenly hit by a deep sense of his own mortality: "Going under a heavy shade tree, I felt the beer come up, not into my throat but into my eyes. The day sparkled painfully, seeming to shake on some kind of axis, and through this a leaf fell, touched with unusual color at the edge. It was the first time I had realized that autumn was close. I began to climb the last hill," he says significantly (a little too significantly; Dickey is usually a good deal more deft in his handling of symbols). Inside his office, Gentry is again overcome by "the old mortal, helpless, time-terrified human feeling": "The feeling of the inconsequence of whatever I would do, of anything I would pick up or think about or turn to see was at that moment being set in the very bone marrow. How does one get through this? I asked myself" (19). "It seemed like everything just went right by men, nothing mattered at all" (29).

Gentry, it is clear, is going through what is commonly called, in these days of pop psychology, a "mid-life crisis." All the classic symptoms are there: the feeling of being trapped ("I was not really thinking about their being my prisoners," he says at one point, referring to his employees, "but of being my own" and the restlessness that accompanies it; the sense that, though he has won all the right prizes—the station wagon, the house in the suburbs, the color TV—his life adds up to nothing, that it is rich in material possessions but empty of meaning. He has a sexual infatuation with a model half his age and a marriage which, though decent and loving, no longer holds much excitement for him (in an early lovemaking scene with his wife, Martha, it is she who takes the active role, manipulates and issues commands, while Ed remains passive and detached, dreaming of the model and commenting on his wife's "practical approach to sex" (29). Everything about his life seems sterile and unfulfilling. Though he works as the art director of his ad agency, for instance, he does not consider himself to be at all creative: "[My wife] insisted on believing that I had talent as an artist, though I had none. I was a mechanic of the graphic arts, and when I could get the problem to appear mechanical to me, and not the result of inspiration, I could do something with it" (28).

This sense of emptiness, meaninglessness, psychic sterility is, Jungians tell us, the result of the one-sided psychological development that social adaptation demands—the necessity for sharpening consciousness while repressing one's instinctive nature. Ed Gentry is a prime example of the civilized man whose superior rationality is "won at the expense of his vitality."[18] He has become dangerously dissociated from his instinctual self, from the primitive energies of the psyche which society forces us to deny. Images evoking the tension between nature and culture abound in the book: a view of the trees in Ed's back yard, "wild, free things...in a domestic setting" (33); a vision of "domestic animals suddenly turning and crushing one against the splintering side of a barn stall" (52); a quick glimpse of the primitive forces "moiling" beneath the tidy surface of a happy suburban household, as Ed's son Dean "playfully" stalks his father with a sheathed Bowie knife after father and mother have made love, and Ed suddenly grows conscious of the vulnerability of his naked genitals beneath his bathrobe.[19] All these things—along with repeated references to the "monkey fur" on Ed's body, the vestigial mark of his animal ancestry— are symbols of the narrator's plight, of his deeply felt distance from the instinctual roots of his being.

What is the answer to this problem? The solution is suggested by the second epigraph which Dickey prefixes to his story: "The pride of thine heart hath deceived them, thou that dwellest in the clefts of the rock, whose habitation is high; that saith in his heart, Who shall bring me down to the ground?" (*Obadiah,* verse 3). While some critics have read this as an allusion to the mountain men who figure in the story ("thou that dwellest in the clefts of the rock"), it makes more sense to me as a reference to Ed, the upper middle class city dweller, a member of the "gentry" (as his name suggests),[20] who must, in order to be cured of his complaint, be "brought down to the ground"—made aware of an important connection to the natural world. Read in this way, the epigraph applies not only to the external action of the story—the "back-to-nature" plot—but also to its psychological action. In psychological terms, the epigraph may be taken to refer to a consciousness which has become too highly developed and must be put back in touch with the "lowly" instinctual level of the psyche from which it has become detached.

How can such a reattachment be achieved? Reestablishing a connection between the various parts of the psyche is precisely the goal of analytical psychology, and is accomplished by means of what is known in Jungian terminology as *individuation*—a process of self-realization which acts "to abolish the separation between the conscious mind and the unconscious, the real source of life, and to bring about a reunion of the individual with the native soil of his inherited, instinctual make-up."[21] And this psychological process is precisely what *Deliverance* portrays. Dickey's novel is essentially a visionary work which depicts a night journey into No Man's Land—"the country beyond the ego"—and the confrontation with the alien powers of the deep unconscious. Moreover, and this is unusual for a work of American fiction, *Deliverance* represents a *successful* hunt for selfhood, a hero's quest which culminates in a genuine rebirth.

"In dreams or myths," writes the Jungian analyst Joseph Henderson, "individuation most frequently presents itself as the lively, urgent wish to undertake a journey"[22]—and in the opening section of *Deliverance,* Dickey introduces us to four Southern suburbanites planning a weekend canoe trip into the backwoods of Georgia. Ed himself expresses a "lively" desire to go—"I...felt ready for something like this" (8)—but the urgency is communicated more by his companion Lewis Medlock, who, playing the role of the mythological "herald," announces his determination to travel down the "wild rippling water" (36) before the river is dammed and the Cahulawasee is transformed into Lake Cahula, a "real estate heaven" of "choice lots...marinas and beer cans" (7). The other two members of the group, Bobby Trippe and Drew Balinger, have reservations about the journey, don't feel any particular need for it. "The whole thing does seem kind of crazy," Bobby says (10). But, like Ahab on the quarter-deck, Lewis goads them on.

There are, as a matter of fact, interesting similarities between *Deliverance* and *Moby-Dick.* In many ways, Drew is just like Starbuck. Staid and steadfast, domestic and devout—"The only decent one; the only sane one" (186)— he is incapacitated by his own normality: a man whose "mere unaided virtue or right-mindedness" affords him no protection against "spiritual terrors" and who is invariably destroyed by the voyage to Hades.[23] Bobby, on the other hand, resembles Stubb, the typical Melvillean bachelor, jolly and obtuse—the clown who can journey into the heart of darkness without understanding anything at all about the experience; whose smug satisfaction with the world is a sign of his spiritual shallowness:

...Bobby, particularly, seemed to enjoy the life he was in. He came, I believe, from some other part

of the South, maybe Louisiana, and since he had been around—since I had known him, anyway—
had seemed to do well. He was very social and would not have been displeased if someone had
called him a born salesman. He liked people, he said, and most of them liked him—some
genuinely and some merely because he was a bachelor and a good dinner or party guest.... He
was a pleasant surface human being (11).

Lewis, the leader of the expedition, is, as I have suggested, similar to
Ahab. Driven, obsessed (12), fanatical (40), "insane" (230), he sees the canoe
trip, not simply as a weekend jaunt, but "A Way"—a quest for immortality:

Lewis wanted to be immortal. He had everything that life could give, and he couldn't make it
work. And he couldn't bear to give it up or see age take it away from him, either, because in the
meantime he might be able to find what it was he wanted, the thing that must be there, and that
must be subject to the will. He was the kind of man who tries by any means—weight lifting, diet,
exercise...—to hold on to his body...to rise above time (12).

Lewis, I believe, is suffering from a neurotically extreme fear of dying. This
may seem strange, given his compulsive daredeviltry. But after all, neurotic
phobias often express themselves in paradoxical ways, so that a person
suffering from a pathological fear of speed, for instance, may never set foot
in a car or, alternatively, may become a professional racer. The two
responses are just the flip sides of a single coin. Lewis' craving for
immortality is simply a desperate desire not to die. At the same time, as Ed
himself is well aware, Lewis' accident-proneness reveals an equally
desperate desire *to* die, as if he is eager to relieve himself of the burden of his
terrible fear (12). After fracturing his thigh in the rapids, however, Lewis
finally comes to "know something that I didn't know before" (194)—"that
dying is better than immortality" (235). No longer compelled to play
superman, he becomes "a human being, and a good one" (235), at peace with
himself at last. Thus, though he and Ahab both suffer crippling leg
injuries—"It feels like it broke off," Lewis gasps (126)—the significance of
the wound is very different for each man: for Lewis, it means the end of his
quest, for Ahab the beginning.

Like Ishmael, who is carried away with the rest of the crew by the
"irresistible arm" of Ahab's rhetoric, Ed listens to his friend and feels
himself "getting caught up...in his capricious and tenacious enthusiasm"
(9). For Gentry, the canoe trip is also "a Way," though not to physical
fitness. Whereas Lewis regards the Georgia wilderness as a testing-ground
for his body, Ed looks at a map of the area and sees something else: "It was
certainly not much from the standpoint of design. The high ground, in tan
and an even paler tone of brown, meandered in and out of various shades of
green, and there was nothing to call you or stop you on one place or another.
Yet the eye could not leave the whole; there was harmony of some kind" (13).
Right from the start, the region of the unknown holds out the promise of
spiritual wholeness, psychic serenity, self-realization, to Gentry. Just as the
narrator of *Moby-Dick* must leave the "insular city of the Manhattoes" and
travel into "the mystic ocean," "the dark side of the earth," to cure his
spiritual sickness—the "damp, drizzly November" in his soul[24]—the
narrator of *Deliverance* is impelled to journey into night country in order to
dispel his *hypos*. Like the schoolteacher Ishmael, whose spiritual quest

unites him with the neglected instinctual side of his psyche, embodied by the cannibal Queequeg, Gentry must make the inner voyage to confront those primitive qualities which, when assimilated, will revitalize his existence.

As he sets out for the valley, Ed expresses some skepticism about the trip. He defends "the way of civilization," of order and comfort and rationality, while Lewis extols nature and asserts that city life is "out of touch with everything")42). "You don't believe in madness, eh?" asks Medlock.

"I don't at all. I know better than to fool with it."
"So what you do...."
"So what you do is go on by it. What you do is get done what you ought to be doing. And what you do rarely—and I *mean* rarely—is to flirt with it."
"We'll see," Lewis said, glancing at me as though he had me. "We'll see. You've had all that office furniture in front of you, desks and bookcases and filing cabinets and the rest. You've been sitting in a chair that won't move. You've been steady. But when that river is under you, all that is going to change" (40).

Ed's reservations about the wilderness experience—"I'll still stay with the city," he insists (46)—reflect the conscious mind's natural resistance to entering the realm of the irrational. But, as all heroes must, Ed responds to the "call" of the unconscious and takes the plunge. That his journey is indeed a dream-trip—a symbol of the descent into the darkness of the unconscious—becomes clear as soon as he enters the river: "A slow force took hold of us; the bank began to go backward. I felt the complicated urgency of the current, like a thing made of many threads being pulled, and with this came the feeling I always had at the moment of losing consciousness at night, going towards something unknown that I could not avoid, but from which I would return" (65-66).

As Gentry travels farther into the woods, he begins to make contact with the alien forces of his psyche—a situation symbolized by a dreamlike experience he has on the first night of the journey. Lying in the blackness of his tent, deep in the forest, he is startled when something slams against the roof. He snaps on a flashlight and runs "the weak glow up from the door...."

I kept seeing nothing but gray-green stitches until I got right above my head. The canvas was punctured there, and through it came one knuckle of a deformed fist, a long curving of claws that turned on themselves. Those are called talons, I said out loud.

. . . .

I pulled one hand out of the sleeping bag and saw it wander fraily up through the thin light until a finger touched the cold reptilian nail of one talon below the leg-scales. I had no idea of whether the owl felt me; I thought perhaps it would fly, but it didn't. Instead it shifted its weight again, and the claws on the foot I was touching loosened for a second. I slipped my forefinger between the claw and the tent, and half around the stony toe (78).

This strange, hallucinatory scene represents, as Donald W. Markos points out, "the penetration of the wilderness into human consciousness"[25]—i.e., the breakdown of the barrier between the ego and the unconsciousness. The owl, a creature associated with night vision and wisdom, symbolizes Ed's increasing insight into the darkness of his psyche.

In a perceptive essay on *Deliverance,* Donald J. Greiner discusses the book in terms of Ed's growing self-knowledge, and maintains that Dickey's central concern is bestiality: "In *Deliverance* Dickey goes beyond the violent action and he-man acrobatics to suggest that each of us harbors in the deepest recesses of himself an unknown part which we are afraid to face because we might be forced to acknowledge our own bestiality." The narrator's spiritual dvelopment, Greiner argues, depends precisely on his ability to accept that "unknown part," to "call forth the monster within...to meet [his buried self] face to face." "The adventure in the big woods teaches [Ed]...that self-awareness means an acknowledgment of and harmonious relationship between the two sides of his nature, the bestial and the human."[26] Though Greiner's approach is not Jungian, his insights correspond very closely to archetypal theory. For according to that theory, self-realization invariably begins with the recognition of "the monster within"—that dark embodiment of bestial qualities which Jung calls the *shadow archetype.* "The meeting with oneself," he writes, "is at first the meeting with one's own shadow."[27] In *Deliverance,* that meeting takes place early in the second day of the trip when, "in the intense shadow" of the woods (98), Ed and Bobby encounter a pair of grotesque mountaineers:

They came forward, moving in a kind of half circle as though they were stepping around something. The shorter one was older, with big white eyes and a half-white stubble that grew in whorls on his cheeks. His face seemed to spin in many directions. He had on overalls, and his stomach looked like it was falling through them. The other was lean and tall, and peered at us as though out of a cave or some dim simple place far back in his yellow-tinged eyeballs (95).

For Gentry, this second man is indeed "the Other"—the Enemy, the Hostile Brother: that figure who represents the hidden side of Ed's personality, "its lower, primitive, instinctual, sensual half."[28] Ignorant, incomprehensibly brutal (98), animal-like (102), "repulsive-looking" (170), he is the personification of the city man's "inadmissable" impulses—of sheer, unbridled carnality and aggression. The utter bestiality of the mountaineers— "Pull your shirt-tail up, fat ass" (99)—is the antithesis of Ed's civilized behavior, of his sensitivity and rather passive sexuality.

Confronted with the horrors of his shadow's repellent urges, Ed resists his insight at first, strives to assert his rationality: "The lean man put the point of the knife under my chin and lifted it. 'You ever had your balls cut off, you fuckin' ape?' 'Not lately,' I said, clinging to the city" (98). It soon becomes clear, however, that, if Ed is to survive, it will be necessary for him not merely to face his shadow but to come to terms with it. In order to be reborn, in order to achieve deliverance, Ed must become a savage himself— i.e., incorporate the shadow archetype into his conscious personality.

The process of accepting his inherent animality, of acknowledging the primitive impulses which constitute the shadow, begins when the first mountaineer is slain and Ed approves Lewis' plan to bury the corpse in the woods. As the four men drag the body upstream, their civilized veneer is stripped away, and Gentry finds himself transformed into a beast: down on all fours in the "squelchy" muck, panting and digging wildly with his hands (117). Ed's metamorphosis is made explicit a few pages later when Drew is (apparently) shot in the head and the canoe overturns, spilling the narrator into the rapids: "I got on my back and poured with the river, sliding over the stones like a creature I had always contained but never released" (124). Attempting to right the canoe, he thinks of himself as "an out-of-shape animal" (127). Here, he is beginning to identify himself with his antagonist, who had leaped into the forest "like an animal" (102) when his partner was killed; an identification which signifies Ed's conscious realization of his shadow side, his recognition of a connection with the archetype. Indeed, as Ed crouches at the bottom of the gorge beside Lewis and Bobby, trying to figure out a way to save them all from the "murderous hillbilly" above (135), his "hidden" personality rises to consciousness and he experiences the Other within:

> "I think," I said, "that we'll never get out of this gorge alive."
> Did I say that? I thought. Yes, a *dream-man* said, you did. You did say it, and you believe it.
> "I think he means to pick the rest of us off tomorrow," I said out loud, *still stranger* than anything I had ever imagined.
>
> ....
>
> "What can we do?"
> "What can do three things," I said, and *some other person* began to tell me what they were. (129-130; my italics)

Liliane Frey-Rohn, describing the emergence of the shadow into consciousness, writes that "In such cases one often has the impression that the psyche is being controlled by a 'stranger' who appears as a 'voice'...."[29] Ed has started to know his shadow, but it still remains an alien entity. His next task, difficult and extremely dangerous, is the full assimilation of the "inner opponent," of the "archetypal figure of the adversary."

Ed's perilous ascent of the cliff "as smooth as monument stone" (141) is a version of an archetypal trial—the fairy tale hero's climb up the crystal mountain to win "the treasure hard to attain." At one point, the experience becomes deeply erotic: desperately fighting for a handhold on the wall, Ed loses control of his bladder and his urine flows "with a delicious sexual voiding like a wet dream" (140). Suddenly, the "immense rock...spring[s] a crack" and Ed crawls inside it, where he lies motionless "as though...in a sideways grave." "I simply lay in nature, my pants' legs warm and sopping with my juices" (145). This episode symbolizes Ed's penetration into the tomb-womb of the great Earth Mother and is an instance of what Jungians call "heroic" or "regenerative" incest: the act of entering into "the Mother"—the maternal unconscious—in order to be reborn through her.[30] That Ed's "heroic incest" with *Magna Mater* does indeed bring him closer to self-realization is indicated by the appearance, at this point in the novel, of the mandala symbol—the magic circle, the archetypal symbol of the Self.

As he begins to "inch upward again," he finds himself "moving with the most intimate motions of my body, motions I had never dared use with Martha or with any other human woman. Fear and a kind of moon-blazing sexuality lifted me, millimeter by millimeter" (151). "Fuck[ing] the cliff for an extra inch or two in the moonlight," Ed suddenly sees some holes in the rocks above him, "and in one of them was a star.... as I went, more stars were added until a constellation like a crown began to form" (151). This circle of light is a vision of wholeness, a prefiguration of the psychic totality which awaits him at the end of his ordeals. "The mountain," writes Marie-Louise Von Franz in her *Introduction to the Interpretation of Fairy Tales,* "marks the place. . . where the hero, after arduous effort (climbing), becomes oriented and gains steadfastness and self-knowledge, values that develop through the effort to become conscious in the process of individuation."[31]

Having conquered the mountain, Ed is prepared for the confrontation with the Enemy. His heroic "effort to become conscious" has brought him to the verge of a critical stage in the individuation process: the full realization of his shadow, of his own capacity for evil. "At a definite moment of time," writes Liliane Frey-Rohn, "the self seems to 'demand' that the personality be made complete *through the recognition of what were up until then hostile, immoral and asocial tendencies.'*[32] This recognition is commonly symbolized by the slaying of the Adversary. "The 'hostile brother' has to be faced, overcome, incorporated into one's own psyche. Only in such a way can the ego evolve from partial self-knowledge to complete assimilation of the unconscious."[33]

Even before Ed kills his enemy, however, their coalescence is nearly complete: setting up an ambush for the mountaineer, the narrator feels "our minds fuse," and imagines himself performing fellatio on the stranger—visualizes a very literal act of incorporation: "If Lewis had not shot his companion, he and I would have made a kind of love, painful and terrifying to me, in some dreadful way pleasurable to him, but we would have been together in the flesh, there on the floor of the woods, and it was strange to think of it" (154). "A peculiar kind of intimacy" has developed between them (163), and when the mountaineer finally appears, he seems different from the utterly repulsive creature that had attacked Ed and Bobby in the forest: "He was looking up the river and standing now with both hands on the gun, but with the attitude of holding it at his waist without necessarily thinking of raising it to his shoulder. There was something relaxed and enjoying in his body position, something primally graceful; I had never seen a more beautiful element of design" (161). Ed's shadow has suddenly assumed another aspect, positive and benign. "Unassimilated, the shadow figure [is entirely] evil," observes John Halverson, "a constellation of all that is demonic in the dark side of the psyche." As the archetype is integrated, however, the shadow begins to play a constructive role—"helping to bring up to consciousness those elements of the unconscious. . . necessary to the wholeness and health of the self"—and the stranger reveals himself to be the hero's helpmate and lover.[34]

The realization of the shadow is achieved with the mountaineer's death. Shooting a razor-sharp arrow through his adversary's throat, Ed becomes fully conscious of his capacity for violence. And when the wounded man crawls off, like an animal, to die in the bush, the narrator acknowledges his own bestiality by "getting down on my hands and knees and smelling for blood"—tracking his quarry "like a dog" (168, 169). When Gentry finally locates the corpse, he even considers cannibalizing it:

I took the knife in my fist. What? Anything. This, also, is not going to be seen. It is not ever going to be known; you can do what you want to; nothing is too terrible. I can cut off the genitals he was going to use on me. Or I can cut off his head, looking straight into his open eyes. Or I can eat him. I can do anything I have a wish to do. . .(170).

"The hero," says Joseph Campbell, "whether god or goddess, man or woman, the figure in a myth or the dreamer of a dream, discovers and assimilates his opposite (his own unsuspected self) either by swallowing it or by being swallowed."[35] While Ed does not commit "the ultimate horror," he *does* have the sensation of "being swallowed" by his shadow, momentarily possessed by his enemy's spirit. Walking "to the edge of the bluff" to see if Bobby has made good his escape, Ed spots the canoe on the river and—furious at Bobby for doing "everything wrong"—picks up the mountaineer's rifle and draws a beat on the "soft city country-club man." "Do it, the dead man said. Do it, he's right there" (171). The incident represents the surfacing of absolute evil in Ed, of the civilized man's most malevolent impulses. But he does not yield to these impulses: "I got around the feeling just by opening my fingers, and letting the gun fall to the ground." While the narrator is now fully conscious of the existence of his shadow tendencies, he does not unconditionally surrrender to them. Rather, he manages to integrate the two parts of his personality, the civilized and the bestial—succeeds, as Jung puts it, in joining the shadow to the light. This psychological condition is symbolized by the actual joining of Ed and the mountaineer: having lowered the dead man down the cliff on a nylon rope, Ed follows after him and, for a while, the two hang suspended in space, connected by a cord (a scene reminiscent of chapter 72 in *Moby-Dick,* where the relationship between Ishmael and Queequeg is symbolized by the "monkey-rope" which ties them together like "inseparable twin brothers").

When the cord suddenly snaps, Ed plunges headlong into the icy river:

I yelled, a tremendous, walled-in yell, and then I felt the current thread through me, first through my head from one ear and out the other and then complicatedly through my body, up my rectum and out my mouth and also in at the side where I was hurt. . . .It had been so many years since I had really been hurt that the feeling was almost luxurious, though I knew when I tried to climb the water to the surface that I had been weakened more than I had thought. Unconsciousness went through me. I was in a room of varying shades of green beautifully graduated from light to dark, and I went toward the palest color. . . .An instant before I broke water I saw the sun, liquid and transformed, and then it exploded in my face (177).

The "black waters of death," writes Jung, are also "the water of life, for death with its cold embrace is the maternal womb just as the sea devours the sun but brings it forth again."[36] Having suffered this ritual death, Ed is finally prepared for his deliverance, and gradually makes his way out of the valley. His reintegration into society completes the mythic pattern which structures his story: separation-initiation-return.[37] And his "trial by landscape" produces a striking transformation. Awakening in a boarding-house room on the morning after his return, Ed examines himself in a mirror and sees an "apparition" that bears little resemblance to the respectable suburbanite who had set out for the river a few days before. Stitched and bandaged, wearing a tattered flying suit with a web belt and a hunting knife, he looks like a wild man, a barbarian—"bearded and red eyed, not able to speak" (207). This savage he sees in the mirror is, of course, his own "inmost part,"[38] the shadow side of his civilized consciousness. Having completed his night journey, Gentry now clearly recognizes the primitive aspect of his personality. More important, he is able to *accept* this side of himself, to say in effect what Prospero says of the brutish Caliban at the close of Shakespeare's *The Tempest:*

> ...this thing of darkness I
> acknowledge mine.

Looking at his reflection, at the image of his violent inner self, Ed smiles "very whitely, splitting the beard" (207). By acknowledging the reality of his instinctual nature, Gentry wins the boon: the harmony he has been searching for.

That the experience in the wilderness does indeed benefit Ed by putting him in touch with an immanent power which enriches every aspect of his life is made clear near the end of the novel:

> Another odd thing happened. The river and everything I remembered about it became a possession to me, a private possession, as nothing in my life ever had. Now it ran nowhere but in my head, but there it ran as though immortally. I could feel it—I can feel it—on different places of my body. It pleases me in some curious way that the river does not exist, and that I have it. In me it still is, and will be until I die, green, rocky, deep, fast, slow, and beautiful beyond reality. I had a friend there who in a way had died for me, and my enemy was there.
>
> The river underlies in one way or another everything I do. It is always finding a way to serve me, from my archery to some of my recent ads and to the new collages I have been attempting for my friends. George Holley, my old Braque enthusiast, bought one from me...and it hangs in his cubicle, full of sinuous forms threading among the headlines of war and student strikes. George has become my best friend, next to Lewis, and we do a lot of serious talking about art...(234).

This activation of Ed's imaginative powers—his metamorphosis from a "mechanic of the graphic arts" into a serious artist—is evidence of his new relation to what Frey-Rohn calls "the creative sources in the psyche." The adventure on the "night river" (235) has produced a significant enlargement of Ed's personality, an "inner transformation and rebirth into another being."[39] Revitalized and self-possessed, he relates more effectively, not only to the inner forces of his unconscious, but to the people around him as well. "Thad and I are getting along much better than before," he says, referring to his business partner, and George Holley, the "Braque man" who had seemed so tiresome to Gentry before the trip, is now the narrator's second-best friend. Thus *Deliverance* is much more than just a simple "adventure yarn"; it is a work in the tradition of the American "dark romance," a mythopoeic novel whose action symbolizes the dangers and rewards of the descent into "the land of impossibility" (235), into the dark, unknown depths of the psyche. "To sojourn in those depths," writes Jolande Jacobi, "to withstand their dangers, is a journey to hell and 'death.' But he who comes through safe and sound, who is 'reborn,' will return, full of knowledge and wisdom, equipped for the outward and inward demands of life."[40]

Notes

[1]This advertisement, which ran in magazines in 1952, has recently been reprinted in *Popular Writing in America,* shorter alternate edition, ed. Donald McQuade and Robert Atwan (New York: Oxford University Press, 1977), pp.26-27.

[2]J.A. Avant, *Library Journal,* 1 March 1970, p.912. Though Avant's remark is obviously intended as a sarcastic "put-down" of Dickey, there actually are several references to Tarzan in the novel which serve a serious thematic function. On pages 90, 91, 213 and 225 of the paperback edition of *Deliverance* (New York: Dell Publishing Co., 1971; all quotations in my text are from this edition), Lewis is either compared to or called Tarzan, and Ed—whose body, we are told repeatedly, is covered with "monkey fur"—is referred to as either Tarzan's son or "Bolgani the Gorilla." These passages all relate to the novel's central theme: the necessity for the civilized man (as epitomized by Ed) to rediscover the animal side of himself, to get back in touch with the instinctual roots of his nature.

[3]See Walter Clemons, "James Dickey, Novelist," *New York Times Book Review,* 22 March 1970, p. 22.

[4]Dickey didn't help matters much either when, some time after the appearance of *Deliverance* he published a perfectly serious article in *Esquire* on the joys of hunting rattlesnakes with a home-made blowgun.

[5]2 May 1970, p. 123.

[6]22 March 1970.

[7]*Southern Review,* 7 (1971), 947-953.

[8]April 1970, p. 106.

[9]Ibid. Geoffrey Wolf, on the other hand, felt that the characters were "limned flawlessly by a few broad strokes" (see *Newsweek* 30 March 1970, p. 94).

[10]*The Amerian Novel and Its Tradition* (Garden City, N.Y.: Doubleday Anchor Books, 1957), p. 13.

[11]*Love and Death in the American Novel,* revised edition (New York: Dell Publishing Co./A Delta Book, 1966), p. 155. *Edgar Huntly* is a book with many striking similarities to *Deliverance.* Brown's novel, like Dickey's, concerns a civilized, sensitive, very rational man who journeys into a nightmarish wilderness, where, after undergoing a series of bizarre ordeals, is temporarily transformed into a murderous savage.

[12]Ibid., p. 156.

[13]"Psychology and Literature," in *Modern Man in Search of a Soul,* trans. W.S. Dell and Gary F. Baynes (New York: Harcourt, Brace & World, Inc., Harvest Books, 1933), pp. 152-172.

[14]"The journey to Hades, or the descent into the land of the dead. 'Nekyia' is a title of the 11th book of Homer's *Odyssey.*" See Jolande Jacobi, *The Way of Individuation* (New York: Harcourt, Brace & World, 1967), p. 154, n. 16.

[15]Walter Clemons, "James Dickey, Novelist," *New York Times Book Review,* 22 March 1970, p. 22.

[16]This introductory section of the novel is omitted from the film version of *Deliverance,* which opens with Ed and his companions on the way to the river. While the filmmakers' decision to limit themselves strictly to the adventure in the woods was undoubtedly a wise cinematic choice—the movie is very fast paced and suspenseful—it also significantly altered the meaning of the original story, as did the casting of younger men in the four lead roles and the changes made in the ending (see below, n. 40).

[17]Frieda Fordham, *An Introduction to Jung's Psychology* (Baltimore: Penguin Books, 1970), p. 78.

[18]C.G. Jung, *Memories, Dreams, Reflections,* ed. Aniela Jaffe, trans. Richard and Clara

Winston (New York: Vintage Books, 1963), p. 245.

¹⁹p. 31. This incident foreshadows the scene in the wilderness when Ed—confronting the unbridled terrors of the id directly—is threatened with castration by one of the mountaineers (p. 98).

²⁰Another possible source for Ed's surname is suggested by the poem "On the Coosawattee" (from *Helmets*), which describes a canoe trip similar in certain respects to the one in *Deliverance* and features a character named "Lucas Gentry."

²¹C.G. Jung, *Psychology and Alchemy, Collected Works* XII, trans. R.F.C. Hull (Princeton: Princeton University Press, 1968, Bollingen Series XX), p. 137.

²²*Thresholds of Initiation* (Middletown, Conn.: Wesleyan University Press, 1967), p. 134.

²³Herman Melville, *Moby-Dick*, ed. Harrison Hayford and Hershel Parker (New York: Norton Critical Edition, 1967), pp. 162 and 104.

²⁴Ibid., pp. 12 and 140.

²⁵"Art and Immediacy: James Dickey's *Deliverance*," *Southern Review*, 7, No. 3 (1971), 951.

²⁶"The Harmony of Bestiality in James Dickey's *Deliverance*," *South Carolina Review*, 5, No. 1 (1972), 44-45.

²⁷C.G. Jung, *The Archetypes and the Collective Unconscious, C.W.* IX, part 1, p. 21.

²⁸John Halverson, "The Shadow in *Moby-Dick*," *American Quarterly*, 15 (Fall 1963), 437.

²⁹"Evil from the Psychological Point of View," in *Evil*, ed. the Curatorium of the C.G. Jung Institute, Zurich (Evanston, Ill.: Northwestern University Press, 1967), p. 162.

³⁰C.G. Jung, *Symbols of Transformation, C.W.* V, p. 224.

³¹Chapter VII, p. 12.

³²"Evil from the Psychological Point of View," in *Evil*, p. 186.

³³Alex Aronson, *Psyche & Symbol in Shakespeare* (Bloomington, Ind.: Indiana University Press, 1972), p. 115.

³⁴"The Shadow in *Moby-Dick*," 438. Cf. Leslie Fiedler's remarks about Chingachgook, Jim and Queequeg in *Love and Death in the American Novel*, esp. p. 369. Ed's uncertainty about the slain man's identity reflects, I believe, the shadow's ambiguous nature. While the shadow figure appears totally evil before it is incorporated, it performs a positive function—and assumes a correspondingly positive image—once it is brought to consciousness. The fact that Ed cannot definitely identify the dead man does not mean that he has shot an innocent person but that his shadow, having been "realized," no longer appears as absolutely "unprepossessing" as it did earlier. Peter G. Beidler points out that "the tall rapist" has "yellow-tinged eyeballs" and a totally toothless mouth, whereas the man Ed kills on the mountain has "clear blue" eyes and only a "partial upper plate." Beidler concludes that Ed "has killed the wrong man" ("'The Pride of Thine Heart Hath Deceived Thee': Narrative Distortion in Dickey's *Deliverance*," *South Carolina Review*, 5, No. 1 [1973], 29-40.) My contention, however, is that these physical discrepancies symbolize the shift in the shadow's nature, the "humanization" of the other.

³⁵*Hero With a Thousand Faces* (Cleveland: World Publishing Co., Meridian Books, 1971), p. 108.

³⁶*Symbols of Transformation, C.W.* V, p. 218.

³⁷See Joseph Campbell, *Hero With a Thousand Faces*, p. 30.

³⁸William Shakespeare, *Hamlet*, III, iv, 20: "You go not till I set you up a glass/Where you may see the inmost part of you."

³⁹C.G. Jung, *The Archetypes and the Collective Unconscious, C.W.* IX, part 1, p. 131.

⁴⁰*Complex/Archetype/Symbol* (Princeton: Princeton University Press, 1959, Bollingen Series LVII, p. 186). The film version of *Deliverance* ends on a very different note: with Ed haunted by nightmares of the slain mountaineer. Unlike his counterpart in the novel, the hero of the movie is unable to accept his shadow. The film's penultimate image—of the hand of the dead man rising menacingly out of the river—suggests that Ed has only repressed his aggressive side again, and that it will reemerge from the depths of the unconscious, a continuing source of trouble. (I should add, however, that in cinematic terms, the shot is very effective, very chilling, and that, had the ending of the movie been as serene as that of the book, it probably would have seemed anticlimactic. So once again—as with the omission of the prologue—the filmmaker's alteration of the original story, while drastically changing its meaning, was valid and perhaps wise, given their decision to make a simple, straightforward thriller.)

Pilgrims in the Waste Land

Russell Kirk

OF ENGLISH POETS, only Byron, waking to find himself famous, more abruptly conquered the realm of letters than did T.S. Eliot. *The Waste Land,* published in 1922, made Eliot the most talked-about poet of his time, not merely in English-speaking lands but everywhere; his supremacy would endure until his death, and as yet no major poet has supplanted him. It is of some interest to examine Eliot's curious popularity and the failure of endeavors to diminish his influence.

If we think of the sales-volume of books, of course Eliot's popularity was relative only. No important poet of the twentieth century appears long on the best-seller lists, if his name is to be found there at all. Eliot did desire to reach a large audience for his poems and verse-plays; he aspired to revive the power of poetry over the popular imagination. If he never succeeded on the scale for which he may have hoped in his earlier years, still he was read by a very large number of educated and quasi-educated people. Phrases or whole lines, images, whimsicalities from *The Waste Land,* "The Love Song of J. Alfred Prufrock" or "The Hollow Men" continue to adorn the speech of people who actually never have read the whole of any of these poems. And for six years I knew well a stalwart hobo, a wanderer in the Waste Land, who quoted Eliot—not so frequently as he quoted Edward Fitzgerald or Thomas Gray, but sometimes. This friend of mine, who had fled from school at the sixth grade, knew who Eliot was and took pleasure in listening to Eliot's recordings of his poems.

Eliot deliberately chose for his exemplars Vergil and Dante. His poems were known to a greater proportion of his contemporaries, presumably, than were Dante's or Vergil's during their own lifetimes. Whether *The Waste Land* will be quoted two thousand or seven hundred years from now, one may doubt; yet that is conceivable. Popularity should be measured not merely by immediate impact, but also by the multitude of readers in later times.

Eliot did not mean to be a poet of the Academy merely, and he did not despise simple popular verse; he said that there should be various cultures within a society, and many different kinds of education for many different kinds of people. During their lifetimes, Edgar A. Guest was read by far more people than was T.S. Eliot. When Henry Regnery, the Chicago publisher, calling on the Pope of Russell Square in the 'Fifties, remarked diffidently to Eliot that he recently had become publisher of Guest's many little volumes of verse, Eliot reassured his visitor. "He smiled in his quizzical, knowing way, and said, 'Don't be ashamed of that. There isn't a publisher in the business who wouldn't be delighted to have Eddie Guest on his list, and, furthermore, he was an honest man, which is more than one can say of many people who write poetry these days.' "

If Eliot's popularity was not precisely that of Edgar A. Guest, still it became tremendous, overnight, in those circles which pay any attention to serious poetry. The prompt success of his long poem surprised its author, who is said to have remarked of *The Waste Land,* years later, "To me it was only the relief of a personal and wholly insignificant grouse against life; it is just a piece of rhythmical grumbling."

Yet this "rhythmical grumbling" swept the field, for the time overcoming all opposition, establishing a new mode and a new purpose in modern poetry—and yet a mode and a purpose drawing from the well of tradition. Eliot deliberately had intended to wrest the poet's laurels from the English Georgian poets and from such representatives of the old order in popular poetry as G.K. Chesterton; from Carl Sandburg and Vachel Lindsay in America. He succeeded beyond his expectation, and indeed by his triumph blocked the way for other new poets who had intended modes very different from Eliot's.

William Carlos Williams was among those undone by Eliot's swift victory; as Williams would write in his autobiography, "Then out of the blue *The Dial* brought out *The Waste Land* and all our hilarity ended. It wiped out our world as if an atom bomb had been dropped upon it and our brave sallies into the unknown were turned to dust." Eliot had handed back poetry to the Academy, Williams would complain; he discerned in Eliot a reactionary innovator. But lamentation was vain.

Even those who had sneered at *Prufrock* were silenced by *The Waste Land.* Of course there was some angry critical opposition to the startlingly long poem; but it is remarkable how heavily this hostility was outweighed by critical enthusiasm, and how very soon the opposition succumbed. It was as if the old-school critics had exhausted themselves in attacking *Prufrock,* five years earlier. *The Dial* had denounced *Prufrock* as plagiarism; under new editorship, *The Dial* launched *The Waste Land.* Arthur Waugh had compared the author of *Prufrock* to a drunken helot; Sir Edmund Gosse's London set, then dominant in criticism, had scoffed at Eliot as a versifier of negation and bad manners. All this opposition soon collapsed. What the rising generation thought of *The Waste Land,* immediately upon its publication, was best expressed by Rose Macaulay.

"Here was a poet," she wrote, long later, "who drew from the dim corridors of the febrile and fantastic human mind, conscious and unconscious, a new wealth of associated and disassociated images, a newly minted litter of notions, emotions, desires, fears, fantastic prodigies and dreams, the fabulous junk that gleams in the mind's cellars and on its peripheries, a shifting kaleidoscopic mosaic of images, enriched and coloured literature of every age."

So it went. The rising luminaries of letters became Eliot enthusiasts, if they were not such already: the Sitwells, Aldous Huxley, Lytton Strachey, many more. The very Georgian poets that Eliot eclipsed promptly became his adulators: as Roy Campbell observes in his autobiography, the whole "England's green and pleasant land" set, "those who were then the most fervent admirers of J.E. Flecker, Brooke, and Lascelles Abercrombie," overwhelmed by *The Waste Land,* shifted from denigration of Eliot to discipleship, so that they turned his "most ardent admirers and imitators.... From then on the infuence of Eliot literally swallowed up many of these minor poets as a blue whale swallows mites of krill."

Ezra Pound, Wyndham Lewis, James Joyce, and other principal literary innovators had been Eliot's friends and allies before *The Waste Land* was published. Now, in 1922, Eliot won over the young radicals, many of them Americans, who talked eagerly in Parisian cafes—even though his character and his cast of mind were very different from theirs.

The Left Bank types did not apprehend clearly what Eliot was engaged upon. Yet those young movers and shakers of 1922 felt a trifle uneasy with the new master. As Malcolm Cowley writes in *Exile's Return* of their reception of *The Waste Land,* "Strangeness, abstractness, simplification, respect for literature as art with traditions—it had all the qualities demanded in our slogans." They found it necessary to champion the strange poem against the passing generation of critics and against popular philistinism. At heart, nevertheless, they were hostile without knowing quite why, Cowley suggests:

When *The Waste Land* first appeared, it made visible a social division among writers that was not a division between capitalists and proletarians.... But slowly it became evident that writers and their theories were moving toward two extremes (though few would reach one or the other). The first extreme was that of authority and divinely inspired tradition as represented by the Catholic Church; the second was Communism. In Paris, in the year 1922, we were forced by Eliot to make a preliminary choice. Though we did not see our own path, we instinctively rejected his.

This instinctive rejection, nevertheless, did not produce a body of adverse criticism from the Left until a decade later. How could innovators on principle set themselves against the triumphant champion of poetic innovation?

Neither the young writers of the Left Bank nor the entrenched critical establishment of 1922 were at all certain what *The Waste Land* was *about;* they knew that it was marvellous, but as for its purpose... Well, was it about personal tribulations? Or was it about the sunken state of society? Or something else altogether?

E.M. Forster and F.R. Leavis soon decided that *The Waste Land* was a personal poem only. Certainly the people whom Eliot called "the sociological critics" exaggerated, from the first, the relationship between the broken inner order of the soul, as Eliot drew it, and the smashed outer order of European society—to which there are obvious references in *The Waste Land.* Yet it will not do to represent the poem, really, as "a personal and wholly insignificant grouse"—not if one takes into account Eliot's accustomed self-depreciation, and his good-natured mockery of many sobersided critics of his poems. The state of the civil social order was for Eliot a burning concern when he founded *The Criterion*—the very period of *The Waste Land.* And it is worth remembering how when he ceased to publish that quarterly review, at the beginning of 1939, he wrote that public disorder had induced in him a "depression of spirits so different from any other experience of fifty years"—a depression equal, apparently, to any private sorrow.

There is not space here to try to penetrate to the inner meanings of *The Waste Land.* Serious criticism of that poem exceeds many times over the whole bulk of Eliot's volumes of verse and prose. (Among the more perceptive detailed analyses of *The Waste Land* are Cleanth Brooks', in his *Modern Poetry and the Tradition,* and C.M. Bowra's, in his *Creative Experiment,* published respectively in 1939 and 1948.) Yet let me touch rashly upon the heart of the matter. If this poem is no social tract, neither is it simply a collection of sentiments of personal suffering. *The Waste Land* is Platonic, in that it relates microcosm to macrocosm, the person to the republic. The disorder of the soul is the cause of the disorder of society—a point Eliot made so very clear, later, in his prose writings that one marvels how critics of the poem still can ignore the connection. Yet the poem is not a kind of obscure allegory of the fate of Europe: Eliot is writing primarily of inner confusion and error, which Europe and the world after the Treaty of Versailles mirrored. The poem arose in part out of private tribulation; but it was not an expression of personal despair; it was an appeal for regeneration. Eliot's own passing experience of an inner confusion, what he described as "an aboulie and emotional derangement," enabled him to discern a more general affliction of the modern mind and conscience: a sickness of the spirit which was communicated to the public order.

That, shortly after publication, *The Waste Land* was mistaken by some for the defiance of Farinata, by others for a wailing nihilism, by yet others for a cry of anguish at the spectacle of Europe ruined—such interpretations are evidence of that twentieth-century aridity of imagination which Eliot was describing. Eliot's search for the seminal sources of wisdom, far from being a declaration of modern helplessness, was a reassertion of hope—and not the delusory hope that came last out of Pandora's box. Life has not always been for all men what it seems to the intellectuals of this century; Saint Augustine and the Buddha were not dupes of false visions that issue from the gates of ivory; though for the time being we shore fragments against ruin, the power to build is not inconceivable. Matthew Arnold and Ralph Waldo Emerson, the feeble nineteenth-century Guardians of the Law, are not the only Guardians humankind has known.

Some of this significance was glimpsed by critics upon the strange great poem's publication; but no one could be sure. The poem's mystery was the greatest of its charms; it is mysterious still, and Eliot declined to unriddle his riddles, in this and his other poems. In a twinkling, Eliot's reputation had risen so high that it would have been imprudent for any Advanced Critic to assail this young colossus. Eliot's humanist friend Paul Elmer More, in his old-school way, told Eliot to his face that *The Waste Land* was abhorrent to him. But the Bloomsbury set, with Leonard and Virginia Woolf at their head, backed Eliot against all comers; soon his *Criterion* was the leading critical journal of the day, publishing both old critics and new. For the time being, *The Waste Land,* reinforced by

"Gerontion" and "The Hollow Men," was unassailable. Some years would pass before elder critics and younger critics would dare to inquire (as Kathleen Nott was to do, mordantly) whether the Emperor Eliot was wearing any clothes.

*   *   *

The concerted assault, when it came, was ideological rather than aesthetic, arising out of the bitter political divisions on the eve of the Second World War. In 1928, Eliot had declared himself a classicist in literature, a royalist in politics, an Anglo-Catholic in religion. That blue flag waved before liberal and radical bulls produced sorrowful cries that Eliot was a lost leader, to Eliot's amusement. And as literary people divided into armed camps, Eliot and the "Criterion crowd" grew isolated. *The Waste Land* and Eliot's other early poems were subjected to most hostile re-examination. If a writer's political opinions are incorrect—why, must not his poetry be contemptible and baneful?

By the middle 'Thirties, Auden and Spender and their set, though still moved by Eliot's style and imagery, were repelled by Eliot's politics. George Orwell, in *Inside the Whale,* describes the climate of opinion: "Between 1935 and 1939, the Communist Party had an almost irresistible fascination for any writer under forty. It became as normal to hear that so-and-so had 'joined' as it had been a few years earlier, when Roman Catholicism was fashionable, to hear that so-and-so had 'been received.' For about three years, in fact, the central steam of English literature was more or less directly under Communist control." For critics who saw no enemies to the Left, it had become necessary to demolish Eliot's reputation.

By 1939, David Daiches, in his book *The Novel and the Modern World,* was declaring, from the postulates of dialectical materialism, that Eliot should have identified himself with the proletarian but instead had involved himself in an incredible religious faith. The world required "alteration of the environment," not personal compensation, Daiches insisted: writers like Eliot and Aldous Huxley were impeding that progress. Edwin Muir replied to Daiches, remarking that "Words like 'compensation' are two-edged; Mr. Daiches' interpretation of Mr. Eliot's experience may be a compensation for not understanding it."

And Louis MacNeice, in his *Modern Poetry,* moved by ideological dogmas like Daiches', proceeded to indict Eliot of *The Waste Land.* Eliot was alleged to have "sat back and watched other people's emotions with ennui and an ironical self-pity. . . . Ten years later less feeble protests were to be made by poets and the human heritage carried on rather differently. . . . The contemplation of a world of fragments becomes boring and Eliot's successors are more interested in tidying it up."

There then took up the cudgel for Eliot that formidable polemicist Orwell—who, in 1940, wrote that Eliot was one of his four favorite living writers. Eliot was right to publish poetry about other things than war and social turmoil, Orwell insisted. (It was the early poems, including *The Waste Land,* that Orwell admired; he was to entertain a very different opinion of *Four Quartets.*) Eliot's politics were not Orwell's politics; but Orwell, for all his insistence that politics and humane letters cannot be divorced, rose superior to ideology.

During those passionate 'Thirties, an aside by Eliot in his lectures at the University of Virginia brought upon his head the wrath of "anti-Fascists" (the quasi-professional breed held in burning contempt by democratic socialist Orwell) and the formidable suspicion of the *New York Times*—this latter a hostility which has endured to the present, despite complete changes of personnel in Times Square. In the first of his Page-Barbour Lectures (1934), soon thereafter published as *After Strange Gods,* Eliot said that in Virginia "reasons of race and religion combine to make any large number of free-thinking Jews undesirable." That single phrase accounts for *After Strange Gods* never having been reprinted in America.

Orwell (and also Herbert Read) defended Eliot against the insulting charge of "anti-Semitism." "Of course you can find what would now be called antisemitic remarks in his early work," Orwell would write to a friend in 1948, "but who didn't say such things at that time?... Eliot's antisemitic remarks were about on a par with the automatic sneer one casts at Anglo-Indian colonels in boarding houses." But the accusation sufficed to rouse a certain body of opinion against Eliot on either side of the Atlantic, for many years later.

A full account of the Left's critical campaign against Eliot just before and during the Second World War could make a rather lively, if unpleasant, small book. The most interesting thing about all this, in the light of our present concern, is that the assault did not seriously impair Eliot's popular reputation as a poet, nor even his reputation as a social thinker. The reason for his relative immunity again is political, in part: Eliot's poetic championship of England during the Second World War, and the courage of his personal conduct in bombed London, "whence all but he had fled"—all other famous poets, that is.

"In the heady days of the Popular Front," J.M. Cameron wrote in 1958, "he managed to keep his balance when many writers lost theirs, and this without yielding to the complacency which marked the Conservatism of Mr. Chamberlain and Lord Halifax." More, Eliot had spoken, as the "incandescent terror" of the bombs had descended upon London, for all that had been high and free in England's historic experience: "History is now and England."

So it was that Eliot's general reputation, in the years after the Second World War, stood higher than ever; and *The Waste Land* seemed undiminished in power. Political attacks on Eliot would continue. In the pages of *The Nation,* Oscar Cargill would declare ominously that Eliot and Frost must mend their politics and become social and economic egalitarians, or else they would cease to be read: neither mended his ways, and neither suffered any diminishing of popularity—quite the contrary.

Eliot's later poetry was received with less cordiality, chiefly because it was suffused with religious conviction. "It is clear that something has departed, some kind of current has been switched off, the later verse does not *contain* the earlier, even if it is claimed as an improvement upon it," Orwell wrote of "Burnt Norton," "East Coker," and "The Dry Salvages."

Other critics declared that, nevertheless, *Four Quartets* was Eliot's supreme achievement. Yet had Eliot there strained poetry to its limits? "When the traditional form of even our central belief has become a problem of intellectual analysis," Anthony Thorlby wrote in 1952, "what should we expect of our lesser forms, the conventions of art and poetry?" He had in mind *Four Quartets.* "The critical answer, if it is only this we are able to understand, and must insist on for our understanding at all, leaves the formal truth still *questioned,* however right our answer shows it to be. . . . Perhaps in our unhappy age the traditional happiness of poetry is no longer possible."

Be that as it may, both the critics' admiration and the popular reputation of *The Waste Land* remained unimpaired at the hour of his death in 1965. Also many of the mysteries of that poem remained unexplained. "In my end was the beginning," was graven upon Eliot's stone in the ancient church at East Coker.

*   *   *

During the five or six years after Eliot's death, the critical studies of his poetry and his prose steadily increased in number: probably no other poet in any time has been the subject of so much close analysis. Nearly a hundred books have been written about Eliot's work, and the number of periodical essays and long reviews must now approach three or four thousand, depending upon what one counts. This mass of criticism, during the 'Sixties, continued admiring and deferential, with few exceptions. Almost no one challenged the power of *The Waste Land.*

As earlier, during this period it was Eliot's politics and his religion, rather than his talents as a poet, which were subjected to attack. An example of this hostility was John Harrison's *The Reactionaries* (1966), with its bitter chapter denouncing Eliot's social writings, particularly *Notes towards the Definition of Culture.* Yet literary critics who disapproved of Eliot's political and perhaps his Christian doctrine—Northrop Frye, for instance—nevertheless insisted that these convictions did not diminish his greatness as a poet.

One might have expected that the resurgent radicalism of the 'Sixties and early 'Seventies would have struck a hard blow at Eliot's popularity. It did not. So far as the general public was concerned, nothing is deader than dead politics. In the eyes of his readers, Eliot stood above party and faction, and it was of small interest what he had thought about Stalin, Hitler, Mussolini, Churchill and Roosevelt. (He had much disliked them all.)

But surely the New Left people of the rising generation must have detested Eliot? Not at all. Dissent from his politics and his religion though they did, still to them Eliot remained the grand innovator in literature, the poet of imaginative vision.

Our best example of this grudging admiration is the chief collective product of the New Left literati, published in 1972, when the "Movement" of the young radicals already was in the sere and yellow leaf: *Literature in Revolution,* edited by George Abbott White and Charles Newman. Just half a century after publication of *The Waste Land,* the New Left contributors to this volume, though they denounced *The New York Review of Books* as a reactionary publication, paid their tributes to T.S. Eliot. For they still were pilgrims in the Waste Land.

Indeed, Eliot haunted these New Left Critics. "Eliot thought that his poetry could be understood by factory workers," Sol Yurick wrote. "...Eliot, damn it, is right. Stalin and Mao on literature are dead wrong." George Abbott White quoted "an ex-president of SDS" (Carl Oglesby?) who confessed his high admiration for Eliot: "Now it strikes me that hardly any American-English poetry has gone beyond him, that in any case he must be absorbed in order to be transcended...."

White himself devoted a large part of his essay about F.O. Matthiessen, "Ideology and Literature," to a running commentary on Eliot: much to White's vexation, he knew that Eliot's communication of the dead was tongued with fire beyond the language of the living. He wished it were otherwise; for, White instructed the readers of this anthology, rather primly, "Eliot, let us say it plainly, with his *very bad politics*," had been an "elitist." (White seemed unaware of Eliot's demolition, in *Notes towards the Definition of Culture,* of Mannheim's concept of elites.)

As their contribution to *Literature and Revolution,* Marge Piercy and Dick Lourie presented a kind of dialogue called "Tom Eliot Meets the Hulk at Little Big Horn: the Political Economy of Poetry." Miss Piercy had been told by an SDS poet "that an individual's aesthetics had to belong to the same world view as his politics: it was senseless to have Che's politics and Eliot's poetics. Equally, I might add, you shouldn't adopt socialist realism unless you dig Stalin's politics too." She hoped for New Left poetry consistent with New Left politics, but she found such aspirations squelched by *The New York Review of Books.* Eliot, confound his Anglo-Catholicism, had been this century's great innovator in poetry; while the dominant left-liberals of the past decade, posing as arsonists, read aloud in the firehouse from the selected poems of Benito Mussolini. Who might redeem us from thralldom to Eliot the revolutionary in literature, Eliot the self-proclaimed reactionary in politics?

The contributors to *Literature and Revolution* shared with Eliot a marked dislike of the present state of society. But they were simplifying theorists, Burckhardt's "terrible simplifiers." Disdaining reforms, they insisted upon revolution—which meant that they got nothing. They had no recent revolution to celebrate, no true revolutionary consciousness to analyze, no style adequate to work a revolution within literature on the scale of the revolution which Eliot had worked fifty years earlier. A weariness ran through these essays, perhaps a fatigue with their own slogans. Knowing Eliot, they could not shut their ears to an insidious whisper:

> This is the way the world ends
> Not with a bang but a whimper.

Someone had come and taken their revolution away. Was Eliot the thief? Indeed, was their intended revolution ever really a practical Marxist revolution? Eliot had known their kind well.

By his literary principles, the Marxist "is compelled to scorn delights, even such moderate ecstasies as may be provoked by the reading of Emerson's Essays, and live laborious days in deciding what art ought to be," Eliot had written in 1937. "For this knowledge of literature he is obliged to apply himself, not to the furtive and facile pleasures of Homer and Vergil—the former a person of doubtful identity and citizenship, the latter a sycophantic supporter of a middle-class imperialistic dynasty—but to the arduous study of Ernest Hemingway and John Dos Passos; and the end of his precipitous ascent will be an appreciation of the accomplishment of Sam Ornitz, Lester Cohen, and Granville Hicks." Since Eliot wrote those sentences, three of those names have become anathema to Marxist orthodoxy in letters, and two have been forgotten. One may expect similar changes in opinion and reputation among the writers of the recent New Left; for many of them read too much Eliot for their own piece of mind.

Literature and society both depend upon faith in a transcendent order, Eliot had argued. "If you will not have God (and He is a jealous God) you should pay your respects to Hitler or Stalin," Eliot had written in *The Idea of a Christian Society,* on the eve of the Second World War. The contributors to *Literature in Revolution,* and most other New Leftists, no longer could stomach Stalin by 1972, or even Mao. So they went adrift in politics, with that abstraction "permanent revolution" for compass; so they foundered in letters, dragged down by the weight of ideologues who had detested literary dilettantes.

Thus the decade-long phenomenon of the New Left on either side of the Atlantic did not impair the dead Eliot's ascendancy as a poet, or even overwhelm his social criticism expressed in *The Idea of a Christian Society* and *Notes Towards the Definition of Culture.* Eliot had argued that the nineteenth-century notion of an illimitable Progress had been a silly delusion; he seemed vindicated by the disasters of the 'Sixties. The New Left writers, like all of us, still were pilgrims in the Waste Land.

*   *   *

As the New Left era in criticism and politics drew to a close, Mrs. Valerie Eliot published *The Waste Land: A Fascimile and Transcript of the Original Drafts, Including the Annotations of Ezra Pound* (1971). This book, from the long-lost typescript, mostly, of the Eliot drafts in 1922, opened the way for a new outpouring of books and essays about Eliot and his most influential poem.

The political assault on Eliot had subsided without really discernible effect upon his reputation, and with little reference to *The Waste Land.* But out of the revived discussion of that poem, or at least about the poem, came a different effort at denigration of Eliot: a curious moralizing movement, bound up with the rising fad of psychobiography.

This commenced with the publication, in 1971, of a thin little book by Robert Sencourt (dead by the time of publication), who had been acquainted somewhat with Eliot: *T.S. Eliot: a Memoir.* This was of small interest, except that Sencourt implied that Eliot had been a homosexual.

The New York Times, hostile toward Eliot for decades, gave elaborate pre-publication publicity to this book—although later the reviewers for that same paper scoffed at Sencourt's memoir. Giggling references to the possibility of Eliot's immorality began to appear in syndicated Sunday supplements of daily newspapers and other quarters which previously had displayed little interest in Eliot's work. By 1977, a book about Eliot's writings was published that solemnly endeavored to relate the whole of his accomplishment to this alleged aberration.

Eliot was a natural target for such inquiries, among people who fancy themselves as psychobiographers. Jealous of privacy, and shy, Eliot wrote more than once that we ought to dissociate the sentiments which a poet expresses from the details of his own experience—which experience, ordinarily, ought to be of no large consequence to anybody. Eliot used to quote Kipling: "Seek not to question other than/The books I leave behind." In his will, Eliot had asked that no biography of himself be countenanced. A curiosity, sometimes purient, about the private lives of literary men is common enough. A dead man cannot sue for libel. Was there not opened up a rich field for new approaches to Eliot—perhaps even a lucrative field?

The Waste Land in particular was searched for evidences of sexual deviation. How about Mr. Eugenides, the Smyrna merchant, "unshaven, with a pocket full of currants"...who "Asked me in demotic French/To luncheon at the Cannot Street Hotel/Followed by a weekend at the Metropole?" And how about Tiresias' sex-change? And how about Eliot's not marrying again for many years after parting with his first wife, Vivienne?

It is possible to find almost anything one seeks in the contrived corridors of Eliot's poems; Eliot expected his readers to find much there which he had not himself intended. Of *The Waste Land* especially, many interpretations of particular passages have been remarkably plausible—yet perfectly absurd. The only trouble with the theory that T.S. Eliot was a pederast, as drawn from *The Waste Land* and other poems by people who never knew Eliot, is that Eliot was *not* a homosexual. Christ came to save sinners, and not the righteous, as Eliot knew so well; but that particular sin was not Eliot's.

The only book as yet published about Eliot's private life is T.S. Matthews' *Great Tom* (1974). Matthews knew Eliot fairly well for a good many years; I myself knew Eliot for a dozen years. I agree with Matthews that the notion of Eliot's alleged sexual deviation—advanced nowadays by some as a clue to the poems—is merely preposterous.

Catholic, royalist, classicist—a writer so bold as to describe himself thus sets himself up as a mark to be shot at by folk who worship strange gods. If only Eliot could be proved a hypocrite! Wasn't he impotent? Better still, mustn't he have been homosexual? Should it be possible to diminish Eliot's personal reputation as a Christian gentleman—why, wouldn't that defamation rub off happily upon Eliot's confounded religion and Eliot's confounded politics? One thinks of Andersen's long tale "The Snow Queen," with its diabolical distorting mirror: "The most beautiful landscapes reflected in it looked like boiled spinach, and the best people became hideous, or else they were upside down and had no bodies....All the people in the demon's school—for he kept a school—reported that a miracle had taken place; now for the first time, they said, it was possible to see what the world and mankind were really like."

That mirror was held up to the dead face of Eliot, but T.S. Matthews flung the mirror aside. Alas for the evangels of Liberation: Eliot was no pathic. Nor was he even incapable of bodily love for woman: he loved not wisely but too well, and within marriage only. One finds actual evidences of this in the poems, most of all in *The Waste Land* and *Ash-Wednesday;* and there are other evidences, summarized by Matthews.

"Eliot's suppressed desire was not for his fellow man but for his wife," Matthews wrote. "...Bertrand Russell said that Eliot was ashamed of his marriage; if so, it may not have been for the social reasons that Russell assumed but because he was disconcerted and abashed by the violence and 'animality' of his passion."

Ezra Pound did good service to Eliot by his amendments to *The Waste Land;* but wretched service by encouraging Eliot to marry Vivienne Haigh-Wood. Still, had there been no profound sorrow, there might have been no high poetry. The bent condition of his world would have oppressed Eliot, melancholy and witty by constitution; yet concern for civilization only might have impelled Eliot to write tracts, not verses.

This endeavor to prove that Eliot was sexually abnormal would not be worth refuting, were it not that it may illustrate the perils of being popular. Envy, in *Doctor Faustus,* cries, "Why shouldst thou sit, and I stand?" To pull down great reputations is a pleasant exercise for a certain sort of psychobiographer. Another writer of that breed recently has published a book to prove that because Edmund Burke sometimes slipped into rages, Burke must have been a homosexual. (This particular biographer forgets that Burke was an Irishman; and that Irishmen who do *not* rage are abnormal.) In so latitudinarian a decade as this, it is somewhat surprising to find critics abruptly turned Pharisees where Eliot is concerned—yet remaining perfectly tolerant toward the open and notorious homosexuality of W.H. Auden and Christopher Isherwood.

No, *The Waste Land* is not a "gay" lamentation over the poet's own unusual erotic preferences. Eliot did not fret about his "lifestyle," which was quite as conventional as it outwardly appeared to be. *The Waste Land* has survived the bombardment of many sorts of critics, and undoubtedly will survive the psychobiographers. Orthodoxy, not perversity, was the doxy of this innovator in poesy. Eliot demonstrated Chesterton's argument that genius really is centric. He was a good man—as Matthews remarks, genuinely kind. Despite that, lifelong he was haunted by a Puritan's sense of guilt, moved by that desire to atone which Celia Coplestone expresses in *The Cocktail Party*—although, like Celia, Eliot had done nothing which the world nowadays considers especially sinful. What oppressed him was not some particular exotic sin, but Original Sin.

That fact distresses the psychobiographers, and not those alone. One still finds some reviewers in the big papers lamenting that Eliot was a lost leader; that he abandoned the deliciously deliquescent negativism of *The Waste Land* (their assessment of the poem, not Eliot's) for the repulsive archaic affirmations of *Ash-Wednesday* and *Four Quartets,* the reactionary notions of *Murder in the Cathedral* and *The Cocktail Party!* If only he had embraced decadence on principle, how great might he have grown! Our Waste Land today, such stubborn critical misconceptions suggest, is as parched as it was in 1922.

*   *   *

At the end of another half-century, how will the popularity of this poem stand? Will *The Waste Land* be regarded as a period-piece, interesting principally as a specimen of the climate of opinion in 1922? Will it be a curiosity of poesy, a stage on the rapid approach to the final exhaustion of all poetry? Will it be analyzed by sociologists (the old literary culture having expired altogether) as the pathetic and unsuccessful reassertion of certain superstitions of the childhood of the race? "Ye unborn ages, crowd not on my soul."

The Waste Land is too long, and requires too much explanation, for anthologies; I suggest that (except for images and phrases that are being embedded in the language) this poem will become less familiar, by the end of the century, than "Gerontion" and "The Hollow Men." "Gerontion" possesses a Jacobean pith of expression unequalled in Eliot's time; "The Hollow Men" is more readily subjected to close analysis. For full expression of Eliot's belief, clearly the *Four Quartets* are superior to *The Waste Land. Murder in the Cathedral* will be read, and perhaps even performed; so, conceivably, *The Cocktail Party.* This much of Eliot will endure a long while. I fear that *Prufrock and Other Observations,* still so much quoted and still best relished by many Eliot admirers, nevertheless may sink gradually from sight, regarded unjustly by some as trivial, and by others (with somewhat better justification) as so many quaint samples of the past irrevocably vanished.

But *The Waste Land?* Yes, already it is something of a period-piece; yes, it is an inimitable curiosity; yes, it goes against the grain of the modern temper; yes, it seems surprising that a poem so obscure and so learned ever could have achieved wide popularity. But it remains relevant.

Relevant to what? Why, to the permanent things, as Eliot called them: to the human condition in every age. I am told that nowadays some undergraduates, as much puzzled by this poem as were their grandfathers, protest sullenly that it is irrelevant—meaning that Eliot (to borrow a phrase, perhaps somewhat to Eliot's disapproval, from D.H. Lawrence) does not chew the newspapers. There's not one word in this poem about Sadat or Begin. But who is relevant—Ginsberg? No, those same students already have forgotten Ginsberg. "Relevance" in the sense of obsession with contemporaneity (an obsession consistently reproached by Eliot) cannot produce poetry at all—only versifying.

The study of poetry is valueless, if poems do not speak to our own concerns; they then become mere grist for degree-mills, in a time when teachers of humane letters are not urgently in demand. But *The Waste Land* remains quick, relevant to our present discontents, much as no history is more relevant to our time than the history of Augustan Rome.

For the Waste Land of 1922 is the Waste Land of this decade. The querulous voices of the displaced and uprooted are louder now; the hyacinth girl escapes us again; Madame Sosostris finds more dupes than ever before; emancipated woman grows shrill in boredom; the ghost Stetson walks, and his name is legion; the river girls and the secretary smooth their hair with automatic hand; Lil has her abortion—now quite lawfully, in London or New York; the hooded hordes march, and cities are consumed; a generation of bats with baby faces glowers at us.

Yet the Thunder still peals above the ruined Chapel, for those who ask the burning questions. Give, sympathize, control: no higher wisdom has been discovered.

And those relevant poets of our decade who say something meaningful to us are the heritors of *The Waste Land*. Take Paul Roche's "Death at Fun City":

> Will skirts be up or down next spring?
> *Chi lo sa*? But what we know is this:
> The wayside will be marvelous
> With bottles, paper, plastic cups, and everything.
> And what of the ecumenic city, Cosmopolis?

* * *

> I must hurt the trees
> Slaughter the last whales
> Butcher polar bears from a chopper
> Slow to a stop
> Photogenesis in the seas:
> If I be denied love.*

The denial of love: that is what *The Waste Land* describes so evocatively, so mordantly, so relevantly. That description is why it has been popular, even with people who have glimpsed its meanings only dimly as in the riddle of a mirror. In the end, Eliot found his way to the intellectual love of God and to the love of created beings. All of us, or nearly all, are pilgrims still in the Waste Land. The dust-devils whirl more furiously than ever about the Red Rock, but because Eliot asked the everlasting questions, some listen to the Thunder. The Fisher King's wound festers unhealed; and so Eliot's probing poem, after more than five decades, has lost nothing of its significance. Nor, so long as many people reflect upon our personal and our public condition in this bent world, will it lose altogether its peculiar popularity.

*From a recording by Mercury Records; quoted by the permission of Paul Roche.

The Enigma of Unpopularity and Critical Neglect: The Case for Wallace Markfield

Melvin J. Friedman

I

WALLACE MARKFIELD is the author of three novels, *To an Early Grave* (1964), *Teitlebaum's Window* (1970) and *You Could Live If They Let You* (1974), a handful of short stories and frequent bits of journalism and book reviewing. His first novel was published by Simon and Schuster and the other two by Knopf. His stories have appeared mainly in prestigious magazines like *Partisan Review* and *Commentary*. His journalistic pieces have graced the pages of *Partisan Review, Commentary* and *Hudson Review* but have also found their way into the more widely circulating *Esquire, Saturday Evening Post, Life* and *The New York Times*.

The above seems to be the publishing profile of an enviably successful writer, appreciated by unlettered as well as highbrow readers. One has reasons to suspect that his books are required reading in universities and that he is the subject of frequent articles in critical quarterlies. Little doubt should remain when one realizes that Wallace Markfield—from his earliest stories in *Partisan Review* in the mid-forties through his 1974 Knopf-published *You Could Live If They Let You*—devotedly tilled much the same literary soil as Philip Roth, Saul Bellow and Bernard Malamud. Their urban Jewish subjects, as most of us know, may seem as irresistible in fictional terms as the dilemma of the American innocent abroad once did to a generation of writers from Henry James and Mark Twain to F. Scott Fitzgerald.

So all indications are that Markfield should be inhaling that "sweet smell of success." The reverse is, unhappily, the case. The 1977-78 edition of *Books in Print* reveals that only one of his novels, *You Could Live If They Let you,* is still in print. The Winter 1978 *Paperbound Books in Print* offers the unsettling information that nothing of his is available in paperback. (The British Penguin Books issued a paperback of *To an Early Grave* in 1968 but that edition, alas, has been out of print for several years.)

Markfield has fared no better with critics or literary historians. Not that he has been roundly castigated or dismissed; he has been merely ignored. Books on the American Jewish scene, like Irving Howe's *World of Our Fathers,* Max Schulz's *Radical Sophistication: Studies in Contemporary Jewish-American Novelists,* or Allen Guttmann's *The*

33

Jewish Writer in America: Assimilation and the Crisis of Identity, give him only passing notice. Alfred Kazin, the distinguished Jewish critic who greeted rather cordially the publication of *Teitlebaum's Window* in the October 18, 1970 *New York Times Book Review,* makes no mention of Markfield in his latest study, *Bright Book of Life: American Novelists and Storytellers from Hemingway to Mailer.* Markfield's name is nowhere to be found either in that monument of literary scholarship, the fourth edition (1974) of the *Literary History of the United States. The Penguin Companion to Literature 3: United States and Latin America,* which has entries on such notable contemporary American writers as Peter Schjeldahl, Frederick Seidel and Robert Mezey (household names all!), ignores Wallace Markfield.

The standard bibliographies, published annually by *PMLA* and *Journal of Modern Literature* and quarterly by *American Literature,* reveal not a single item on Markfield. This last discovery is perhaps the most baffling and disconcerting of all. At a time when young academics are fighting for tenure and find that the most manageable area for research and writing is contemporary American fiction, one has to wonder how Markfield has eluded their grasp.

Some sort of evil demon seems to accompany Markfield's career; he is clearly the hard-luck figure in contemporary American literature. He appears to have the formula for popular and critical success, yet both have proved to be beyond his reach.

II

In an excellent essay on Erskine Caldwell, Jay Martin observes that in his work "two impulses have equal primacy. One is the experimental, modernist impulse. And the other is the influence of journalism and popular writing.[1]" These words could easily have been written about Wallace Markfield. Indeed Markfield has read the great experimental, modernist writers—like Joyce, Eliot and Hemingway—and used them and their artistic devices to great advantage in shaping his own work. He is also tuned into the rhythms and special pulse beat of popular culture. An examination of his fiction reveals the extent to which the "two impulses" exist together in relative ease and harmony from the early stories through *You Could Live If They Let You.*

An early piece like "Notes on the Working Day" (*Partisan Review,* September-October 1946), more a vignette than a story, already makes clear the debt to Joyce; one doesn't have to be much of a Joycean to catch these echoes from *Finnegans Wake* and *Ulysses:* "There goes Everyman, Here Comes Everybody, the H.E.C. of our culture-lag." "Leopold Bloom of the garment center...." "Leopold fat-belly Bloom...." (p. 462) Published exactly a year later, another *Partisan Review* story, "Ph.D.," reveals some of the same modernist impulses. This is a brief sketch of a self-conscious history graduate student ("marginal man of the initial") whose mind wanders through the groves of academe, CCNY style. The main character, known only by the surname Auerbach, seems a younger version of the four Volkswagen riders who occupy our attention in Markfield's first novel, *To an Early Grave.* The subway, a haunting presence in this novel, is constantly on Auerbach's mind: "He remembered now, Auerbach, the time he had once been in a subway and the train had emerged from the tunnel....The train had passed a large expanse of vacant lots, and suddenly it was as if the concept of time and movement had been lost....Each day in the subway, for months afterwards, Auerbach sought the conclusion, sometimes in the tunnel lights which flashed past him as the train rose on the elevated above the city streets." (p. 468) The sense of epiphany, "a sudden spiritual manifestion" (as Joyce characterized it in *Stephen Hero*), seems to have grabbed hold of Auerbach just as it will act crucially on later Markfield subway riders.

The New York subway—that artifact of popular culture—is entirely central to the best known of Markfield's stories, "The Country of the Crazy Horse" (*Commentary,* March 1958).[2] This story owes its modest reputation to a passing remark made by Philip Roth in *Portnoy's Complaint:* "The novelist, what's his name, Markfield, has written in a story somewhere that until he was fourteen he believed 'aggravation' to be a Jewish word."[3] "The Country of the Crazy Horse" is the monologue of a New York Jew who traces his Saturday morning subway ride from Manhattan to Brooklyn to visit his parents. Two stops from his destination he engages in a conversation with a woman who graphically describes her *tsuris,* her brother-in-law's recent operation. The exchange reveals Markfield's "gifts of mimicry" (Alfred Kazin's words):

"They opened him up, they took a look, and they sewed him up again. And you know what he got it from? From one thing only. Aggravation."
  "Oh yes, oh yes," I chant liturgically. "I can imagine, I can believe it. Aggravation...." Till the age of fourteen I had been certain it was a Yiddish word. (p. 238 *Commentary;* p. 101 *Jewish-American Literature)*

The story further describes the narrator's visit to his parents (who sound like echoes of the woman on the subway) and his subsequent departure, shopping bag overflowing with food (predictably!) by his side. The New York Jewish scene, with all its props and stage effects, has never been more faithfully rendered.

"The Country of the Crazy Horse" offers easy access to Markfield's first novel, *To an Early Grave.* The Volkswagen seems to have replaced the subway here as the means of transporting those heroic urban types who must negotiate the seemingly impossible distances separating the boroughs of New York City. Yet, interestingly, *To An Early Grave* begins with the frame character, Morroe Rieff, dreaming of being on a subway. He is awakened with a start by the ringing of the telephone—a phone call which announces the unexpected death of his friend, Leslie Braverman. The early part of the novel brings together first Morroe with the estranged widow, Inez Braverman, and then Morroe with the three friends who accompany him to the funeral in the Volkswagen. Much of the novel is the dramatization of the funeral "expedition"—very cinematic in shape[4]— which has certain of the mock-archetypal characteristics of that curious burial procession in Faulkner's *As I Lay Dying.* Yet it is something quite different, with its distinctly urban rhythms and its marvelous admixture of high and popular culture.

Stanley Edgar Hyman was quick to point out Joycean strains in his review of *To an Early Grave:* "Markfield has clearly taken *Ulysses* as his model, but instead of trying to duplicate that encyclopedic masterpiece, he has aimed more modestly at writing just Mr. Bloom's Day in Brooklyn." At least two other reviewers seemed aware of *Ulysses* when they discussed Markfield's first novel: Charles Shapiro, in the June 6, 1964 issue of *Saturday Review,* referred to Morroe Rieff as being "not exactly a Leopold Bloom" (p. 38); Jeffrey Hart, in the August 25, 1964 *National Review,* saw it all as "a kind of Eighth Street Bloomsday" (p. 735). Indeed one can enlarge these optics somewhat and say that Markfield shares in a vast Joycean legacy which has made *Ulysses* and *Finnegans Wake* virtually "conduct books" for a generation of American Jewish writers which includes Henry Roth, Saul Bellow and Leslie Fiedler, among many others.

One should go beyond the tentative though useful *apercus* of Hyman, Shapiro and Hart and suggest that *To an Early Grave* offers a kind of gloss of the sixth ("Hades") episode of *Ulysses.* Joyce's "creaking carriage" of June 16, 1904 has fittingly been replaced by a 1960s Volkswagen; Paddy Dignam has turned into Leslie Braverman; and the four mourners who attend the Dignam funeral, Martin Cunningham, Leopold Bloom, John Power and Simon Dedalus, give way to the more literary foursome of Morroe Rieff, Holly Levine, Felix Ottensteen and Barnet Weiner. Hades is surely very much on Markfield's mind as he plots the course of the Volkswagen, with its four mourners, making "the *descent* to Brooklyn"[6] (my italics) on the way to Braverman's funeral.

To an Early Grave, like *Ulysses,* takes place in a single day—in this case a Sunday. The unexpected early death of Braverman brings together the four New York Jewish intellectuals who occupy our attention through most of the novel. The conversation on the way to the cemetery reflects the urban chic of their milieu, with its mixture of modernist literary habits and concerns and a fanatical devotion to popular culture. These ingredients seem to have something to do with those "two impulses" which Jay Martin found in Erskine Caldwell.

The conversation reflects Markfield's "uncanny ear"[7] for sounds and verbal rhythms. He is clearly tuned into the resonances of a generation of New York City intellectuals who have read *The Waste Land* and *Ulysses* ("Da dayadhvan...Stately plump Buck Mulligan....)" at the feet of Lionel Trilling and Richard Chase at Columbia University.[8]

Before the group assembles for the funeral drive, we get a privileged view of the Volkswagen owner, Holly Levine, alone in his apartment trying to get into a book review which he is preparing for one of the prestigious quarterlies. He manages a pompous opening sentence which he proceeds to revise and torture to death in his typewriter. At one point, "he went to his bookshelves and at the bottom of the vertically stacked *Kenyon Reviews* found the one *Playboy* and, though fighting not to, shook out and inspected from many angles the center fold." (p. 62) This wonderfully comic moment creates a kind of "tension" between the highbrow and popular which carries through much of the novel.

Levine announces some twenty pages later, when they are gathered in the Volkswagen, that he will probably be giving a popular culture course in the fall. This produces an elaborate exchange which involves a commingling of the popular (comic strip characters, old movies, old radio programs) with the academic (articles in critical quarterlies, the university scene dominated by Lionel Trilling and the New Critics). The precise English of the intellectual is liberally sprinkled with Yiddish expressions and occasional solecisms in most of the conversation. The following exchange is fairly typical:

> "I? I?" Weiner said softly. "*Nahrisher kint!* Except..." He scratched behind one of Levine's ears. "Gaah, I don't know. Is that for you? Is it, like they say in the quarterlies, your metier?"
> His color deepening, Levine answered, "My piece on John Ford has been twice anthologized. Twice!"
> "Granted, granted. Your grasp of the gap between low-middle and high-middle culture—perfect. Your cinematic depth analysis—I don't think I would want better. But when it comes to comic strips and such—unh, unh, man, you doan know shit!" And Weiner shook his head in the slow mournful rhythm of an old darkie.
> Levine pursed his lips, as though sucking through a straw.
> "Maybe I'm wrong," Weiner placated. "Maybe I am being less than fair. In which case, answer me this: Who used to say, in moments of *Angst*, 'Golly Moses, I got the whim whams all over'?"
> "Rooney, Rooney, Little Annie Rooney!" Levine looked around as if for applause.
> "Don Winslow of the Navy—his rank!"
> "Commander!"
> "Now the nemesis of Bim Gump!"
> "Wait, wait! She wore a veil...she would always drug him...MADAM ZENDA!"
> "And the protectors of Daddy Warbucks?"
> "Punjab," Levine said, delightedly. "Punjab and the Asp."
> "The Rinkeydinks," Weiner came back, relentless. "Who and from where?"
> "From 'Winnie Winkle.' The club. And there was Perry, the little brother. And there was Spud....There was Chink...." (pp. 82-83)

Markfield is obviously at home in this world and tuned into the precise cadence of its speech.

One of the problems with *To an Early Grave* is to decide where the comedy and satire end and the pathos begins. When the Volkswagen finally arrives at a chapel, Braverman's four friends are treated to an elaborate funeral oration by a rabbi (whose pomposity and bloated syntax recall the rabbis of Philip Roth and Bruce Jay Friedman), only to discover, after examining the corpse, that they have attended the wrong funeral. After this comic interlude, the four do finally arrive at the right cemetery in an almost anticlimactic gesture. The novel ends with the most sympathetic of the mourners, Morroe Rieff, breaking into tears following his return home; the last line strikes a genuinely pathetic note: "And he began to cry freely and quietly." Yet the comic seems to endure beyond the fleeting attempts at tragedy.

How good a novel is *To an Early Grave*? Does it survive its attempts to be another *Ulysses* on a smaller, less mythical scale? I should say that it is both an accomplished novel and one which gains a new dimension by virtue of its kinship with Joyce. Novels which get too close to the raw nerves of

Joyce's masterpiece have a way of being deeply scarred by the encounter. Here, for example, is a convincing description of Ross Lockridge's 1948 novel, *Raintree County*: "It is as if someone had read Stuart Gilbert's exposition of *Ulysses,* and the files of the *James Joyce Quarterly,* and then confidently set about to write the original novel. But a *Ulysses,* without the richly realized creation of Leopold Bloom, and Molly, and Stephen, and the rest of them, and without the vibrantly keen-eyed and keen-eared verbal presence of Joyce, would be an utterly dead thing."[9] Markfield may well have read Gilbert's study and some of the early issues of *James Joyce Quarterly* as well as *Ulysses* itself on the way to writing *To an Early Grave,* but he emphatically did not produce "an utterly dead thing." His is a lean and tidy novel of less than 200 pages (not a thousand-page blockbuster of the order of *Raintree County*) which exudes wit, vitality and an unerringly right sense of place and timbre.

<h1 style="text-align:center">III</h1>

Teitlebaum's Window is twice the length of *To an Early Grave* and is somewhat bloated and large limbed where the earlier novel is spare and even svelte. The Rabelaisian proportions of *Teitlebaum's Window,* however, seem precisely suited to this Brighton Beach-Coney Island version of the *Bildungsroman,* which records the coming of age between the Depression years and the beginnings of World War II of the Jewish boy Simon Sloan. *Teitlebaum's Window* is clearly more experimental than *To an Early Grave* although it is also less Joycean. Joyce enters Markfield's second novel rather obliquely, mainly as an inspiration for certain techniques and patternings rather than through frequent echoes and analogies.

The narrative of *Teitlebaum's Window* proceeds in a vastly complicated way, with traditional storytelling methods frequently giving way to clipped diary notations, letters, classroom notes (liberally borrowed from those Markfield took himself when he was a history major at Brooklyn College?) and snatches of monologue. There is also some small emphasis on the visual, especially toward the end of the novel when, for example, a childish drawing of a face makes several appearances. Many of the chapters begin with an immense, convoluted sentence, which may go on for several pages: dating the events, reintroducing characters, referring to celebrities in the political, film and comic book worlds, and quoting the signs in Teitlebaum's window—for example, "('There will always be an England but there will not always be such a low low price on belly lox')." [10] These long sentences act rather like the interchapters in Virginia Woolf's *The Waves* or the vignettes separating the stories in Hemingway's *In Our Time.* What Hemingway said about his vignettes applies tellingly to these runaway sentences: they "give the picture of the whole between examining it in detail." The techniques of modernism have clearly informed Markfield's verbal maneuverings.

Teitlebaum's Window, even more than *To an Early Grave,* shares many of the concerns of the type of American Jewish novel which came into prominence around 1960, the year Philip Roth won the National Book

Award for *Goodbye, Columbus.* Simon Sloan's growing up is intimately linked with the intruding presence of his mother—who induces the usual amounts of Portnoyesque guilt and frustration.[11] Her syntax and logic are peculiar to the species of Jewish mother: "Mom said Believe me, you look around and its all over and a person is a big big dope if she puts off her youthful dreams and thats why if God spares us, we should live and be well and she should feel better than she's been feeling on her dropped stomach we're all three going before Pesach to see Ohrbachs." (p. 138) This sentence—if that's what it is—brilliantly avoids logical and syntactical structures and twists and turns like a snake.

Teitlebaum's Window is the seemingly unedited record of a decade in the early life of a New York Jewish boy; it captures the urban experience of the pre-World War II years quite as faithfully as any contemporary American novel I can think of. It seems to be fashioned along the same large lines as the most recent work of Bellow, from *Herzog* through *Humboldt's Gift*—which earned their author two National Book Awards, a Pulitzer, and eventually a Novel Prize.[12]

IV

You Could Live If They Let You is less closely plotted than either of the previous novels. It offers what is probably, at least according to reviewers, another version of the Lenny Bruce saga. Earlier in the year in which this novel appeared, Markfield reviewed Albert Goldman's *Ladies and Gentlemen, Lenny Bruce!!* for the *New York Times Book Review* (May 26, 1974). One of Markfield's sentences performs double duty in characterizing the peculiar gifts of Lenny Bruce as well as those of his own fictionalized Bruce character, Jules Farber: "It's enough for Goldman that Bruce at his best was the greatest stand-up comic—'Shpritzer'—of his time, that Bruce milked language till it bled, till language turned into song, and that song a recital of the 'Jewish blues'." (p. 2)[13]

You Could Live If They Let You is dedicated to "the wisest men of our time—the stand-up comics" and its narrative captures the staccato verbal habits of a Lenny Bruce or a Woody Allen. The Yiddish clashing with the English at every turn and supplying it with a quite new dimension creates a special style of its own. Markfield's is not a classic Yiddish, acquired from textbooks or evening courses at Brooklyn College or Columbia University, but rather a part of his "residual memory," closely linked to the "collective unconscious."[14] It is interesting to note that the title of his latest novel is probably a variation on the Yiddish expression *M'ken leben ober m'lusst nisht* (you can live but they won't let you) which Markfield is fond of using.

Farber's stand-up comic delivery—like that of Bruce, Allen, Henny Youngman and so many other practitioners of the trade—favors the incongruous, the unexpected: "Plehnt hah tree in Eretz Yisroel for Norman Vincent Peale"; "Readings from Kierkegaard, Kafka and Julia Child"; "it's Bobby Fisher's end game and Thomas Aquinas quoting from William Buckley and Bella Abzug buying two-and-a-half pounds of the best flanken...."[15] This rhetoric, which favors the odd juxtaposition, is consistently irreverent as it takes on every variety of adversary including the Anti-Defamation League, American rabbis, the Modern Language Association of America and the world of popular culture.

We not only hear the voice of Farber but also that of Chandler Van Horton (his Boswell) and that of Farber's sister, Lillian Federman. Here is Chandler Van Horton, in a dialogue with Farber, bringing together the popular with the highbrow:

Van Horton: If I consult my impressions I have more than once caught in your voice throbbings of glory and wonder and danger when you pronounce—no, call up—Brooklyn and Flatbush. I take the name of Edmund Wilson less poignantly than you take the name of Ocean Parkway. As I might speak of E.E. Cummings' enormous room or Swann's madeleine you speak of Dubrow's cafeteria and Mallomars. You manage to arouse in me contempt—I hope it is no worse than contempt—for my lackluster past, my well-scrubbed personal history—(p. 151)

The nostalgic takes over here, as it did in *To an Early Grave* and *Teitlebaum's Window,* for those who grew up in Brooklyn before and during World War II: Markfield once again displays virtually "total recall" of an era and a place—of which he has, in a sense, become the ideal chronicler.

Farber's life is eventually fleshed out in bits and pieces as we find out about his autistic son, Mitchell, and his Christ Therapist estranged wife, Marlene. (Marlene is not unlike Bellow's Madeleine Herzog, whose name is mentioned once in the novel.)

You Could Live If They Let You has many of the urban Jewish concerns of the earlier novels. One of its eminently quotable one-liners has relevance for all of Markfield's work: "When you're in love the whole world is Jewish; and perhaps, in fact, even when you're not in love." (p. 71) This aphoristic turn deserves a place next to Malamud's more famous "all men are Jews." When Farber proclaims early in the novel, "I got a terminal case of aggravation," (p. 12) we are reminded of a succession of other Markfield characters who suffer from a similar illness.

V

As we examine Markfield's career we find it to be very much of a piece. All that he has written till now offers an urban Jewish world view, with its curious hybrid language which makes use of Yiddish, the idiom of popular culture, and a literary vocabulary deeply informed by the presence of Joyce, Eliot and the other essential figures of Modernism and New Criticism. His journalism, which includes essays with titles like "The Yiddishization of American Humor" (*Esquire,* October 1965), "Oh, Mass Man! Oh, Lumpen Lug! Why do You Watch TV?" (*Saturday Evening Post,* November 30, 1968) and "By the Light of the Silvery Screen" (*Commentary,* March 1961), reinforces his fiction at every turn and reveals his continuing commitment to popular art forms.

Among Markfield's most recent publications is *Multiple Orgasms,* which the author describes as the opening segment of an unfinished novel. This was brought out late in 1977, in a very limited edition of "350 numbered copies, signed by the author," by Bruccoli Clark Books in Bloomfield Hills,

Michigan. It is not likely to attract much attention! A stroke of irony found Markfield, in November 1977, contributing an "afterword" to a new edition of a novel by Peter Martin, *The Landsmen,* in a series published by Southern Illinois University Press entitled "Lost American Fiction." Quite like Markfield's own novels, *The Landsmen* was cordially received by reviewers but allowed unceremoniously to go out of print. It would not, alas, seem too far-fetched to imagine *To an Early Grave* one day joining *The Landsmen* in the "Lost American Fiction" series.

In a letter received from Markfield, dated February 17, 1978, he mentioned in passing: "Here's a footnote on the future to help you along in your piece: I'm working on a thriller. Only one Jew who speaks not a word of Yiddish is soon gone." This could suggest a fresh departure in his work. Still the hope is that it will not stifle that rare and genuine talent which produced those three novels and the handful of short stories—all delicately balanced between the popular and the highbrow, as they assess the condition of urban Jews in our time.

Notes

[1]Jay Martin, "Erskine Caldwell's Singular Devotions," in *A Question of Quality: Popularity and Value in Modern Creative Writing,* ed. Louis Filler (Bowling Green, Ohio: Bowling Green University Popular Press, 1976), p. 53. All subsequent references will be to this edition.

[2]This story has been reprinted in *Jewish-American Literature: An Anthology of Fiction, Poetry, Autobiography, and Criticism,* ed. Abraham Chapman (New York: New American Library, 1974), pp. 99-108.

[3]Philip Roth, *Portnoy's Complaint* (New York: Bantam, 1970), p. 107.

[4]The novel was made into a highly effective, modestly successful film, *Bye, Bye Braverman*—which periodically makes the rounds of college film clubs. Markfield, incidentally, served a term as film critic for *The New Leader* (1954-55) and has written impressively on various aspects of the cinema over the years.

[5]This review is most readily available in Hyman's *Standards: A Chronicle of Books for Our Time* (New York: Horizon Press, 1966), pp. 214-218. The quotation appears on p. 218.

[6]Wallace Markfield, *To an Early Grave* (Harmondsworth, Middlesex, England: Penguin Books, 1968), p. 89. All subsequent references are to this edition.

[7]The expression appears in Marion Magid's review of *To an Early Grave* in the November 1964 issue of *Commentary,* p. 81.

[8]Witness the following passage from *To an Early Grave:* "And he [Holly Levine] hissed softly, 'Trilling...Leavis...Ransom...Tate...Kazin...Chase...' and saw them, The Fathers, as though from a vast ampitheater, smiling at him, and he smiled at them." (p. 62)

[9]Lawrence Jay Dessner, "The Case of *Raintree County,*" in *A Question of Quality: Popularity and Value in Modern Creative Writing,* pp. 217-18.

[10]Wallace Markfield, *Teitlebaum's Window* (New York: Knopf, 1970), p. 269. All subsequent references will be to this edition.

[11]Robert J. Milch made a useful comparison in his review of *Teitlebaum's Window* in the November 28, 1970 *Saturday Review:* "Because both deal at length with the problems of Jewish-American adolescents, *Teitlebaum's Window* will inevitably be compared with *Portnoy's Complaint.* Markfield's is a far better book, not least because Simon Sloan, for all his uniqueness, is a fundamentally decent person with whom many readers will be able to identify, while Alex Portnoy is a study in ugly, neurotic selfishness." (p. 37) Milch's interesting judgment, alas, has not stopped *Teitlebaum's Window* from going out of print and *Portnoy's Complaint* from setting records in sales and popularity. Markfield, in a sense, plays Dick Cavett to Roth's Johnny Carson.

[12]I must say that *Teitlebaum's Window* does not especially recall to me any single work of

Bellow. Markfield probably comes closest to Bellow in "A Season of Change" (*Midstream, Autumn 1958*). Monroe Krim in his story reminds one on occasion of Tommy Wilhelm in Bellow's *Seize the Day*. Krim's relationship to his friend Portnoy (is this where Philip Roth got the name?) is not unlike Wilhelm's curious dependence on Dr. Tamkin. Markfield offers a succession of father-figures who serve much the same function as Wilhelm's father, Dr. Adler.

[13]In a two-year period Lanny Bruce and the type of the stand-up comic were very much in focus. Aside from Goldman's study and Markfield's novel, there were Bob Fosse's film *Lenny* and Irvin Faust's 1975 novel, *A Star in the Family*—which reviewers found to be "astonishingly similar" to Markfield's *You Could Live If They Let You*.

[14]This is the way he described it to me in a telephone conversation.

[15]*You Could Live If They Let You* (New York: Knopf, 1974) pp. 25, 14, 131. All subsequent references will be to this edition.

Hemingway and Ethnics

Paul Marx

WITH THE OUTBREAK of World War I the period of mass, unrestricted immigration into the United States was at an end. The mass immigration of the previous three decades had changed the character of the country. America was no longer a huge, underpopulated nation of small towns and rural villages. It was no longer a country whose elite—white, Protestant, predominantly Anglo-Saxon—could be sure of itself. As a result of the great waves of immigration, the values and the culture of thousands of relatively homogeneous communities across the spread of the continent were being replaced by the varying values and numerous cultures of the cities into which the immigrants thronged.

For the old elite the city was becoming the stronghold of the enemy. The culture of farmers and small businessmen was being undermined by the alien, hybrid cultures found in the cities. As John Roche puts it, spokesmen for the old elite "echoed Thomas Jefferson's detestation of these sores on the body politic and his fears that urbanization in the New World would lead to the demoralization of the populace and the degeneration of the democratic way of life."[1] The fifty years between 1880 and 1930 were expansive and exciting, but for some they also were terrifying. For those who were rooted in the country for two or three generations and for whom a sense of national and community unity was important, the new people of many different languages and variety of complexions and physiognomies could be the cause of deep resentment, fear and hatred. For many new Americans also, these years were terrifying, for they were the frequent victims of blatant attempts at repression. For both older Americans and new the 1928 candidacy of Alfred E. Smith, a Catholic and a wet, was of profound symbolic importance. For the underdogs in the fight against the old elite, Smith was the challenger whose victory would be a great step toward liberation and equality. For the farmers and businessmen of the towns and villages, the candidacy of Al Smith represented a grave threat to the sturdy, orderly nation that had been built on the severe but sensible and proven values that were the legacy of the Puritan founders.[2] Hemingway's story "Wine of Wyoming" is set in 1928, and the candidacy of Al Smith is a central metaphor. The main character does not believe Smith will be elected.

The writers of the Twenties whom we admire today knew that the old Jeffersonian society was doomed, that the old elite had to give way. Nevertheless, if they were a part of or if they were close to the old elite they could not altogether escape from absorbing some of the bigotry with which those who felt threatened allayed their fears. The most common forms such bigotry took were jokes based on nationality or race and the easy use of racial and ethnic epithets. And so it is not unusual to find people who were otherwise admirable easily using such epithets. In the literature of the period it is not unusual to find sympathetic characters using such epithets. For sometimes the epithets are but one component of language that is used not to express hatred or contempt but manliness, worldliness or even, ironically, affection. Ethnics and epithets turn up in a number of Hemingway's short stories. One cannot read for very long in Hemingway's short stories without running into kikes, micks, niggers, bohunks, swedes, polacks, wops, spicks or squaws.[3] That is not the case with the novels, with the exception of *The Sun Also Rises*. In *The Sun Also Rises* a black American boxer taken advantage of by an Austrian promoter is treated sympathetically. Robert Cohn, of course, is treated hostilely, so hostilely that it is futile to try to argue that the anti-semitism is not really the author's. In any case it is interesting to consider what might have been some of the cultural influences shaping Hemingway's attitudes toward American minorities.

Hemingway, it should be remembered, was born in 1899. He grew up in Oak Park, Illinois, a town on the edge of Chicago, a town sometimes known as "the middle-class capital of the world." Hemingway did a stint as a reporter on the Kansas City *Star* following his graduation from high school in 1917. In June of 1918 he arrived in Europe for service with the Red Cross. He was severely wounded in July, and was back home in Oak Park in January, 1919. Married to Hadley Richardson of St. Louis, Hemingway returned to Europe in December of 1921. During the almost three years he was back in the States a lot happened in regard to American minorities.

The summer of 1919 was a season of race riots—25 to be exact.[4] The Ku Klux Klan, which had been revived in the South during the war, grew rapidly throughout the Midwest and in rural sections of the East, spreading poison against blacks, Jews, Catholics, Asians—all the foreign born. Resonating with the bigotry being spread by the Klan were the ideas of Henry Ford. Ford bought the weekly newspaper, the Dearborn *Independent* in January, 1919, and turned it into the *Chronicler of the Neglected Truth*. Two notions predominated in the pages of Ford's *Independent*: the sinfulness of big cities and anti-semitism. Keith Sward, in *The Legend of Henry Ford*, writes that "as an antidote to the debauchery of city life, the Dearborn *Independent* advised solid Americans to go to church and to keep their boys down on the farm....After all, the paper insisted, 'The real United States lies outside the cities. When we stand up and sing, My Country Tis of Thee,' it said, 'We seldom think of the cities'."[5]

In promulgating an anti-semitism that has been surpassed only by the Nazi propaganda ministry, Ford was cultivating a native strain of Jew-baiting that had long associated the Jew with money changing—from high finance to the pawnshop. Ford's editors at the *Independent* obtained a copy of the infamous *Protocols of Zion* and adapted it to the American scene. Beginning with the issue for May 22, 1920 and continuing for 91 consecutive issues, the *Independent* told of a Jewish plot to conquer the world and destroy Aryan culture by fomenting every social malady known to man.

The *Independent* amplified a thousand-fold the anti-semitism that for a long time had been a stock item in such popular journals as *Puck* and the *Police Gazette,* which week after week ran lurid cartoons showing Wall Street as a gigantic Jewish pawnshop.[6] As a boy in high school, Hemingway had had great fun calling himself "Hemingstein"—sometimes "Stein" for short. He called a couple of his pals Goldberg and Cohen. And on their three adjacent lockers he chalked the balls that are the sign of the pawnshop. "We deal in funds," Hemingway said. "We don't lend. You lend to us. We promise to use any money anyone wants to contribute and we promise never to return it."[7]

Among the hundreds of ways the Dearborn *Independent* accused Jews of despoiling American life was the corruption of baseball. There was a germ of truth to this charge. The involvement of a couple of Jews in the Black Sox scandal of 1919 undoubtedly was the source of the *Independent's* charge. The Jewish involvement in the scandal may have been a crucial factor in determining the way Hemingway was to portray Jews. Hemingway's interest in baseball went back at least to the spring of his twelfth year when he wrote a poem commemorating the first game of the new season for the Chicago Cubs.[8]

Perhaps the biggest news in the sporting world in 1919, at the beginning of which Hemingway was back in Oak Park from Europe, was the great success of Chicago's American League team, the White Sox. Their starting team was an interesting collection of Americans, a small melting pot. Several ethnic groups had players on the Sox. Americans of German stock could identify with the centerfielder from Milwaukee, Happy Felsch, and with the catcher, Ray Schalk. Scandinavians could identify with the shortstop, "Swede" Risberg, Italians with the star pitcher Eddie Cicotte, Irish with the Collins at second base and another Collins in right field. "Shoeless" Joe Jackson in left and the other big pitcher, Lefty Williams, represented the poor South. Old-stock Americans could latch onto Buck Weaver at third and Chick Gandil at first.

This White Sox team was supposed to walk away with the World Series against Cincinnati. At almost every position the Sox player was superior to Cincinnati's. But despite the inequality of the teams, the country awaited the Series with great anticipation; it was the first World Series since the end of the war. Every pitch of every game would be telegraphed into meeting halls in 250 cities. Betting on sports was at its peak. In the Chicago area, huge sums were bet on the Sox, who looked like a sure thing. In Cincinnati and in New York, however, the professional gamblers were putting their money down on Cincinnati. Word had been passed among them that the Series was fixed.

With the end of the war and a new devil-take-the-hindmost attitude running through the country, betting was rampant. And fixes were not infrequent in baseball, boxing and horse racing. Before Judge Kenesaw Mountain Landis became baseball commissioner in 1920, gamblers had easy access to players and boxers. That easy access made for frequent suspicion of fixes. But those who should have been concerned to protect the sanctity of sporting events chose to ignore unequivocal evidence that fixes were in the making. Americans were enjoying sports too much for anyone to want to disturb it all with charges of corruption.[9] Nevertheless, talk of fixes was always in the air. Fixes are mentioned in at least five of Hemingway's stories set during the Twenties.[10]

Following the White Sox loss in the Series, there was a certain amount of commentary in the press about whether there had been a fix. Hugh Fullerton, sports columnist for the Chicago *Herald and Examiner,* wrote several pieces in which he asserted that the Series had been suspicious and called for an investigation. He implied that the Series had been tampered with to enrich the gamblers. As a result, Fullerton was attacked for besmirching the integrity of the national pastime. In the ensuing polemics, an opposition came to be developed between baseball, which was wholesome and American, and the professional gamblers, who were un-American parasites, usually Jewish. *The Sporting News* took offense at Fullerton's allegations and came to baseball's defense this way: "Because a lot of dirty, long-nosed, thick-lipped, and strong-smelling gamblers butted into the World Series—an American event, by the way—and some of said gentlemen got crossed, stories were peddled that there was something wrong with the way the games were played...."[10]

Eight of the 1919 White Sox were ultimately indicted by the State of Illinois for conspiracy. At the trial in 1921 a jury acquitted them of the conspiracy charges, despite the fact that there was no disputing that seven of them had accepted money to throw the Series. Among the names that figured prominently at the trial were Arnold Rothstein, the millionaire gambler of New York, and Abe Attell, the former featherweight champion who had fallen in with gamblers. During his years as a fighter, Attell was known as "The Little Hebrew." It was Attell, who, knowing that the key players on the Sox were willing to throw the Series, had gone to Rothstein to get him to put up $100,000 to finance the fix.[11] Although the idea of fixing the Series had originated with Sox first baseman Chick Gandil and his first contact was with a Boston gambler named Sport Sullivan and although a number of others who helped arrange the fix were not Jews, in the mind of the public it was Attell and Rothstein who corrupted baseball. And thus the famous scene in *The Great Gatsby* in which Gatsby introduces Nick Carraway to Meyer Wolfsheim—"a small, flat-nosed Jew...with two fine growths of hair which luxuriated in either nostril." When Gatsby tells Nick that Wolfshem is "the man who fixed the World Series back in 1919," Nick is incredulous. "The idea staggered me. I remembered, of course, that the World Series had been fixed in 1919, but if I had thought of it at all I would have thought of it as a thing that merely *happened,* the end of some inevitable chain. It never occurred to me that one man could start to play with the faith of fifty million people...."[12]In Hemingway the fictional counterpart of Arnold Rothstein is Happy Steinfelt, a "big operator" in the story "Fifty Grand."

Hemingway's fascination with boxing surely had a lot to do with his interest in ethnics. Hemingway began to box when he was 16. He and his neighborhood pals are said to have improvised gymnasiums and rings. He apparently went into Chicago often to the gyms of Kid Howard and Forbes

and Feretti.[13] He claims to have sparred with some of Chicago's leading
boxers. He wrote a boxing story for the high school literary magazine. It
was a humorous story in the manner of Ring Lardner, whose columns in
The Chicago *Tribune* Hemingway kept up with. The story was called "A
Matter of Colour." In it, "the Big Swede" is hired to stand behind a curtain
on one side of the ring and knock out with a baseball bat the black man who
is fighting a white man. The Big Swede knocks out the wrong man. When
cussed out, the Big Swede explains he got mixed up because he's color
blind.[14]

At any rate, the boxing world of Hemingway's boyhood, adolescence
and young manhood was another melting pot. The black man in "A Matter
of Colour" was given the name Joe Gans. Joe Gans happened to be the name
of a real fighter, a black man who fought as a lightweight during the period
of Hemingway's boyhood. Joe Gans and Battling Nelson, known as "The
Durable Dane," fought spectacular fights in 1906 and 1908. In 1916, when
"A Matter of Colour" was written the Jewish lightweight Benny Leonard
was coming into prominence; in 1917 he was to win the title from the
Welshman Freddie Welsh.[15] The featherweight division had quite an ethnic
mix during this period. Jewish Abe Attell won the title in 1908 from
Irishman Tommy Sullivan. As champion, among others, he fought The
Durable Dane and Jem Driscoll, the British champ. Attell lost the title in
1912 to Irishman Jimmy Kilbane. One of the best featherweights and
lightweights of the period was Italian-born Johnny Dundee, known as "The
Scotch Wop." It was not unusual during this period for a fighter in the
American ring to have been born in Italy, Ireland, Denmark, France or in a
Russian state.[16]

Perhaps the greatest cause of racial and ethnic feeling during the period
was the winning of the heavyweight championship in 1908 by a black man,
Jack Johnson. For the next seven years there was a frantic search for a
"great white hope" who would win the title back from Johnson. Johnson's
ostentatious living and his succession of white wives made it a national
compulsion that he be whipped. An earlier champion, James J. Jeffries, was
urged to come out of retirement to do the job. One of those who urged him to
do so was his friend Jack London, the writer. Jeffries was badly beaten. The
cause of white pride was even taken up by a middleweight, a Pole,
Stanislaus Kiecol, better known as Stanley Ketchel. Johnson toyed with
Ketchel for a while, then knocked him out.[17] Much of the dialogue in a later
Hemingway story, "Light of the World," is about Ketchel and Johnson.

Boxers, championship bouts and baseball were very much at the center
of the national folklore during the period of Hemingway's youth. The
appearance of so many ethnic types in the stories of the Twenties suggests
how alert and well tuned in the young Hemingway was. But as an old-stock
American with few heroes who clearly represented him Hemingway was
somewhat confused by all the excitement and fervor.

In Hemingway's stories, the most fascinating treatment of ethnics
occurs in "The Killers." Hemingway's contempt here is directed at the small
town bigot. Let us take a close look at this story.

The killers, you will remember, are a couple of gangsters who come to a small town lunchroom in order to murder Ole Andreson, a former heavyweight boxer. The story is told from the point of view of young Nick Adams, who is at the lunchroom counter when the killers arrive. When Ole fails to show up at the lunchroom and the killers leave, it is Nick who goes to Ole's rooming house to warn him. Two-thirds of the story, however, consists of dialogue between the killers and George, the counterman. Before George has any idea of why the two men, who are obviously city types, have come to the lunchroom, antagonism quickly develops among them over what is available to eat. In the talk that follows, George, it seems to me, is being portrayed as a complacent, bigoted small town type. Contrary to what most commentators have asserted, I believe that it is not George from whom Nick Adams is supposed to learn, but the killers and Ole, the former fighter and associate of gamblers and criminals. The story is a progressive disarming, an unmanning even, of George and an affirming of both the killers and their intended victim as representatives of manhood more worthy of Nick's emulation. Nick's decision at the end to leave town represents more than just a manifestation of fear. In deciding to leave Summit, Nick is rejecting the way of life of the Georges of the world in favor of that of the story's dual heroes, Ole and the killers. "Soldier's Home" has a similar ending. In that story, Krebs returns to his Oklahoma hometown from the war and finds that his parents and his fellow townsmen are complacent, middleclass hypocrites. At the end of the story, Krebs leaves for Kansas City, just as Nick leaves Summit, presumably for Chicago.

When the killers first enter Henry's lunchroom they are concerned only with getting something to eat. George, though, makes this very difficult for them. The two men are obviously strangers in town, but George will not deviate from his usual, familiar greeting. "What's yours?" he asks them, and in so doing implies that they can have anything they want. But then to Al's order George replies that it isn't ready yet, and makes no further explanation. Al presses him, however, and finally George says, "That's the dinner. You can get that at six o'clock." At this point George thinks he has the upper hand—the two strangers are dependent on him for their food. George will not volunteer any information; instead, he makes the strangers ask. Knowing the clock behind him reads twenty minutes past five, George tells them that it is five o'clock. And again only when Al presses him does George explain that the clock is fast.

Now Al and Max are quick to realize the kind of game George is playing with them. They have been confronted with this kind of presumption before. When Al orders a second time, and once more gets the answer, "That's the dinner," the whole situation is very very familiar to him. "Everything we want's the dinner, eh?" he says, "That's the way you work it." "That's the way you work it"—could any remark better typify the bitter resignation of a person who is habitually subjected to high-handed, arbitrary treatment, of a person convinced that no matter what he wants (here, simply a dinner) someone will try to block his way?

To the two gangsters, George quickly comes to stand for the kind of person who has blocked their entry into the mainstream of American life. George is one of those who look down on people who have not been completely melted into Americans. Al and Max clearly are different from George and the kind of people who ordinarily patronize the lunchroom. Probably they are Jewish (the significance of Max's crack about a "kosher convert"). Hemingway also has made the doomed boxer in the story an ethnic. He is called Ole Andreson rather than Jim Anderson because Hemingway wants him recognized as a "Swede." When Max tells George what he and Al are about he says: "We're going to kill a Swede." This ethnic differentiation accounts for Al's animosity to Nick Adams. He asks Nick his name and the answer he gets is "Adams"—a good, solid American name. Al classifies him immediately: "Another bright boy." "The town's full of bright boys," Max says.

With everything George does or says during the almost two hours the gangsters are in the lunchroom, they—but Max more than Al—become increasingly aware of him as a symbol of the small town. After they finish their meal the gangsters begin setting up the lunchroom for the murder of Ole, but now, aware of the danger to himself, George suddenly changes his tune. He tries to curry favor with the killers by turning his bigotry upon someone else. When he is asked who is in the kitchen he answers: "The nigger." He uses this term, apparently, in order to elicit from the killers the feeling that in spite of their differences there remains at least one very significant bond between them, contempt for the Negro. But the killers refuse to play along with George. "What do you mean the nigger?" Max asks. A question that George answers with, "The nigger that cooks."

As the killers prepare for Ole's appearance, it is very obvious that they know their work. Nick and the cook are put out of the way by being bound and stowed in the kitchen. Max remains at the counter trying to give the place an air of normality by talking to George. Al looks the scene over from the kitchen. Like a photographer he poses the two of them along the counter; then, with his derby tipped back, he sits on a stool beside the wicket to the kitchen, rests the muzzle of his sawed-off shotgun on a ledge, and waits patiently. There is a very definite purpose in this depiction of the killers' skill at their job, and it is to contrast their skill with George's relative lack of skill at his job.

Max, across the counter from him, knows exactly what George is. He wants to impress upon George that now *he* is in command and that he knows more about what is to happen in the lunchroom than George does. This is a reversal of their earlier roles. Max now cannot resist being ironic about all he knows and all George does not know; his belligerent, staccato questions are intended to show George how ignorant he is. Similarly, this is what causes Max constantly to refer to George as "bright boy," to call him "a regular little gentleman," and what causes his ironic explanation to Al that it isn't because of the shotgun that George is cooperative: "No...it ain't that. Bright boy is nice. He's a nice boy. I like him."

By the time Nick leaves Ole's room after telling him about the killers, he has seen the complacent George become submissive; he has seen the gangsters calmly and efficiently prepare for a killing "just to oblige a friend," as Max says; and he has seen Ole face impending death without a whimper. Nick does not know what George and the killers represent, but he does sense something significant in the conflict that develops between them.

When Nick returns to the lunchroom to tell George about his visit with Ole, George is his old self again. Nonchalantly wiping his counter, he answers Nick with meaningless platitudes and pretends to understand everything. When Nick wonders what Ole has done, George knows: "Double-crossed somebody. That's what they kill them for." When Nick suddenly says that he is going to get out of "this town," George again sounds like a man much taken with his own wisdom. " 'Yes,' George says, 'That's a good thing to do'." That is very ironic. For it *is* a good thing for Nick to do, not because Nick is in danger, as George apparently thinks, but because he has outgrown his former aspirations. Having seen the Swede's stoicism and the killers' deliberateness and cool competence, Nick senses the inadequacy of Summit to provide him with models after whom he might pattern his life.

Notes

[1]The Quest for the Dream (New York: Macmillan, 1963), p. 5.

[2]Edmund A Moore, *A Catholic Runs for President: The Campaign of 1928* (New York: Ronald Press, 1956), pp. 101-102.

[3]Ethnics and epithets can be found in "Wine of Wyoming," "The Light of the World," "After the Storm," "The Killers," "Ten Indians," The Battler," "The Gambler, the Nun, and the Radio," "God Rest You Merry, Gentlemen," "Fifty Grand."

[4]Roche, *The Quest for the Dream*, p. 82.

[5]*The Legend of Henry Ford* (New York: Athenaeum, 1968), p. 144.

[6]Sward, *The Legend of Henry Ford*, pp. 146-151.

[7]Carlos Baker, *Ernest Hemingway: A Life Story* (New York: Bantam, 1970), p. 30.

[8]Baker, p. 25.

[9]Eliot Asinof, *Eight Men Out* (New York: Holt, Rinehart and Winston, 1963), p. 135.

[10]"The Killers," "My Old Man," "The Three-Day Blow," "The Gambler, the Nun, and the Radio," "Fifty Grand."

[11]Asinof, p. 28.

[12]F. Scott Fitzgerald, *The Great Gatsby* (New York: Scribner's, 1925), p. 74.

[13]Baker, p. 34.

[14]Baker, pp. 34-35.

[15]Sam Andre and Nat Fleischer, *A Pictorial History of Boxing* (Seacaucus, N.J.: The Citadel Press, 1975), p. 292.

[16]Andre and Fleischer, p. 329.

[17]Andre and Fleischer, p. 86

"Would 25-Cent Press Keep *Gatsby* in the Public Eye—Or is the Book *Unpopular?*"

Barry Gross

"WOULD THE 25-CENT PRESS keep *Gatsby* in the public eye," Scott Fitzgerald lamented to Maxwell Perkins in May, 1940, "or is the book *unpopular?* Has it *had* its chance? Would a popular reissue...make it a favorite with classrooms, profs, lovers of English prose—anybody?"[1] One popular reissue had already flopped: in 1934 *Gatsby* was reissued in a Modern Library but was eventually withdrawn because it didn't sell.

In 1940 Fitzgerald was not worried about the *novel's* chance; he was worried about *his* chance for survival. He was forgotten, nothing was in print. He thought *This Side of Paradise* and *The Beautiful and the Damned* were as dead as the twenties, he felt he had made serious—and ultimately fatal—errors with *Tender is the Night,* he had high hopes for *The Last Tycoon* but it was still only a fragment. He had, however, the same opinion of *The Great Gatsby* that he had had in 1925—that it was "something really [his] own,"[2] that it had "something extraordinary about it," that it was "marvelous."[3]

In 1925 a number of critics agreed—William Rose Benet, Carl Van Vechten, Gilbert Seldes, Conrad Aiken, Heywood Broun—but many did not. The reviewer for *Life* wrote, "After, you feel as if you'd been some place where you had a good time, but now entertain grave doubts as to the quality of the synthetic gin." John Kenney in *Commonweal* thought it "inferior...considered from any angle whatsoever." L.P. Hartley in *The Saturday Review* called it an "absurd story,...a piece of mere naughtiness." Ruth Hale in *The Brooklyn Eagle* detected "not one chemical trace of magic, life, irony, romance, or mysticism in *The Great Gatsby."* Isabel Patterson in *The New York Herald Tribune Book Review* considered it "an imponderable...trifle,...neither profound nor durable."

Most damaging, H.L. Mencken, the critic whose approbation Fitzgerald most craved, wrote in *The Baltimore Evening Sun* that *The Great Gatsby* was "certainly not to be put on the same shelf with, say, *This Side of Paradise* " because despite the novel's "fine texture," its "story is obviously unimportant," is "no more than a glorified anecdote." Complaining that Fitzgerald "does not go below the surface," Mencken concluded that what ailed *The Great Gatsby* was "its basic triviality."

West of the Hudson the reviewers were downright hostile: "Strip this story of the Fitzgerald cleverness and you have merely the drunkenness,

51

adulteries, and sudden deaths from speeding that are the sordid ingredients of any Smart Set story" *(Cleveland Plain Dealer)*; "A spectacle of fast-living people who care nothing for conventions and know no loyalty except to their own vices" *(Columbus Dispatch);* "A jazz novel in every sense of the word— confusion, harsh screaming sounds jumbled together with an occasional thread of continuity evident after a time" *(Indianapolis News)*; "Highly sensational, loud, blatant, ugly, pointless" *(Dallas News);* "As permanent as a newspaper story, and as on the surface" *(Milwaukee Journal).*

It was clearly a case of the hinterland rising up on its collective hind legs and bellowing in protest against a corrupt and decadent East, presumed spiritual seat of drinking and adultery, of fast cars and faster people, of jazz, of The Jazz Age itself. But Eastern critics who knew better didn't like the novel either. Those who disdained it employed the same synonyms for the same sentiments, regardless of region: synthetic, feeble, melodramatic, naughty, slight, negligible, unimportant, anecdotal, trivial, dime-novelish, minor, pointless, impermanent, shallow, superficial, transitory. Even Conrad Aiken, who admired it enormously, felt impelled to point out that *Gatsby* was not a "great" or "large" but "a highly colored and brilliant *little* [my italics] novel."

Fitzgerald had anticipated—and feared—just such a reaction. He had warned Perkins not to advertise the novel as " 'a picture of New York life' or 'modern society' " because "so much superficial trash ha[d] sailed under those banners."[4] Some of it, Fitzgerald might have added, of his own creation in the pages of *The Saturday Evening Post.*

The main flaw, it seemed, was Gatsby himself. Mencken thought him a "clown" with "the simple sentimentality of a somewhat sclerotic fat woman." Kenney in *Commonweal* complained that "the Great Gatsby wasn't great at all—just a sordid, cheap little crook." Eagleton in *The Dallas Morning News* wrote "Mr. Fitzgerald thinks, quite obviously, that Gatsby is a great and tragic figure, but he merely succeeds in making the reader see him as a rather unbalanced young man who has become a crook." Kerry Scott in *College Humor* called the novel "a tragedy of a nobody." Clifford Trembly in *The St. Paul Daily News* termed Gatsby "a weird character [not] worth so much effort." And Laurence Stallings in *The New York World* argued that *The Great Gatsby* was "not a great novel or even a fine one" because of the title character's "lack of breadth."

This, too, Fitzgerald had anticipated. Perkins had commented on Gatsby's insubstantiality when he first read the manuscript and Fitzgerald's "first instinct after [Perkins'] letter was to let [Gatsby] go and have Tom Buchanan dominate the book"; Buchanan was, Fitzgerald thought, "the best character [he'd] ever done."[5] Gatsby, on the other hand, was, Fitzgerald admitted to John Peale Bishop, "blurred and patchy" because he had "started out as one man" Fitzgerald knew "and then changed into" Fitzgerald. "The amalgam was never clear in [Fitzgerald's] mind," he "never at any one time saw [Gatsby] clear."[6]

Fitzgerald was right, the critics were wrong. *The Great Gatsby* is marvelous, is extraordinary. Time has proved it to be both permanent and profound, durable and important. And precisely because Gatsby is so "blurred and patchy." What Fitzgerald meant when he wrote Perkins in 1924 that "Gatsby's vagueness is O.K,"[7] I don't know but it is precisely his insubstantiality that permits him to embody an attitude, a state of mind—that "heightened sensitivity to the promises of life," that "responsiveness," that "extraordinary gift for hope," that "romantic readiness," that beating on against the current in search of something commensurate to one's capacity for wonder, in search of the orgastic future.

It is the condition of youth itself, what Fitzgerald called in "The Diamond as Big as the Ritz" "youth's felicity," an "inability to live in the present," an insistence on "measuring up the day against its own radiantly imagined future—flowers and gold, girls and stars, they are only prefigurations and prophecies of that incomparable, unattainable young dream." If *The Great Gatsby* has proved to be "a book for the ages" it is because each generation is, for a brief moment, the Dutch sailor, is Gatsby—for all it knows, unprecedented, outward and upward bound for that incalculable future that is surely theirs, to that secret place across the seas, the secret place above the trees.

My generation, at least that small, New York, middleclass subsegment of it that entered its teens in 1950 and came of age just in time to vote for John Kennedy in 1960, discovered Fitzgerald before our professors *re*discovered him. Perhaps it was because we had no real literature of our own: the war novelists spoke for the generation just prior to ours, the contemporaries—Bellow and Baldwin, Miller and Malamud, Ellison and Williams, Kerouac and Ginsberg—were too remote from our middleclass lives. For us there was only Jerome David Salinger but I think we knew, even as we adoringly devoured them, that *The Catcher in the Rye* and *Nine Stories* were not enough. There came a point when, however regretfully, we had to leave Holden behind; we may have been as reluctant to grow up as he was but most of us, in fact, did, or tried to. At some point in the decade Holden had to become our past: the man, not the adolescent, sentimentalizes boyhood.

I think it was when we had to turn from Salinger and to a future that we found Fitzgerald. We flattered ourselves that there was an affinity between his generation and ours—the fifties also followed upon yet another Great War; it, too, was a time of economic prosperity and political reaction. Attracted to the *idea* of burning the candle at both ends, the *idea* of a generation lost, we turned to the twenties. We didn't know what had been lost, we simply sentimentalized the *notion* of loss and romanticized it a la Thomas Wolfe, prefacing it with a sigh, following it with an exclamation point: they were the "O Lost! Generation," *lost* meaning lovely, the "lovely light" of Millay's poem (did it have a title? were there three lines?).

It was an identification we were not entitled to. True, we, too, found all gods dead, all wars fought, all faiths in men shaken—as Fitzgerald so eloquently put it in *This Side of Paradise*. But what gods, what wars, what faiths we couldn't say. We had never gone through any process of loss. We had not become disillusioned. We were merely—and not even tragically, but pathetically—*un*illusioned. The disillusion in that decade was not ours but our elders', especially our teachers who *had* worshipped gods, fought wars, clung to faiths for which they were now being punished. They communicated their disillusion to us by what they did *not* say, what they did *not* tell us to do, out of love, I think, to spare us their pain.

We were not like that lost generation at all. We were "The Silent Generation," not because we had nothing to say but because we were hesitant, we were cautious. Where they were wild, we were solemn. What passions we had we kept in check. No climbs to secret places, no journeys to fresh, green breasts of new worlds for us. We would cultivate our meager gardens, modest plots in fenced-in yards. It was Eliot who really summed us up. We were premature Prufrocks, afraid to presume, afraid to disturb the universe, afraid to force a moment to its crisis, politic, cautious—sensible.

But not *in*sensible. We *did* hear the mermaids singing, each to each, *did* see them riding seaward on the waves. We longed, we yearned, we wanted. Could the Bellow of *Henderson,* the Baldwin of *Notes,* the Ellison of *Invisible Man,* the Mailer of *Deer Park,* the Miller of *Crucible,* the Williams of *Cat* and *Camino,* the Ginsburg of *Howl,* the Kerouac of *On the Road* have pointed a way? But that would have involved a risk, the risk, quite precisely, of involvement. Far safer—and I think we craved safety most of all, though from what we didn't really know—to turn to a past that could make no claims on us.

For it is the peculiar charm of nostalgia that it is safe, undemanding— voyeurism without penalty, no fear of failing or being caught. We were parasites, feeding off another generation's life—or, rather, what our adolescent notion was of that life—because we despaired of living our own. We turned deaf ears to the aggressive rhythms of rock 'n' roll and resurrected Cole Porter, the Gershwins, Rodgers and Hart. We snubbed the dangerous Presley in favor of the sophisticated Sinatra. We kept *The Boy Friend* and *The Three-Penny Opera* running for years. We discovered the old films, made cult figures of Davis and Bogart, Hepburn and Tracy, memorized *Maltese Falcon,* catechized *Casablanca.*

And we found Scott Fitzgerald. Not the Fitzgerald of "The Crack Up" or *Tender is the Night,* but the Fitzgerald of *The Great Gatsby,* or, rather, one *Great Gatsby.* For we *were* Nick Carraway, "inclined to reserve" everything, full of interior rules that acted as brakes on our desires, simultaneously within and without, repelled by the inexhaustible variety of life but enchanted by it too, and wanting desperately to overcome the repulsion, to give in to the enchantment.

Ask your students how old Nick is and they will tell you, oh, twenty. They cannot spot the J. Alfred Carraway who foresees down "the portentous, menacing road" of his thirties "a decade of loneliness, a thinning list of single men to know, a thinning briefcase of enthusiasm, thinning hair" ("They will say: 'How his hair is growing thin!...But how his arms and legs are thin!' "). They cannot understand the Nick Prufrock who decides that Gatsby paid too high a "price for living too long with a single dream" ("Do I dare Disturb the universe?...How should I begin...And how should I presume?") or who concludes that, though "we beat on, boats against the current," we are "borne back ceaselessly into the past" ("I grow old...I grow old...I do not think that they will sing to me.").

Our students can't imagine thirty, much less thinning enthusiasm or thinning hair. Nor can they believe that "the dream" is "behind." For them there is nothing behind. There is no past for them to be borne back into. There is only orgastic future, not the future that "year by year recedes" but "tomorrow," that "one fine morning" when, having finally run fast enough and stretched out their arms far enough, they will stand "face to face...with something commensurate to [their] capacity for wonder."

Our students' Nick is searching for something commensurate to *his* capacity for wonder: the "restless" Nick who returns from the war to find his native "Middle West...the ragged edge of the universe" ("...formulated, sprawling on a pin"); the romantic Nick who hears in Daisy's voice "a singing compulsion, a whispered 'Listen,' a promise that she had done gay, exciting things just a while since and that there were gay, exciting things hovering in the next hour" ("I have heard the mermaids singing, each to each."); the hungry Nick who picks out "romantic women...from the crowd" and follows them, in his mind, "to their apartments on the corners of hidden streets" ("Let us go then, you and I,...through certain half-deserted streets"); the enchanted Nick who sees in New York the "promise of all the mystery and the beauty in the world," the promise that "anything can happen...anything at all" (" 'Do I dare?' and, 'Do I dare?' ").

In short they see Nick as one of them—young, inexperienced, restless, expectant, ready for excitement and fulfillment, for something to *happen,* anything at all. Enter Jay Gatsby, unwitting tutor, bestowing on the initiate a smile "of eternal reassurance" that "faced...the whole external world for an instant, and then concentrated on *you* with an irresistible prejudice in your favor," that "understood you just as far as you wanted to be understood, believed in you as you would like to believe in yourself and assured you that it had precisely the impression of you that, at your best, you hoped to convey."

If Jay Gatsby is something more than "the proprietor of an elaborate road-house," it is because Nick wants him to be, because Nick wants Gatsby to be "a person of...consequence." That is why Nick suppresses his laughter at the "threadbare...phrases" of Gatsby's preposterous autobiography, why his "incredulity [is] submerged in fascination" and finally in faith: "It was all true," Nick concludes, because he wants desperately to believe. Gatsby comes "alive to [Nick], delivered suddenly from the womb of his purposeless splendor" because Nick wants him to. The critics were right: Jay Gatsby is not great. He is great only because Nick thinks he is.

Gatsby's unwitting effect on Nick is salutary. A phrase begins to beat in his "ears with a sort of heady excitement: 'There are only the pursued, the pursuing, the busy, and the tired'." Realizing that he is none of these, that "unlike Gatsby, [he has] no girl," Nick commits himself, ever so tentatively, to Jordan Baker. He is more emotionally involved when he plays Pandarus to Gatsby's Troilus and Daisy's Cressida, perhaps because he is half in love with Daisy himself. On the day of the trust he admits to being "a little harrowed." Listening to Daisy's voice he hears "the loud beating of [his] own heart," feels the "deep tropical burn" of his face.

Ultimately, however, Nick's deepest emotional commitment is to Gatsby. When Gatsby admits he attended Oxford on a G.I. bill, Nick has "one of those renewals of complete faith in him that [he's] experienced before" and wants "to get up and slap him on the back." He has a similar renewal when Gatsby tells him he will take the blame for Myrtle's death. The next day Nick doesn't "want to leave Gatsby." He finally does, but before he goes he stops "reserving judgments" and shouts across the lawn, "you're worth the whole damn bunch put together."

After Gatsby's death Nick finds himself "on Gatsby's side, and alone." The Buchanans have skipped town, leaving no address; Wolfsheim can't get "involved"; the more-or-less permanent boarder Kipspringer calls about the tennis shoes he left behind. The dead Gatsby whispers to him, "I can't go through this alone," and Nick knows he must be "responsible," must be "interested...with that intense personal interest to which every one has some vague right at the end." He takes care of Gatsby's father, arranges the funeral, buries Gatsby in the rain.

On his last night in the East, after erasing the "obscene word scrawled by some boy...on the white steps" of Gatsby's house, Nick locates a greatness in Gatsby comparable to the Dutch sailor's search for "something commensurate to his capacity for wonder," a similar "sensitivity to the promises of life," a similar "gift for hope." Gatsby, Nick concludes, "turned out all right at the end; it is what preyed on Gatsby, what foul dust floated in the wake of his dreams that *temporarily* [my italics] closed out [Nick's] interest in the abortive sorrows and shortwinded elations of men." Nick turns out all right at the end, too, because at the end, he affirms those dreams, he shares those sorrows and elations. When Nick first settled on West Egg "some man more recently arrived" stopped him on the road one morning and asked him how to get to the village. Nick told him and suddenly felt he "was a guide, a pathfinder." He wasn't then, but he is now.

In 1960 we found our own Jay Gatsby. Not that John Fitzgerald Kennedy *was* Jay Gatsby, or even *a* Jay Gatsby, though there were Meyer Wolfheims lurking in the background and there was something Daisy-like about the wife and he frequently gave the impression of not being much more than "an elegant roughneck," but that we responded to him as Nick responds to Gatsby, found in him what Nick finds in Gatsby, and for similar reasons. We awakened to the promises of life, we overcame our repulsion and gave in to enchantment, we satisfied our need to believe.

It seemed, suddenly, that anything could happen, anything at all. "Gay, exciting things" seemed to hover in the next hour. There was music from our neighbor's house and something was going on under the twinkling stars.

But it ended, as we should have known it would. Hadn't we already seen "that ashen, fantastic figure gliding toward him" with gun in hand? We might "still hear the music and the laughter, faint and incessant, from his garden, and the cars going up and down his drive" but we knew "the party was over." America became "haunted" for us, "a night scene by El Greco," the sky "unfamiliar," the leaves "frightening," the rose "grotesque," the sunlight "raw." We closed out our "interest in the abortive sorrows and shortwinded elations of men," we wanted "no more riotous excursions with privileged glimpses into the human heart," we wanted, rather, "the world to be in uniform and at a sort of moral attention forever."

But no more than Nick really can, we could not go home again, home to our basements underground. We had come face to face with something commensurate to our capacity for wonder and had thus earned our credentials, become American, not in that "transitory enchanted moment" but in the passing of it. We had lost, and now we too could "carry well-forgotten dreams from age to age," now we too had a past to be "borne back ceaselessly into."

It was then that we discovered the other Fitzgerald and the other *Great Gatsby,* the ones the young can't know or understand. In a thoroughly negligible *Saturday Evening Post* story called "Diagnosis" Fitzgerald has a character compare the Taj Mahal and the Pantheon and Notre Dame to the "scarcely built" skyscrapers of New York which "not a single generation saw...before we ceased to believe...in the future, in our destiny, in the idea." It is the American dilemma—our beautiful things achieve transitory enchanted moments of splendor and glory and then fail and fade away. That is what Fitzgerald meant when he said, "There are not second acts in American lives." That is what he meant when he lamented in a poem, "To turn the calendar at June and find December on the next leaf!"

The Great Gatsby is two novels, really, and it is Fitzgerald's extraordinary achievement to have combined the both in one. One is a novel for the young about running faster and stretching farther, about the dreams ahead and the orgastic future. The other is a novel for the...not-so-young about the "future that year by year recedes before us" and the dreams that lie behind. It is two novels throughout, but only in Fitzgerald's splendid and paradoxical last line do we realize that.

> So we beat on, boats against the current,
> borne back ceaselessly into the past.

Notes

[1] *The Letters of F. Scott Fitzgerald,* ed Andrew Turnbull (New York: Dell Publishing Co., 1963), to Maxwell Perkins, May 20, 1940.

[2] *Letters,* to Maxwell Perkins, Oct., 27, 1924.

[3] *Letters,* to John Peale Bishop, April, 1925.

[4] *Letters,* to Maxwell Perkins, March 31, 1925.

[5] *Letters,* to Maxwell Perkins, c. Dec. 20, 1924.

[6] *Letters,* to John Peale Bishop, Aug., 9, 1925.

[7] *Letters,* to Maxwell Perkins, C. December 20, 1924.

Chester Himes' Harlem Tough Guys

John M. Reilly

THOUGH CHESTER Himes disavows any innovation in detective story writing ("...when I went into it...I was just imitating all the other American detective story writers, other than the fact that I introduced various new angles which were my own."[1]), his "new angles" mark important adaptations of the American Tough-Guy story illustrating both the continuing possibilities of the genre for social commentary and the rich contribution to be made to yet another portion of popular American culture by the expression of an artist's Black experience.

Given the characteristics of Tough-Guy fiction, it's a wonder, as Himes says,[2] that there haven't been many stories of Black detectives. Tough-Guy fiction in viewpoint or setting reflects conditions produced by the class and caste system. In the manner of Naturalism it depicts character as the product of social conditions, and from the standpoint of an outsider it provides a guide to the disorder of American civilzation, making clear that the cause of it all is eventually located in the practices of the dominant class.[3]

Considering the number of Black authors practiced in Naturalism and the congeniality of the Tough literary perspective to Black experience, one might imagine many Tough-Guy stories written by Blacks and at least a few written about Black experience by whites. For all we know, of course, there were a number of such stories that crossed authors' minds or got into outline, but the white face of American publishing no doubt discouraged their completion and publication, for the fact is that before Himes only one Black writer used Black culture as a setting in a full-length published mystery novel. That was Rudolph Fisher whose novel *The Conjure Man Dies* appeared in 1932.[4] While it details the lives of the folk who reside in its Harlem setting, using superstition and sexual rivalry as motives for plot, Fisher's book is a novel of detection, a whodunit flavored by the exoticism of the Harlem Renaissance, rather than Tough-Guy fiction. As for white authors of mystery and detective fiction, until recently they have used Black Americans either as incidental characters or in ridiculously stereotyped roles. The recent appearance of Black detectives in serious roles has been the result of a popular interest in Black people brought about at last by more than a decade of the most eloquent and militant demands of Blacks themselves, thus serving to reinforce the point that American publishers have found it profitable to issue books that take Blacks seriously only when such books can be labeled as dealing overtly with the "Negro Problem."

Chester Himes began writing Tough-Guy fiction in 1957, however, and the most striking of his "new angles" is the fact that his stories take place almost entirely in Black America. The detectives, the setting, the themes, the plots, and the viewpoint are all Black. The recent acceptance of Black detectives in popular fiction has still not produced work of Himes' comprehensiveness. That deficiency, the past resistance of American publishers to unconventional Black books, and Himes' decision in the 1950s to live and write in exile from the United States explains why, for a period of twelve years, his American Tough-Guy novels had the curious distinction of appearing originally in foreign translation.

Himes began writing in the Tough-Guy genre with *La Reine de Pommes,* which appeared in the French Serie Noire-Gallimard. The novel's success earned it the Grand Prix de Litterature Policier for 1958 and Himes a contract with Marcel Duhamel, the editor of Serie Noire, for additional novels. To date he has published nine Tough-Guy novels. While the books began appearing in American paperback editions, over which Himes apparently had little control, as early as 1959, only *Blind Man with a Pistol* was published originally in an American edition and in English.

Himes was an accomplished Naturalistic writer years before he began his series of Harlem detective stories. In 1945 he published his first novel, *If He Hollers Let Him Go,* narrating the effects of pervasive racial discrimination in a California shipyard upon the psyche of a protagonist who despite his manual and intellectual skills remains as boxed in as Bigger Thomas.[6] *Lonely Crusade* in 1947 extended the protest to the practices of labor unions and the political left.[7] The story of a convict's five year sentence for armed robbery provided the substance of *Cast the First Stone,* which Himes published in 1952.[8]

To one degree or another each of these novels is autobiographical. Himes worked in shipyards, served a prison term, was acquainted with Communist activity in California, and was no more able than any other Black American to escape racial discrimination. Not surprisingly he shared the feeling of some other Black writers that they had to leave the United States in order to concentrate upon writing, and, like at least some other writers, Himes has maintained himself in exile, except for brief visits to the United States, since his departure in 1953.

Expatriation for Black American writers has different results from those for white American writers. Among whites there has developed a variety of international fiction recording the conflicts and congruences between the values of Americans of European descent and their ancestral homeland. In Black fiction there is nothing like that, even though some Black authors have given foreign settings to some of their writing.[9] It is easy enough to suggest a reason for the difference. Perhaps all American authors who go to work in Europe do so with the hope that the European culture will be more congenial to their art than American culture had been, but whites are likely to feel their alienation from much of American culture constitutes freedom, and the possibility of having to retreat into their own personalities because they can never fully assimilate themselves into European culture either does not occur to them or does not threaten them. Black American authors, on the other hand, are unlikely to feel positively about personal alienation. On the contrary, most seem to wish a connection with the popular life of Afro-America and want to emerge into the social world; therefore, while expatriation gives an international cast to the writing of white Americans, Black American expatriates more than likely will express a continued interest in the experience of living in the United States, even though they have had to forego the experience for the sake of their creativity and peace of mind.

Himes' career epitomizes this Black expatriate's concern with the experiences that shaped his consciousness. In the two years after taking up residence in Europe he published two additional novels about Black life in the U.S.: *The Third Generation,* which traces, from heavily autobiographical sources, the disintegration of a Southern Black family, and *The Primitive* concerning the destruction of an inter-racial personal relationship.[10] Then, in 1957, he brought his abilities as a Naturalistic writer to bear upon the special experience of the capital of Afro-America, Harlem, and began the series of Tough-Guy novels that adapt the genre to anatomizing the racism of his native land.

II

In several ways Himes' nine Harlem novels constitute a cycle. Characters reappear, predominantly his two police detectives, Coffin Ed Johnson and Grave Digger Jones, similar events occur, and incidents and persons in one novel are referred to in others. Fundamentally, however, the stories form a cycle because they are controlled by Himes' perception of Black American life, a perception that can be readily outlined by a brief examination of the works making up the cycle.

Himes' prizewinning initial novel, *La Reine de Pommes,* appeared in the United States under the title *For Love of Imabelle.* It was reissued as *A Rage in Harlem,* and currently is identified once again as *For Love of Imabelle.*[11]

The plot of the novel originates in an attempt to defraud a gullible Harlemite eager for quick riches. The victim, a man named Jackson who works as a driver and helper for H. Exodus Clay the undertaker, has given $1500 to Hank and Jodie who promise to "raise" each a ten dollar bill to a hundred by a mysterious process in which they insert the bills wrapped in chemical paper into cardboard tubes and bake them in an oven. The fraud, which the reader learns is a routine known as "the blow," occurs when the oven explodes and Hank, Jodie and Jackson's girl-friend Imabelle escape with the money they had previously pocketed.

Relying on predominantly visual description, Himes sketches the scene of "the blow" in a fast moving opening chapter akin in style to the physical comedy of a slapstick movie. Subsequent chapters describe Jackson's efforts to regain his lost money by playing numbers, shooting craps and visiting a minister who makes a hasty prayer before rushing to dinner. The help he really depends upon to be forthcoming, though, is that of Sister Gabriel, a familiar figure it turns out, often seen soliciting money in the city. Jackson's hope lies in the fact that the Sister is actually his own blood brother who, because of his own successful con game, is knowledgeable about the comings and goings of other crooks.

After establishing through Jackson's experiences that Harlem is the setting of repeatedly unexpected occurrences, Himes introduces his arbiters of the norm, the detectives Coffin Ed Johnson and Grave Digger Jones. Though members of the police force, they are only technically enforcers of the law made outside Harlem. Their loyalty runs first of all to the Black community. Himes' assignment of his tough guys to the police force makes a commentary on the difficulties of moral survival in the community. The tough guys need the protection of police sanction, for were they private eyes inevitably they would offend the people who profit on Harlem's fundamental misery as much as they offend small time crooks. From their realistic perspective, and Himes', Coffin Ed and Grave Digger are necessarily uninterested in fighting the established underworld that caters to "the essential needs of the people—gamekeepers, madams, streetwalkers, numbers writers, numbers bankers," but they are "rough on purse snatchers, muggers, burglars, con men, and all strangers working any racket." (p. 59)

Details of character behavior in combination with the wild sequence of events convey Himes' essentially violent view of Harlem reality. Grave Digger and Coffin Ed are a basic part of the scene, using violence themselves to get information and to catalyze events. Their tough behavior encourages the belief among Harlem's citizens that they would "shoot a man stone dead for not standing straight in line." (p. 52) Whenever they want to control people they draw their long barreled nickel plated guns while Grave Digger shouts "Straighten Up!" and Coffin Ed adds, "Count Off!" Their complicity in violence is undeniable, but their use of it contrasts with others in that their purpose is to introduce order.

From that perspective the organized underworld is not their problem, since it functions in a predictable fashion most of the time, but small time hoodlums and strangers working a con game disrupt people's lives excessively. In such circumstances morality is situational, and the Good often becomes a matter of choosing lesser evil, because the environment of Harlem determines people to live on an elemental level: gray rooftops distort the perspective like the surface of a sea. Below the surface, in the murky waters of fetid tenements, a city of black people who are convulsed in desperate living, like the voracious churning of millions of hungry cannibal fish. Blind mouths eating their own guts. Stick in a hand and draw back a nub. (p. 111)

Even though Harlemites prey on one another, their elementally violent life connects with life elsewhere. The fraud of the bill "raising" and other cons are images of capitalist business and a version of the American dream of quick riches. Likewise, physical murder is the overt complement of the social violence that maintains a cramped ghetto where human misery, denied a salutary assault upon its cause, turns in frustration upon the nearest vulnerable people. In conjunction with these points of theme Himes' prolific use of visually comic scenes becomes very serious business. Those scenes depend upon exaggerated action and unexpected slapstick, and with their violent content they appear to be almost sur-real. But they are in no way incongruous, for actual life in Harlem, as Himes describes it, has the significance of profound absurdity.

Himes' second Tough-Guy novel appeared in the United States under the title *The Real Cool Killers*.[12] A hasty reading of his first novel might fail to reveal the connections between life in Harlem and its external causes, but in *The Real Cool Killers* the connections are inescapable. A white man is shot on a Harlem street apparently by a youngster high on grass. Investigation reveals that his gun shoots only blanks. There is no easily available culprit, so white newspapers and public officials are outraged. Grave Digger and Coffin Ed, as experts on Harlem events, know that, no matter how whites may view it, someway or another exploitative sex is involved in the murder of any white man in Harlem. Nevertheless, the murder introduces disorder and must be reckoned with, because as Grave Digger tells a white patron in a barroom conversation, "If you white people insist on coming up to Harlem where you force colored people to live in vice-and-crime-ridden slums, it's my job to see that you are safe." (p. 66)

The wrap-up chapter of the novel underlines the significance of the caste and class patterns of Harlem crime. When events have run their course, newspapers and police officials by and large still show interest only in the sensation of the white man's death. A more incriminating point comes with the disclosure that the dead man indulged his sadistic sexual desires in a bar where a number of people knew what was happening. He obviously was protected, but nobody could say by whom. The lowest predators, socially speaking, can be uncovered, but the higher and more culpable ones whose power encourages predatoriness never appear in the story.

By the time of his third Harlem Tough-Guy novel, *The Crazy Kill,* Himes had his formulas well established.[13] An opening scene of violence rendered in predominantly visual terms depending upon the unexpected physical event, as in film comedy, involves a number of Harlem characters in a crime that is apparently inexplicable. The remainder of the novel then reveals the motives that explain the crime and relate the characters to one another. While the motives are often psychological in nature, they are intensified and complicated by their presence in residents of Harlem; therefore, they must be interpreted by Coffin Ed and Grave Digger who understand that the conditions of Black life give rise to unique social relationships. As they put it, people in Harlem do the same things other folk do—deceive, rob and kill—but for different reasons and in different ways.

As in all Tough-Guy fiction, physical description of environment in Himes' work explicates events. The metaphoric description of Harlem as a sea full of hungry cannibal fish in *For Love of Imabelle* is one example. More direct portrayal occurs in the description of a "street of paradox" in *The Crazy Kill*:

unwed young mothers, suckling their infants, living on a prayer, fat black racketeers coasting past in big bright-colored convertibles with their solid gold babes, carry huge sums of money on their person; hardworking men holding up the buildings with their shoulders, talking in loud voices up there in Harlem where the white bosses couldn't hear them; teen-age gangsters grouping for a gang fight, smoking marijuana weed to get up their courage; everybody escaping the hotbox rooms they lived in, seeking respite in a street made hotter by the automobile exhaust and the heat released by the concrete walls and walks. (p. 71)

The interplay of life on the street shows how irrelevant abstract categorical morality is when people haven't the luxury of compartmentalizing their lives. If one is constantly a victim, one is conversely a potential predator.

Run Man Run, Himes' fourth Tough-Guy novel, omits Coffin Ed and Grave Digger and transfers the crime to downtown New York, but despite that the story retains the characteristic viewpoint that links the novels in a cycle.[14] In particular this novel underlines Himes' perception of the risky life led by Blacks in a white society.

A drunken racist policeman kills several Black porters at a downtown cafeteria early one morning. One porter who escapes finds everyone thinking him crazy when he accuses the policeman of the killings. The fact that the porter is an ambitiously studious man living a self-regulated life makes Himes' point that whites simply cannot take Black people seriously, because they are unable to shed the preconceptions that abstractly categorize them.

The white murderer is eventually shot by his brother-in-law, also a policeman, but not before other characters are shown to be infected by racist virus. Even the wounded porter's Black girl-friend, the person who knows him best, has doubts of his sanity. To her, as to themselves, white people always appear to be reasonable. They can exploit Blacks (the white murderer has sexual intercourse with the girl-friend), but somehow they seem right, while a shadow of doubt always clouds Black people's veracity.

Besides the tough guys themselves another notable omission in *Run Man Run* is the visual comedy. But Himes' intention cannot be taken as different on that count. The novel follows closely upon the white murderer as he wages a war of nerves on his accuser and attempts to engage his brother-in-law in clearing him. The story, thus, takes place in the context of white society where the appearance of categorical reason is a chief value rather than in Black Harlem where unexpected slapstick physical action is the objective correlative of the disorder induced by racial oppression.

One of the intrinsic interests of Naturalistic fiction for the reader is the detail of workaday life. In Tough-Guy fiction the work is often illegal, and in Himes' works enormous ingenuity marks the big and little rackets that consume the energy of the characters. *The Big Gold Dream,* his fifth Tough-Guy novel, is especially full of such detail.[15] There is, for example, the racket of Sweet Prophet Brown whose followers boast that he is richer than either Father Divine or Daddy Grace. Himes shows his particular scorn for religious charlatans by portraying Sweet Prophet's exploitation of people's desire to believe in the transcendental as outright theft. He sells crumbs of bread to the faithful, charges exorbitantly for baptism, and as his part in the central plot of the novel attempts to hypnotize a female follower to make her contribute the nearly thirty thousand dollars she has won on the numbers to his church.

As usual, the theme of *The Big Gold Dream* concerns exploitation of little people, and, as we have come to expect, Coffin Ed and Grave Digger tolerate the underworld figures who can be counted on to behave more or less consistently. Even a pimp named Dummy they tolerate, not because they approve of his activity but because he could do worse things. This is not intended to be mere cynicism on the detectives' part. Dummy, a has-been boxer deafened by too many fights, has been primed by "do-gooders" to testify before a Senate investigating committee. The consequences of his acting for other people's morality was having his tongue cut out by gangsters. In a kind of economy of wrong-doing Ed and Digger allow him to pursue his trade, since, as they see it, the whores would work for somebody, and at least Dummy treats them better than most pimps would.

A reader can't help but notice that women consistently appear in secondary, dependent roles in these, as in all, Tough-Guy novels. Ed and Digger express sympathy for some women, but generally they display the insensitivity of the creed of machismo they share with other Harlem males. One wishes it were otherwise, but Ed and Digger's participation in the local value system to the extent of accepting the bad as well as the good reminds us that Himes' toughs are only a few degrees more free of their determining environment than the Harlem underworld characters.

The sixth Tough-Guy novel, *All Shot Up,* varies Himes' formula only with the introduction of a prominent national political figure into the cast of characters.[16] There is an exploration of the Gay sub-culture and a series of complicated impersonations emphasizing the dubiousness of reasonable order, but had Himes ended his Harlem cycle in 1960 with *All Shot Up* one might have thought that he had lost interest in the Tough-Guy Form.

True, the possibilities for telling stories of people involved in fraud seem innumerable, but Himes has always been intensely concerned with conveying social themes and while the cumulative effect of the first six novels provides readers a strong commentary on the conditions of Harlem, the vehicle that carries those themes has become too formulized. Moreover, there is a danger of readers becoming insensitive to the characters Himes hopes will embody his vision of Black life, because the violent events that are structured as unanticipated happenings nevertheless satiate our capacity to react. As I say, had Himes ended his cycle with six novels we might have concluded that he saw little possibility for further originality, but he did not end his cycle. The result of his continuation has been the production of what are possibly the most interesting of his Harlem Tough-Guy stories. Doubtlessly the cause of their interest in their topicality. In a burst of social creativity Black Americans have built a liberation movement and invigorated a culture to carry its message. Himes could not fail to be affected by this, and in consequence his three most recent Tough-Guy novels have been devoted to commentary on issues of the sixties.

As an example, *The Heat's On* concerns itself with the alarming rate of heroin addiction in Harlem.[17] Coffin Ed and Grave Digger are suspended from the police force for brutality. They have beaten a pusher forcing him to vomit the heroin decks he has swallowed before questioning, and when the pusher dies there is demand for reprisal. An assistant D.A. lectures the detectives on the distinction between officers who are meant to maintain the peace and courts that punish offenders. By violating this distinction they have killed a man suspected of only a "minor crime." In the anger of Harlem-bred knowledge they vehemently reject the notion that pushing heroin is a minor crime: "All the crimes committed by addicts...All the fucked-up lives...All the nice kids sent down the drain on a habit...Jesus Christ, mister, that one lousy drug has murdered more people than Hitler." (p.60) The reference to Hitler enforces their conviction that since heroin addition is particularly rife among Black people, its distribution is genocidal.

Though suspended, Ed and Digger resolve to follow-up a killing that seems connected with heroin peddling. In the process of describing their activity, alone now without police sanction, Himes' characterization of his detectives becomes fuller, because they are animated by broader moral convictions than in earlier novels. It's as if Ed and Digger had raised their intuitive loyalty to Black people and their commitment to order up to the level of a conception and begun to develop the general principles of their actions and commentary.

The best known of Himes' Tough Guy novels must be *Cotton Comes to Harlem*.[18] In 1966, the year of its publication in America, Sam Goldwyn, Jr. acquired film rights to the novel and six others, and in 1970 it was released as a movie starring Godfrey Cambridge and Raymond St. Jacques in the roles of the detectives.

The events in the story are a projection of Himes' belief that Blacks must make their way in the culture in which they find themselves, that is to say, neither in Africa nor in the idealized past but in present day Afro America. Himes appreciates the importance Marcus Garvey's nationalist movement of the 1920's once had for urban Black people, but the Reverend Deke O'Malley in *Cotton Comes to Harlem,* like the other prophets and faith healers that people Himes' books, seeks only personal profit by offering the vision of a return to Africa to people understandably desirious of escaping American racism. Ironically, despite his professed intention to lead people to Africa, Deke is entirely American in seeking riches by the up-to-date means of exploiting psychic needs, which fact helps make clear Himes' contention that like it or not Harlemites are Americans. The less serious option for the residents of Harlem is a Back to the Southland movement that emerges in the novel under the direction of a white Southern Colonel. This movement has a limited life because it was begun mainly to obtain a bale of cotten stuffed with money that is lost somewhere in Harlem. Nevertheless, both the Back to Africa movement and the Back to the Southland chicanery are viewed by Coffin Ed and Grave Digger as frauds well beyond the "blow" or even Sweet Prophet Brown's pitch. In other words, the detectives themselves, as much as their creator, view the operation of Deke O'Malley on the level of a social problem, as well as a police matter.

Satiric tone is the indicator of this view of O'Malley's Back to Africa movement. Comic physical scenes and irony in the earlier novels interpret, but they do not ridicule. In *Cotton Comes to Harlem* the pairing of a Back to Africa movement with a Back to the Southland movement makes it impossible to imagine a serious ideal behind the phoniness.

A further development in the character of Ed and Digger that accompanies Himes' introduction of specifically topical material is their appearance as appreciative commentators on Black culture. As defenders of Black people and interpreters of their ways, they have been appreciative of course, but in *Cotton Comes to Harlem* a reader begins to notice scenes with the purpose of involving Ed and Digger in Black cultural life. For example, they stop at Wilt's Small's Paradise Inn simply to hear the music:

> Then the two saxes started swapping fours with the rhythm always in the back. 'Somewhere in that jungle is the solution to the world.' Coffin Ed said, 'If we could only find it.'
> 'Yeah, it's like the sidewalks trying to speak in a language never heard. But they can't spell it either.'
> 'Naw', Coffin Ed said. 'Unless there's an alphabet for emotion. The emotion that comes out of experience. If we could read that language, man, we would solve all the crimes in the world.' (pp. 45-46).

Less "philosophical" than the discussion in Wilt's is the familiar scene of the detectives enthusiastically eating Mammy Louise's soul cookery and their wonder at Black people's ingenuity ("If our people were ever let loose they'd be a sensation n the business world, with the flair they got for crooked organizing." pp.71-72), but in sum these and other similar passages show Ed and Digger articulating the pleasure they feel in being Black in the sixties.

With the publication of his ninth Tough-Guy novel *Blind Man With a Pistol* Chester Himes fulfilled the internal logic of his Harlem cycle by bringing the American racial conflict that underlies each of the books into the story as the explicit principle of structure and theme.[19] Structurally the book is composed of three simultaneous plots linked physically by Coffin Ed and Digger's involvement in each.

One plot concerns the killing in Harlem of a white theatrical producer who is evidently involved in an inter-racial homosexual ring. There is no evidence of empathy for homosexuals in Ed and Digger's behavior, but one can suggest that Himes' reference to homosexual "rings" in his novels is less an equation of homosexuality with social corruption than it is an oblique commentary on the code of respectability maintained by white people and their law. Sexual orientation is a person's own business, but if the abstract law of morality tolerates just one variety of heterosexuality (monogamy), many people are forced to illegality. Sooner or later, then, some end up in the city of outcasts—Harlem-and introduce disorder.

Some support for this interpretation of a part of Himes' view of the inhumanity of white morality is provided by a scene in the novel when Ed and Digger go to the East Village. As a setting for dropouts from the morality of respectability, the East Village is populated by damaged people. So is Harlem, of course, but the detectives observe a difference. In the East Village people look "more lost". People in Harlem seem to have some purpose, whether good or bad. But the people down here seemed to be wandering around in a daze, lost, without knowing where they were or where they were going...rejecting reality, rejecting life." (pp.168-169) It would seem that Harlem has the cohesion of a community viewpoint, embodied for us in the novels by the detectives themselves and modifying to a degree the bleak physical conditions in which they act.

The second plot structuring *Blind Man With a Pistol* concerns a killing that occurs in the context of a plan to defraud an aged numbers man by providing him a rejuvenating potion. This plot, which like the first comes to no reasonable resolution, functions to retain the substance of earlier novels in *Blind Man with a Pistol*.

But the third plot represents Himes' fullest exploration of race politics. The plot involves a collection of fools and charlatans offering the people of Harlem competing solutions to the "Negro Problem." The fools are Marcus Mackenzie and his Swedish female companion. From his experience growing up Black in America Mackenzie had come to feel that Christian love would bring the races into harmony. Martin Luther King beat him out with that solution. Himes says, but when Mackenzie met Brigit in Europe he came up with an alternative, brotherly love, stimulated by her constant affection for the Soul brothers, any of them. In the Army Mackenzie learned lots about marching, so he has come to Harlem with Brigit to organize an inter-racial march for brotherly love.

Meanwhile, the charlatan Dr. Moore is working his pitch. He and a staff raise funds for Black Power in the poorest sections of Harlem, and in other sections of the city collect for racial integration. They, too, plan a march under their Black Power banners. The opportunities for clever promotion in the field of solutions to the problem cannot be monopolized, however, and yet a third leader enters. He calls himself General Ham and operates out of the Temple of Black Jesus. His idea is to collect ministers together and march with their statue of Black Jesus under the banner "They Lynched Me." All three groups choose Nat Turner Day, July 15, as the date for their marches.

Himes' satiric description ridicules these non-revolutionary panaceas for American racism simply by describing them. The coincidence of their marches prepares for a hugely comic scene. When the inevitable meeting occurs, however, a riot erupts. At that point the ridiculousness of the groups of marchers becomes less important than the social setting in which they appear. Police officials assume the riot has been caused by instigators. Ed and Digger are more concerned with the origins in color discrimination. They amplify the cause for themselves with the observation that a younger generation of Blacks takes equality seriously whereas earlier generations, like their own, had been resigned to their condition. A talk with Michael X of the Black Muslims certifies this perception. The Muslims receive no ridicule from Himes or his detectives: they are genuinely committed to their people. So when Michael X says that what Whitey doesn't understand is "that there are Negroes who are not adapted to making white people feel good." (p.221). it's an accurate analysis of the mood of the streets.

The three plots of *Blind Man With a Pistol* are narrated in alternating chapters, so that the absence of resolution in each reflects on the others. In addition, Himes provides "Interludes" throughout the book describing Harlem scenes, all of which related to the theme of white racism. To conclude the story Himes tells a parable-like incident involving a blind man aggravated to try to kill at least one white man. Trapped as he is in blindness he shoots instead a Black minister who is admonishing the whites and Blacks to behave like brothers.

The parable relates to many other episodes in the Tough-Guy novels. The rapid sequence of unanticipated violence is on one level comic. On a more profound level the absurd actions are understandable consequences. Himes extends the significance of the parable further, though, by a brief preface to the novel in which he explains that an anecdote told him by Phil Lomax about a blind man with a pistol made him think of "some of our loudmouthed leaders urging our vulnerable soul brothers on to getting themselves killed," and "further that all unorganized violence is like a blind man with a pistol."

The operative word in the preface is *unorganized*. The violence throughout Himes' Harlem cycle and the violence of riots is defensive. It has been forced upon Blacks. The Black community, after all, is where it takes place, and the investigation is clearly from the white community.[20] In an interview with John A. Williams Himes made clear his belief that a change to organized violence would be salutary:

It's just an absolute fact that if the blacks in America were to mount a revolution in force, with organized violence to the saturation point, that the entire black problem would be solved....So the point is that the white people are jiving the blacks in America....Whites want the blacks to find a solution where the blacks will keep themselves in a secondary state.[1]

In light of these remarks Himes' Tough-Guy novels must be seen as an effort to describe necessity. Upon reflection one finds no reason for surprise at Himes' convictions about violent Black revolution. To resist the possibility that the books would be read for titillation (according to Williams this is Himes' favorite word to describe the usual white response to Blacks), he has included the full measure of the volence he perceives in America and tried to demonstrate that it is congenital. In the three most recent books he has become more explicit and increased the topicality, because like other Black Americans he grows justly impatient.

Perceiving the stories of the Harlem detectives as a cycle allows us to see that the commentary Himes intends in *Blind Man With a Pistol* is implicit throughout the cycle. Sometimes critics confuse a Naturalistic writer's credo with his technique and take his intention to describe things the way they really are, to him, as indication that his narrative will provide uncritical portrayal for its own sake. Truly, writers themselves will add to the confusion by their insistence upon their own dispassion or their bleak representation of helplessly determined characters, and it must be said that some of the earlier novels in the cycle independently appear to stress the detectives' coolness and the hopelessness of life in Harlem. Read as cycle, however, Himes' Tough-Guy novels demonstrate how every detail of Naturalistic writing can make an assertion. His descriptions of physical setting, the overcrowded decaying buildings, the rooms filled with the cast-off furnishings of white people or over-priced junk, and the paradoxical streets, emphasizes the status of Harlem as an internal colony. The characters reduced to elemental living or channeling their virtues of loyalty and organization into a struggle for survival represent social relations determined by exclusion and oppression. The plots initiated by fraud or delusion and proceeding through a sequence of unanticipated violent events represent the experience of living in a contradictory world where, on the one hand the majority espouses equal social mobility, and on the other hand actually grants the power of self-determination according to the pattern of rigid castes. Together these essentials of his Tough-Guy novels add up to Chester Himes' assertion of the true nature, not just of Harlem, but the entire American culture of which Black society is inextricably a part.

Notes

[1] John A. Williams, "My Man Himes, An Interview with Chester Himes," Amistad, 1 (New York: Vintage Books, Feb. 1970), p. 49.

[2] Amistad, 1, p. 48.

[3] For discussions of the characteristics of tough guy fiction, see David Madden, ed. *Tough Guy Writers of the Thirties* (Carbondale, Ill.: Southern Illinois University Press, 1968) and David Madden, "James M. Cain: Twenty-Minute Egg of the Hard-Boiled School," *Journal of Popular Culture* 1 (Winter 1967), 178-192.

[4] Rudolph Fisher, *The Conjure Man Dies* (New York: Covici-Friede, 1932).

[5] A complete bibliography of Himes' work appears in Amistad, 1, pp. 92-93. References in this article come from that listing.

[6] *If He Hollers Let Him Go* (New York: Doubleday-Doran, 1945).

[7] *Lonely Crusade* (New York: Knopf, 1947).

[8] *Cast the First Stone* (New York: Coward McCann, 1952).

[9] Only I am responsible for my statements about the causes of differences between white and Black expatriate writing.

[10] *The Third Generation* (Cleveland: World Pub. Co., 1954); *The Primitive* (New York: New American Library, 1955).

[11] *La Reine des Pommes* (Paris: Noire-Gaillimard, 1957); *For Love of Imabelle* (New York: Gold Medal Books, 1959); *A Rage in Harlem* (New York: Avon Books, 1964); *For Love of Imabelle* (New York: Dell Pub. Co., 1971). Citations from all novels appear in the text and unless otherwise indicated refer to the most recent American edition.

[12] *Il Pleut des Cours Durs* (Paris: Noire-Gallimard, 1958); *The Real Cool Killer* (New York: Avon Books, 1959; rpt. New York: Berkley Medallion Books, 1966). Citation in text from Avon edition.

[13] *Couche dans le Pain* (Paris: Noire-Gallimand, 1958); *The Crazy Kill* (New York: Avon Books, 1960; rpt. New York: Berkley Medallion Books, 1966).

[14] *Dare Dare* (Paris: Noire-Gaillimard, 1959); *Run Man Run* (New York: G.P. Putnam's Sons, 1966; rpt. New York: Dell Pub. Co., 1969).

[15] *Tout pour Plaire* (Paris: Noire-Gallimard, 1959); *The Big Gold Dream* (New York: Avon Books, 1960; rpt. New York: Berkley Medallion Books, 1966).

[16] *Imbroglio Negro* (Paris: Noire-Gallimard, 1960); *All Shot Up* (New York: Avon Books, 1962; rpt. New York: New York: Dell Pub. Co., 1968).

[17] *Ne Nous Everons Pas* (Paris: Noire-Gallimard, 1961); *The Heat's On* (New York: G.P. Putnam's Sons, 1967; rpt. New York: Dell Pub. Co., 1968).

[18] *Retour en Afrique* (Paris: Libraire Plon, 1963); *Cotton Comes to Harlem* (New York: G.P. Putnam's Sons, 1966; rpt. New York: Dell Pub. Co., 1967).

[19] *Blind Man With a Pistol* (New York: William Morrow & Co., 1969).

[20] Amistad, 1, p. 46.

[21] Amistad, 1, p. 62.

Larry McMurtry: The First Phase

Patrick D. Morrow

LARRY MCMURTRY has now written six novels, and this seems a reasonable moment in time to examine and judge his artistry, to consider the question of his quality. McMurtry's first three novels were tales of nostalgia, satire, cultural criticism and barbed wire phrases that condemned the modern West. *Horseman, Pass By* (better known as *Hud*, 1961) and *Leaving Cheyenne* (1963) were both cowboy stories of initiation, disillusionment and generational conflict set in Texas. *The Last Picture Show* (1966) was thematically similar and also set in Texas, but small town life rather than ranch life, formed the center for this novel. All of McMurtry's novels have sold at least reasonably well, but *Hud* and *Picture Show* not only have been best-sellers and frequent college texts, but were made into distinguished and very successful films. After these early successes, McMurtry may not have been a household name, but he was an established young writer—and a popular one too, especially with his skill at adapting his fiction into screenplay form.

Then, McMurtry's career took a surprising turn. Rather than continue writing screenplays, he retreated to Houston and then Washington, D.C. and during a low-profile past decade he has been engaged in writing a complex and lengthy trilogy. Demanding skill and time from the reader, the trilogy gradually revealed a chronicle—in panoramic vistas and through several generations—of the quest for moral maturity by a fascinating group of diverse Texans. These three thick volumes demonstrated an involved artistic consciousness, a well-wrought ambiguity in values, characterization and form. McMurtry has succeeded in producing a first-rate group of serious novels.

But appreciation for the magnitude of McMurtry's accomplishment in his trilogy was no means immediate. McMurtry's fiction has always polarized critics somewhat,[1] but the first volume in this new direction, *Moving On* (1970), drew intense critical scorn. Some reviewers damned the book's length (at 794 pages, *Moving On* is over five times *Hud's* length), and few critics could take seriously the protagonist—narrator, Patsy Carpenter. Quite pleased with the earlier short and schematic novels, many reviewers refused to believe that McMurtry could be capable of writing a profound statement on the human condition. Two short excerpts from many angered reviews indicate a pervasive sense of disappointment, perhaps even betrayal. "Tedious," "wrongly conceived," and "flat-surfaced" noted Elroy Bode in *Southwest Review;* "an obese catastrophy," claimed L.J. Davis in *Bookworld.*[2]

However, with the publication of the trilogy's second volume, wryly titled *All My Friends Are Going to Be Strangers* (1972), the critical crying out lessened in favor of some understanding praise. This was fortunate for the author because McMurtry clearly was not going to be deterred from writing a new kind of McMurtry novel. By the release of the last volume in the trilogy, *Terms of Endearment* (1975), critical acclaim was considerable. Leslie B. Mittleman's enthusiasm was by no means atypical. "In *Terms of Endearment* he [McMurtry] creates fully detailed, exuberant personalities who are so charged with the spontaneity of life that they seem to burst from the pages of the book.... Because of his concern for meaningful values, McMurtry is a writer whose best fiction teaches the reader how to live."[3]

McMurtry's literary reputation now has a reasonable amount of security with an increasingly widespread approval and understanding of his trilogy. The trilogy and McMurtry's earlier novels are so different in form and content that any lengthy comparison would be arbitrary and forced. Thus, the key question for this collection of essays appears to be: after some years for perspective, how high *does* the literary quality of his greatest popular successes, *Hud* and *The Last Picture Show,* measure now? This question deserves a fresh approach, and for an answer, two issues need to be explored: first, what was McMurtry's artistic strategy in these two popular novels; and second, where were his successes and failures in these books? Let us begin an exploration by a consideration of *Hud.*

Hud is a successful novel for a number of reasons. By an antiphony/response technique, the novel undercuts, without becoming mannered or silly, the all-time classic Western formula novel, Jack Schaefer's *Shane.* This technique enables McMurtry to maintain a tension between the ideal (past) dream and the nightmare (present) reality, all aimed toward the goal of dramatically rendering the theme of disintegration replacing progress in the modern, mechanical West. McMurtry also demonstrates in *Hud* a stunning talent for making the grotesque and the caricatured intensely, disturbingly real. (This talent has virtually become the author's trade mark.) Lonnie, the young narrator-protagonist of *Hud*, has a Holdon in a Chevy Pick-up quality, but an audience can still take this character seriously. He is an inventive and effective window into Texas as Hell.

Larger than life, villain Hud is an even more successful creation. He is entirely convincing as the Satanic figure who feeds his enormous appetite with an enormous greed. Hud is Emersonian self-reliant man as destructive maniac in the pose of self-justified victim-rebel. He is one of several such figures to appear in anti-establishment novels of the 1950s and '60s; a group which includes Dean Moriarity *(On the Road),* Gnossos Pappadopoulis *(Been Down so Long It Looks Like Up to Me),* and Sebastian Dangerfield *(The Ginger Man). Hud,* then, may have been widely popular because McMurtry uniquely ranges into the tradition of mainstream literature while writing an essentially anti-formula novel. This technique is expanded upon even more successfully in the author's other great popular success, *The Last Picture Show* (1966).

In both form and theme, *Hud* is a direct attack on *Shane.* What Schaefer mythologizes McMurtry annihilates, and in such a punishingly extensive antiphony/response relationship that the parallels can hardly be accidental. The narrative mode of *Shane* is a dual first person voice. An older man (Bob Starrett) recollects from his childhood perspective an inspiring episode in the saga of how those 1880 era homesteaders won the West. This narrative voice, both on the scene and removed in time and space, creates a nostalgic mythology that views continuous masculine violence and continuous feminine security as the expected norm of life. *Hud* is also told in the first person, but the action is immediate and seen from the perspective of Lonnie, a sensitive, misfit adolescent. The beautiful in *Shane* has become the grotesque in *Hud*. *Shane* takes place in a long, lush valley at the base of Wyoming's breathtaking Grand Tetons. The air is clear, the weather bracing, the summer seemingly endless. The town in *Shane* is picturesque frontier frame, populated by helpful older businessmen and hard, tight-lipped ranch hands. *Hud* takes place on the depressing, arid expanses of wind-blown north Texas. It is the early 1950s, and the town consists of a few ramshackle buildings populated by a demoralized confederation of losers whose idea of a good time is getting together for coffee, cherry pie, jukebox listening and reminiscing at a run-down roadside cafe.

Character parallels between *Shane* and *Hud* also exist in a similar golden to brazen antiphony/response. Among the minor characters, Chris in *Shane* and Jesse in *Hud* are parallel. Young and optimistic, Chris succeeds Shane as the hired hand on Starrett's expanding farm. Broken-down Jesse, mainstay of Homer Bannon and his collapsing ranch, has about reached the end of a long and undistinguished cowboy career. The major character parallels are even more pronounced. Joe and Marian Starrett are Bob's concerned, work ethic parents in *Shane*. Joe is mature and reliable while Marian couldn't be more pleased in her role of wife and mother. They are, after all, building their sacred dream on a new land. It is impossible to imagine Joe and Marian (even their names suggest holiness) having an argument. *Hud* presents no such idealized nuclear family. It is not that Lonnie's parents are evil; rather, he has no parents. The parental generation that should be controlling the novel's action and values has vanished or been killed off. A generation gap is emphasized with the entangled ralationships of two widely separated groups—the old (Grandpa Bannon and Grandma) and the young (Hud and Lonnie). Grandma is sick, Grandpa is senile, Hud is greedy and Lonnie is confused. Tension, not nostalgia, establishes the tone of *Hud*.[4]

Both novels are strongly dominated by their leading male characters, Hud and Shane. Hud is a diabolical and vengeful bully, a clear-cut parallel and foil to Shane, whose heroism becomes increasingly Christ-like as the novel progresses. Shane is a mysterious stranger who arrives in the golden valley without explanation but with the ominous air and equipment of a professional gunfighter. However much a killer, he takes readily to home cooking and hard work at Starrett's place, although he insists on facing the front door while eating meals. A displaced Southerner (the true Western hero since Wister's Virginian), Shane is adored by Bob, supported by Marian and inspired by Joe. The symbolic Prodigal Son takes on a cause larger than himself in this novel as he endeavors to help Joe drive Fletcher's powerful and evil cattle monopoly out of the valley. In this parabolic conflict, Shane is reformed evil who restores the right of individual enterprise before vanishing back into the mountains. In the novel's climactic gunfight scene, Shane is wounded, but kills Wilson, Fletcher's hired killer. Wilson looks and dresses enough like Shane to be his double, but Wilson is self-serving, thus evil. (*Hud* reads a great deal like a sequel to *Shane* if Wilson had won the gunfight.) *Shane* defines good in terms of just causes, with no amount of violence wrong in the service of such a cause.

However, violence is the means, not the end in *Shane*. The real substance of *Shane* rests in its theological vindication of the American Dream. Even Bob realizes that "What happened...was beyond me in those days."[5] As mysterious stranger, Shane is both martyr and savior, the final gun wound in his side establishing beyond doubt his selfless, Christ-like significance.[6] In a key passage, Shane explores his theology for Father Starrett:

"I can't really explain it, Joe. But I just know that we're bound up in something bigger than any one of us, and that running away is the one thing that would make it worse than whatever might happen to us. There wouldn't be anything real ahead for us, any of us, maybe even for Bob, all the rest of our lives." (p. 93)

The sacred Manifest Destiny in jeopardy, Shane successfully rises to the rescue.

In *Hud*, villain and hero merge into one figure, the Western hero corrupted into the Western outlaw. *Shane* offers a positive parable of theologically-based Manifest Destiny, but in *Hud* the forces are daemonic, dominated by Hud himself. While Shane is a man of skill, few words and good intentions, loudmouth rebel Hud expresses resentment about what a rotten deal life, with its knaves and fools, has given him. When Grandpa Homer Bannon realizes the consequences of his ill-fated Mexican cattle investment, Hud unleashes his profane theology of a personal manifest destiny. His philosophy is,as he demonstrates in one instance:"Who gives a shit," Hud said. "I'm gonna be boss."[7] While Shane exemplifies the highest law of moral right, Hud operates, without persecution, beyond the law. Hardly the tight-lipped stoic, Hud feels that everyone has treated him unjustly, so he is owed the right to rip-off whatever he can get. Through the novel's course, Hud trades in his bronc for a smashed-up Cadillac, and hustles a distinctive Stetson, then a frizzy, rich blonde, in addition to obtaining a questionable deed to Homer's ranch.

Running through *Shane* is an undercurrent of sexual tension. Shane is attracted to more about Marian than her cooking, and Marian, bred to please, blushes, giggles and says of Shane, "I never saw a man quite like him before." (p. 8) This issue reaches a climax when Shane, ready to fight for the homesteaders, knocks out the foolish Joe who is about to be ambushed by Fletcher. Shane turns to Marian. She says: "We have battered down words that might have been spoken between us and that was as it should be. But I have a right to know.... Are you doing this just for me?" (p. 105) Shane hesitates, and then "...he was looking only at mother and she was all that he could see. 'No, Marian. Could I separate you in my mind and afterwards be a man?' He pulled his eyes from her....you were scarce aware that he was moving[;] he was gone into the outer darkness." (pp. 105-6)

Duty before dishonor is not, however, a theme in *Hud*. McMurtry uses sex and violence as the primary means for exploring man's capacity for evil in the modern, corrupt West.[8] In this latter-day frontier, justice is power, so Hud pretty much seizes what he wants. Hud rapes Halmea, the black, Dilsey-like housekeeper, explaining that she deserved it ("Now, you bitch..." [p. 93]), and that he alone had the guts to enact what the other young men were content to dream about.[9] Hud is also his own hired killer. In a state of total horror, Lonnie listens to Hud's justification for running over Homer, raving and helpless in a ditch, with his Cadillac:

"You listen to me," he said. "No shit, it was best. I ain't lyin' now. Homer wanted it....He was bad off, Lonnie...Tryin' to get to them goddamn dead people a his. I thought if he wanted to get to 'em so bad I'd just let him go. He always liked them better than us that was alive, anyhow....He was just an old worn-out bastard." (pp 128-29)

Shane ensured Bob's future; Hud successfully wipes out Lonnie's past and future.

Two contrasting, parallel scenes from *Shane* and *Hud* further illustrate the grotesque corruption of Western promise. Early in *Shane*, Starrett and Shane successfully remove an enormous stump which Starrett alone has failed to budge. The scene demonstrates the power of brotherhood, cooperative effort for the triumph of homesteading over nature. Starrett wants to clear the land for crops, and Shane wants hard work to redeem his past. Marian and Bob are an audience enthralled with their powerful men. This scene foreshadows, of course, the more important uprooting of Fletcher. Shane gives the final push that dislodges the stump, just as he gives the final push (killing Wilson) that rids the valley of the Fletcher menace. But in the contrasting analogous scene from *Hud*, Homer Bannon's cattle herd is plowed *into* the ground. In a blow of cosmic justice rendered as a Western formula fiction cliche, Homer learns that his entire herd is infected with hoof-and-mouth disease. No amount of noble intentions, productive hard work or brotherhood can establish success here. The benevolent forces in *Shane* have turned into impersonal, all-powerful and often hostile forces in *Hud*. Fate and the government conspire not only to destroy Homer and the herd, but also to wipe out the Western dream of progress through homesteading that *Shane* proffered. Under supervised governmental direction, Homer's final act as a rancher is to corral his cattle—even his aged prize longhorns—into an enormous pit and shoot every last one of them. "Don't take very long to kill things." Grandpa sadly philosophizes, "Not like it takes to grow." (p. 103)

A government agent offers an optimistic interpretation of this tragedy. The herd's destruction is actually a blessing in disguise because now Homer can convert his land into oil leases. But Homer reacts with absolute scorn because that is not his kind of money: "Piss on that kinda money." (p. 88) Leader in the impersonal new order of mechanical land rape for profit, Hud intends to do just what the government agent suggests.

While *Hud* is a jaundiced response to the ideal world of *Shane*, McMurtry does not limit himself to producing merely an anti-formula novel. Occasionally a sentimental moment or phrase drifts into the action of his novel. Certainly *Shane* and *Hud* share many of the same ideals, including a belief in individual freedom and the sacredness of the land. But Schaefer stresses the notion that mankind is fundamentally good; that heroes will emerge, and that in a crisis they will bravely fight for their high ideals, ultimately gaining them. McMurtry studies man's depravity, not offering inspiring solutions, but posing disturbing questions. For example, most of Hud's criticisms against Homer are justified. Grandpa did want to make a cheap, easy, illegal deal on the Mexican cattle, and he was caught in the vice of a punishment far exceeding the crime. Hud continually shocks and intimidates Lonnie, but after Halmea is raped, Lonnie must admit that Hud *is* merely carrying out an action Lonnie has thought about many times. McMurtry's Texas is a brutal, mutilated world. Like Alex in *A Clockwork Orange,* Hud (the anti-Shane) acts on the premise that the only sane response to such a world is to be strong and self-serving, immune to feelings or weaknesses. These issues, explored in some depth and with a distinctive voice, along with the moving portrayal of Lonnie's painful adolescence, place *Hud* beyond the parameters of anti-formula writing.

Hud also has a definite dimension of literary self-consciousness beyond formula Westerns.[10] McMurtry positions the spectre of an aged William Butler Yeats hovering over his novel. Certainly Hud dramatically illustrates those famous lines from "The Second Coming": "The best lack all conviction while the worst / Are full of passionate intensity."[11] The original title of *Hud* was *Horseman, Pass By,* a phrase from Yeats' epitaph and the concluding lines of his poem "Under Ben Bulben." This original title brings to mind the Four Horsemen of the Apocalypse, a sense of the past's passing, and a plea for sanctuary. Yeats' words are an appropriate epitaph to the Western dream of the noble and successful self-made man.

The Last Picture Show is an even better book than *Hud.* Certainly *Hud* is successful, but the novel is more *tour de force* than substantial accomplishment. The anti-formula schemata is sometimes too much a self-conscious virtuoso piece of modeling; there is flight rather than growth on Lonnie's part; there is the triumph of evil Hud, who succeeds so easily because McMurtry has provided no competent, admirable foils. *Hud's* one-dimensional characters and values are refreshing at first reading, but they pale with closer scrutiny. *Picture Show* reads as a much more complex and risky book. Something of a bantam black humor *Tom Jones,* this novel moves by the episodic and satirical to establish the moral growth and self-awareness of hero Sonny Crawford. Faced with some potent threats, including his own inadequacies, Sonny learns to perceive and accept his situation, rather than fleeing. Much of the ugly critical commentary against this book came about because it was misread as a filthy, funny and frightening tall tale posing as reality without any moral quest.

Considering McMurtry's career to date, we can see that *The Last Picture Show* is a transitional work, experimental and often exciting in its sense of self-discovery for author, protagonist and audience. The novel is also flawed with excess episodes—Joe Bob's morality trial seems repetitive as well as preposterous—and a failure to more fully realize thematic implications. But in another way, this is also McMurtry's most balanced book in its movement from anti-formula statement to personal statement, its blend of formula convention and artistic invention. In the mode of Kafka's *Trial* or Paddy Chayefsky's *Network,* McMurtry forces an audience into a confrontation with their values. *The Last Picture Show* convincingly dramatizes the idea that reality imitates art, that satire can be reality. McMurtry here establishes and sustains a marvelously comic tone.

While incident and plot development are emphasized in *Hud,* characterization dominates in *Picture Show* as it does in succeeding McMurtry novels. Set in a small isolated north Texas town in the early 1950s, *The Last Picture Show* bears little resemblance to the Sinclair Lewis-Sherwood Anderson school of small town exposes from the first quarter of this century. *Main Street* and *Winesburg, Ohio,* for example, depict their authors' outrage at the insensitivity and hypocrisy of the American small town. McMurtry points no accusing finger and only occasionally muckrakes with glee a dirty, smelly truth of rural reality underneath the American Dream. Rather, what Lewis and cohorts discovered, uncovered and made into a formula, McMurtry accepts in calm irony, articulating a comedy of further depravity with a fatigued shrug of "so it goes." The novel teases its audience: are we to take all this as modern realism, satire or some new hybrid?

McMurtry's characterization in *Picture Show* is more advanced than in *Hud,* both in terms of depth and range of types. It is primarily through characterization that McMurtry paradoxically compounds stereotypes to move beyond formula in *Picture Show.* Therefore, an ideal way to understand this novel is to trace its character development and interaction from simple beginning to complex finale. *Picture Show*'s characters have the same division found in *Hud*—two conflicting groups, the adolescents and the adults—but this later novel centers on the problems of community involvements and conflicts, rather than problems with evil taking over on an isolated ranch.

The teens in *Picture Show* have their values and life styles built on an image of Hollywood celluloid, a vast romantic adventure played out in great sweeping heroic triumphs. The teens face two tragedies in *Picture Show,* the closing of the town's only movie theatre and the waning months of their senior year. As the novel progresses, this group becomes increasingly disoriented and disillusioned, a confusing on-going identity crisis which results in a bizarre series of shifting feuds and entangled alliances. The adults are set in their ways of disillusionment and impotence. Their problem is not recovering a lost or slipping romantic identity, but living out their mature years without becoming completely insane. They see motion pictures as a stimulating but cruel lie, and have turned to television, forcing the theatre's closing. The adults are happily tranquilized and addicted to this colorless narcotic as narcosis, much to the disgust of their offspring. At the end of the novel, all but one of the adolescents have forsaken the town in search of a stage on which a lost Hollywood romanticism can be recovered and acted upon.

The Last Picture Show is told from an omniscient third person point of view and centers around the activities of several members of Thalia (Greek for paradise) High School's senior class of 1951, particularly one Sonny Crawford. The novel opens on a bitter cold day, the morning after Thalia High has lost the season's last football game. The novel's first sentence effectively sets the book's tone, a mixture of comedy, ignorance and self-pity: "Sometimes Sonny felt like he was the only human creature in town."[12] In the beginning he is a relatively carefree individual who attends school only because of the sports and that activity's correlative, the girls. Estranged from his alcoholic father, Sonny lives in a run-down rooming house with classmate-athlete star Duane Moore, his best friend. Sonny earns money by driving a butane truck for Frank Fartley. Sonny is dissatisfied with all his pasttimes.

Quarterback Duane's true love, Jacy Farrow, is the town's richest girl and the school beauty queen. Jacy, spoiled, selfish and madly in love with herself, ranks near the top of the list of recent literature's most frightening and insightful caricatures. She is first and foremost a performer, a show-off who hates to be considered "backward and country," whose largely realized ambitions are to be first in good looks, first in exciting experiences and first in the minds of admiring others. She is Daisy Miller reincarnated as an authentic mass media symptom—the would-be superstar.[13] Like her high school peers, Jacy is strongly theatrical, influenced most of all by what she sees in the movies.

A self-created "virtuous martyr," her greatest concern is her image, the construction around her person of a legend, an aura of wonder which will be secure for all time in Thalia. This means that Duane is to her little more than an extremely devoted but stupid tool. Sonny is a virtual nonentity. "He [Sonny] admired her extravagantly, but had no money and had not been in the backfield, so he really just didn't count." (p. 71)

The climactic senior class bus trip to San Francisco, wherein the Texas students are ironically cautioned by their teachers to be wary of "lurking preverts," (sic) is the occasion of Jacy's maidenhead sacrifice, said act motivated by her desire to participate fully in the revelry of her sophisticated friends in nearby Wichita Falls. She decides to use the hapless Duane to gain experience, planning to dump him when she returns home as a Woman of the World. She maps out her "seduction" with cunning ("It was the way things were done"), and when Duane's 2,000 mile case of anticipatory erection gives way to sudden impotence at the Crucial Moment, she is furious because her carefully laid plans seem thwarted. "What'll we say?.... The whole class knows what we were going to do!" (p. 147) Appearances must and can be preserved, so when the other girls eagerly come to her room afterwards for an account of the proceedings, Jacy lies in bed, "calm, replete, a little wasted even," and says, "I just can't describe it in words." (p. 148) She enacts reality into movie myth with golden articulation. Jacy's inability to talk about this experience establishes with total certainty for her audience the validity of her deeply-felt passion. Later in the trip Duane finally manages to perform, and to his bewilderment finds himself abandoned upon the return to Thalia. He had always felt that "you were supposed to get whoever you really loved. That was the way it worked in movies." (p. 150) Distraught, he leaves town at the end of the summer to join the army, trading Texas for Seoul and In-Chan.

The Romantic as rip-off artist, Jacy exploits all the reasonably attractive males in Thalia, then moves on to be a star performer with the fast rich set in Wichita Falls. But one night in Thalia, shortly before she takes off to conquer the college set at Southern Methodist, Jacy receives her comeuppance from the novel's best exploiter. This is the oil driller Abilene, an efficient mechanical extension of Hud. Abilene is probably the town's richest man by virtue of his nightly victories at the pool table, a battlefield over which he is so completely in command that his forays on it can only be considered mythically heroic. Extracting a total deference from everyone in Thalia, he epitomizes the modern cowboy after the conquest, the man in control whose hands and clothes never get dirty, and who never has to associate with horses and cattle. His freedoms have been redefined, and his personality and values have mutated from the ideal to fit these new freedoms. He specializes in cool insensitivity, getting what he wants, being exempt, and everyone fears, hates and envies him. Abilene is also the lover of Jacy's mother. On a warm, late summer evening, Jacy unwittingly allows Abilene to seduce her on top of a snooker table. "He played her out as recklessly as he had played the final ball, and when he did she scattered as the red balls had scattered when the white one had struck them so hard." (p. 174) Jacy is undone only for the moment by this well-rehearsed exhibition of Abilene's perfect technique and total disdain. It is Jacy's mother Lois who is really wounded.

Lois Farrow is the town's strongest person, admired and desired by all the men because of her good looks and wildness. A cynical alcoholic who is very bored and unhappy with her life, Lois uses her liquor as an anesthetic for her boredom; and because she is dependent on no one, she is able to dominate nearly all: "If there was anything in the world she was scared of no one knew what it was...she was not in the habit of walking around anyone." (p. 35) Prime time television makes the perfect complement to her alcoholism. As a young woman "she had more life than just about anybody" but years of *ennui* have deadened her somewhat. She fails in her various attempts to implant some vestiges of reality into her daughter's plastic psyche. She enunciates the new ethos of the townsman, and her own, when she says that the land is too tough; that instead of "fighting the hell out of it" one merely acquiesces and does whatever one can to make existence more accommodating. The only thing for Lois to do is grow older and die, a process shunned and endured by everyone but Sam the Lion and Sonny. "Everything gets old if you do it long enough," she tells Jacy. (p. 43)

The book's wisest man, its "old order" representative, is Lois' one-time lover, Sam the Lion, venerable and grizzled owner of the pool hall and theatre (the town's main social centers), and guardian of the faithful and retarded adolescent, Billy. Much of Sam's mental acuity seems to have grown out of the terrible tragedy of his life: a well-known hell-raiser as a youth and later a prominent rancher, oilman and auto dealer, he has seen all three of his sons die violently, following which his wife went insane.[14] A traditional old-timer who fears the mechanical world which has repeatedly tried to destroy him (something like *Hud*'s Grandpa Bannon), Sam becomes known as "the man who took care of things, particularly of boys," (p. 7) and he emerges as Sonny's closest counselor. The latter asks, "Is growing up always miserable? Nobody seems to enjoy it much." Sam replies, "Oh, it ain't necessarily miserable. About eighty percent of the time, I guess." Growing old is one hundred percent miserable, however, and Sam's entreaties echo those of all the adults when he says, "Goddamit! Goddamit! I don't want to be old. It don't fit me!.... Being a decrepit old bag of bones is what's ridiculous." (pp. 123-4) Sam's sudden death, upon which Sonny inherits the pool hall, theatre and Billy, removes the last example of wisdom and perspective from Thalia.

Old or young, the issue of sex cements the generation gap. Sonny's sexual frustrations, while severe, do not drive him to the extreme of most of the other boys, for whom frequent public and private masturbation and regular couplings with heifers, sheep, dogs and even (for variety) geese are not uncommon. Instead, Sonny begins a chance affair with Ruth Popper, the homely wife of Thalia High's football coach. Her forty years of life and twenty years of marriage to this Good Ole Boy have left her devoid of either sexual or emotional fulfillment. Lonely, consumed by an unending depression, enduring an existence for which death would seem a welcome relief, Ruth eagerly jumps at the opportunity of an affair with Sonny because he can bring her companionship, can make her feel needed, wanted and useful. When they first meet she tells him, "Loneliness is like ice" (p. 102), but his presence melts that ice by allowing her—for the first time in her life—to feel a measure of happiness and satisfaction, even though she knows that Sonny comes to her only for sex. For Sonny, "it was an adventure to have slept with someone's wife...it was sort of a feather in his cap." (p. 98) He feels strangely pulled by her, is confused by the emotive processes of her awakenings, and is unable to communicate with her any way except physically. He becomes "everything" to her, what "made the days worth confronting," but after a time he begins feeling "washed out and restless" because he fears the responsibility that her dependence on him seems to imply. Sonny turns from Ruth to Jacy when the beauty queen suddenly becomes available and shows an interest in him. After their abortive elopement, a quite willing Sonny is seduced by Lois Farrow, who philosophizes: "Your mother and I sat next to one another in the first grade.... We graduated together. I sure didn't expect to sleep with her son. That's small town life for you." (p. 201)

Comedy and characterization are so successful in *The Last Picture Show* that some of the novel's other accomplishments may be overlooked. Similar to *Hud*, McMurtry places the hostile environment in the foreground. Few characters can forget that they are stuck and isolated in a vast, flat space and that the town is dying. An omnipresent wind emphasizes an irrecoverable loss. Symbol of angst and time, the "northers" blow everything away from Thalia except the adults, and none of them is in the twenty to forty age range except Abilene (cf. *Hud*). Winds of change accompany the several furtive trips the adolescents take in an attempt to escape the area's oppression and perplexing older generation. The wind motif works well in tandem with the major thematic pattern of illusion/reality, which centers around Sonny. This pattern is a more complex and versatile development of the antiphony/response sequence in *Hud*.

At first Sonny perceives this pattern in terms of bad fate, such as the theatre's closing, and the actions of other, more powerful characters upon him. Like also-ran Duane and others, Sonny has endured years of humiliation and resentment. Several incidents illustrate this victimization. One example would be the scene where, in a fit of rage, best friend Duane blinds Sonny's eye with a broken beer bottle. Duane becomes insanely angered not because Sonny is keeping company with Jacy, but because she revealed the secret that Duane is a woefully inept lover. Jacy also wounds Sonny by setting him up on the fake elopement that successfully enrages her parents enough to send her to chic, expensive Southern Methodist.

But in learning through this painful experience, Sonny outgrows being a pawn and scapegoat. Bright, sensitive and increasingly honest, Sonny gradually realizes that *he* is primarily responsible for his problems. Three episodes point to Sonny's increasing maturity. When he, Duane and several other boys publically humiliate Billy, it is Sonny who accepts Sam's punishment and seeks his forgiveness. Inheriting the pool hall upon Sam's death, Sonny is too slow to realize that this position involves more responsibility than opening, closing and presiding over the town's recreation center. Billy, sweeping the street at dawn when he should be inside and looked after, is run down by a semi loaded with cattle. Sorrowful beyond words, Sonny accepts his part in Billy's death.

Sonny must also take the blame for silently forsaking Ruth Popper who relapses into a helpless loneliness. In the most poignant scene in the novel, Sonny returns to Ruth. He gets no further than her dirty kitchen. Understandably bitter, overcome by betrayal and fast retreating into hopelessness, she cannot face being either happy or vulnerable again. In an angry denunciation she throws a coffeepot at Sonny, who remains calm, needing. Her anger dissolves into tears, and she makes the novel's finest statement in an ambiguous one: "Honey, never you mind...." (p. 220) All the adolescents have made a mess of their lives, but only Sonny has the courage to stay, to see the pointlessness of leaving Thalia to escape himself and the consequences of his actions. Unlike Lonnie, who runs away at the end of *Hud*, Sonny remains behind, sliding into an unarticulated but admirable existential acceptance. He at least passively realizes that wherever he is he must accept his fate, and Thalia is a comfortable known evil. By the end of *Picture Show* a father-son reconciliation is no longer an impossibility. Sonny has been pointed in a direction McMurtry will pursue in much more depth and direction throughout his trilogy.

Perhaps McMurtry has always been more of a cult figure than a popular writer. Muted now, his mass appeal came not so much from his fiction as from two fine films based on his fiction, made some time ago. I would speculate that at present he is a cult figure of the Eastern literary establishment. If his trilogy turns into a successful film or television series, then his broad-based popularity may return. Assuming McMurtry was a cult figure before the film success and his initiation into the highest literary circles, who believed that *Hud* and *The Last Picture Show* were outstanding books? Certainly not the millions who adore Louis L'Amour. Probably not the readers, writers and critics of "serious" Western literature who typically prefer Edward Abbey, Frank Waters or even Eugene Manlove Rhodes as candidates for major recent Southwest writers. "McMurtry just doesn't say much to us here," Tom Lyon, the editor of *Western American Literature* (based at Utah State University in Logan) wrote me some years back. Indeed.

Both *Hud* and *The Last Picture Show* can be seen as Westerns for people who have left the rural West (at least in spirit) in favor of urban life and values (anywhere). Perhaps guilty and unforgiving about their origins and amply large enough for a cult, such an audience would see, especially in *Picture Show*, a fine justification for "moving on," better than a summer vacation "back home" to renew their faith in how rotten their roots really were. Certainly Thalia bears little resemblance to, say, Petticoat Junction or Andy Griffith's Mayberry.[15] This anti-local color dimension may explain why so many urban readers of *Picture Show* I've encountered have been so taken with the novel's "amazing realism." *The Last Picture Show* successfully articulated a generation's feelings about their origins and youth, establishing a theme and tone which can be seen in *American Graffiti,* an imitation even more famous. But *Hud* and *The Last Picture Show,* although flawed, are also good works of literature that deserve serious, attentive reading. They are solidly in the twentieth century tradition of the experimental *bildungsroman* that has produced such great works as Lawrence's *Sons and Lovers* and Joyce's *Portrait of the Artist as a Young Man.*

While it is to McMurtry's credit that his artistry markedly improved this past decade, he has also suffered an important loss. There is much to be said for those novels which have a mission to articulate—with a shock of recognition—our perception of the American scene, the American experience. Larry McMurtry has become the spokesman of his own vision at the expense of continuing his career as an authentic American *vox populi.* With the trilogy behind him, it would be fascinating to see what kind of a Western novel as cultural statement McMurtry could produce now.

Notes

[1]Critics tend to avoid impartiality with McMurtry in favor of either adulation or condemnation. Thus, most articles are justifications thinly disguised as explications, perhaps because the longest standard treatment of McMurtry is harsh. This is *Larry McMurtry* (Austin, Texas: Steck-Vaughn Southwest Writers Series, No. 23, 1969) by Thomas Landess.

[2]Elroy Bode, "Moving On...and On...and On," *Southwest Review,* 55 (1970), p. 427; L.J. Davis, *"Moving On* by Larry McMurtry," *Bookworld* (June 21, 1970), p. 6.

[3]Leslie B. Mittleman, *"Terms of Endearment,"* in *Literary Annuals, 1975,* ed. Frank McGill (Englewood Cliffs, New Jersey: Salem Press, 1977), pp. 317, 320.

[4]Is it coincidence or design that the late Brandon de Wilde played both Bob and Lonnie in the film version of these novels?

[5]Jack Schaefer, *Shane* (Boston: Houghton-Mifflin Co., Riverside Reading Series, 1964), p. 84. Further page citations from this work appear in this text. *Shane* was first published in 1949.

[6]For a full and excellent treatment of Shane as Messiah, see Michael T. Marsden, "Savior in the Saddle: The Sagebrush Testament," *Illinois Quarterly,* 36 (Dec., 1973), pp. 5-15. The definitive treatment of the religious impulse in Western literature is still Max Westbrook's "The Practical Spirit: Sacrality and the American West," first published in *Western American Literature,* 3 (Fall, 1968), pp. 193-205.

[7]Larry McMurtry, *Hud* (New York: The Popular Library, 1961), pp. 67-68. All subsequent page references are from this edition and are included in the text. *Hud* was originally published by Harper & Row in 1961 under the title *Horseman, Pass By.*

[8]McMurtry's frequent scenes of sexual explicitness may partially account for his popularity as well as, to some, his offensiveness.

[9]The grim allegory of this scene was side-stepped in the screen version of *Hud.* There, the Halmea character won an Oscar as played by Patricia Neal, carefully made up in a whiter shade of pale.

[10]As Eliot noted in "Tradition and the Individual Talent," one of the hallmarks of quality literature is its reliance upon past major works and recognition of innovation in genre development.

[11]M.L. Rosenthal, ed., *Selected Poems of William Butler Yeats* (New York: The Macmillan Co., 1962), p. 91.

[12]Larry McMurtry, *The Last Picture Show* (New York: Dell, 1966), p. 5. Further important quotes from this novel will be identified by page numbers in the text. *Picture Show* was first published by The Dial Press in 1966.

[13]Cybil Shepherd played Daisy and Jacy in film versions of these novels, both directed by Peter Bogdanovich. Ms. Shepherd, of course, is Jacy's projection of her ideal self, not what she actually is.

[14]With the names, insanity, retardation, enslavement by the land and culture, *and* death of the older order, it is difficult to miss Faulkner's presence in *The Last Picture Show.*

[15]The Pasadena of *Family* (ABC) might also qualify.

Ken Kesey, John Updike
and The Lone Ranger

Andrew S. Horton

THE LONE RANGER has been one of the most popular mythic heroes of this century. The Masked Rider and Tonto, his incredibly faithful Indian sidekick, first appeared as a Detroit radio program in 1933 and quickly became the most popular half-hour program in radio history.[1] As early as 1940 the Ranger was a million-dollar business spread over five media: radio, movies, comic strips, comic books and novels. Even in the fifties millions of Americans and foreigners around the world thrilled to the adventures of this dauntless duo. Recently senators and congressmen went on record as stating that only the single-minded efforts of the Lone Ranger could see swift justice done in the Watergate Scandal. Today, however, the Ranger's entertainment power has evolved into advertising power. Now we laugh to see the once great figure shaving or selling cars on TV, or posing as an insurance agent in a magazine ad. To many Lone Ranger fans such a shamelessly capitalistic transformation must seem the beginning of the Masked Rider's end. But from another point of view the appearance of the Lone Ranger in recent advertisements is testimony to his staying power. Certainly Madison Avenue would not dare to spoof a loser. What is it about the Ranger that accounts for his past and his present popularity?

George Trendle, the Detroit business man who thought up the Lone Ranger, has said that he wished to create a new hero who embodied the best of Robin Hood and Douglas Fairbanks in *Mark of Zorro* (p. 134). Surely the resulting character's success must have surprised Trendle and surpassed his original models. I believe there are at least six traits the Ranger possesses that help explain his mythic power: 1) he is a defender of Virtue and Justice; 2) he is a man of action; 3) he is a cowboy; 4) he is a masked man; 5) he is white; and 6) he is an American. Other mythic heroes of popular culture may boast of exhibiting some of these qualities, but none can support such an impressive combination. Robin Hood defended the poor and down-trodden, Zorro and Superman hid behind their disguises, and all of the comic book heroes (until recently) were white men of action, but the Lone Ranger managed to be all of these things and an American cowboy as well.

In this way the Ranger has become much easier for Americans in particular to identify with. He is the American Dream, seen in terms of an Old West that never existed; the West of fiction and Hollywood where life is reduced to the readily identifiable forces of good and evil. Violence seems to be the only law, but we all know that the good guys will clobber the bad guys in the end. Tarzan, Superman and Bat Man are heroes too, but Africa, outer space and Bat Caves lend these characters an air of being somehow too "un-American" to attract the following the Lone Ranger has commanded.

If much of the Masked Rider's appeal is attributed to his red-blooded American persona, how is it possible that the Ranger has outlasted other Western heroes, real and imaginary? It is impossible to completely explain away the mystique of a popular hero, but I feel there are some traits that make the Ranger unique among Western gunfighters, sheriffs, cowboys and dudes. Combining the first two points mentioned above, we can state that the Lone Ranger has both right and might on his side. But unlike many good Western cowboys who have some humanizing weakness to counterbalance their virtue, the Ranger is lily white. He never shoots to kill, he defends the middle class institutions of marriage, the home and womanhood, and he is "fair" to all racial and religious groups. He is, therefore, as his creator intended him to be, appealing to parents as well as children who regard him as "wholesome" entertainment with a solid moral overtone.

And yet while the Ranger defends the bourgeois justice and status quo, he himself is removed from the rest of society. He is not married and he has no home. He is very much in the tradition of the wandering loner (of course Tonto is always by his side, but since Tonto is an Indian, this still leaves the Ranger "alone"). Unlike many Western figures, particularly sheriffs like Matt Dillon and Wyatt Earp, who are primarily identified as working for one specific town, the Ranger is his own man on nobody's payroll and, one supposes, with no social security number. In this sense the Ranger's appeal is paradoxical. Parents may find the Lone Ranger good for their children because of his uprighteous nature, but the irony is that this man who solves the problems the other "good" people in society have is himself an outsider. After listening to a number of shows or reading some of the Ranger novels, one has the definite impression that the wronged citizens are incapable of solving life's problems by themselves. If this masked knight-errant didn't happen by in the nick of time, the implication seems to be that society would collapse under the crafty schemes of the bad guys. And conversely, these tales indicate that the Ranger could never settle down and function effectively at a nine to five job in some crossroads cow town.

As a masked man the Lone Ranger is even further removed from the humdrum of daily existence. The problem for many people is that they see too much of each other. The result is that they are bored or jealous; in the first case they remain good citizens and, in terms of the Ranger's West, in case of jealousy or anger, they become outlaws. But the Lone Ranger avoids both extremes by preserving his private identity while serving a public function. In this way he enjoys the best of both worlds. The masked identity is also a practical plus for the Lone Ranger film, TV and comic book industry because there is never any question of audience disappointment between the way he looked in this film or book and the way he appeared in that other one. Thus the Ranger's mask insures the possibility of numerous actor switches without the loss of continuity. Such, of course, has not been the case with James Bond, for instance, who is and probably always will be in most people's minds, Sean Connery.

The fact that the Ranger is a white man must not be overlooked. Certainly he is a good white man who treats Tonto with great respect, especially since Tonto saved his life, but there is never any doubt that Tonto must play Sancho Panza to his Don Quixote. Thus Tonto is even more isolated from his society than the Ranger is from white society. Tonto must stick by his friend as he battles the criminals in the Ranger's society, turning his back on his Indian background. But Tonto is important to the Ranger legend even if at times he seems to be a shadow and not an individual. He serves to make the Ranger even more unique by demonstrating a harmonious relationship between a white and a red man at a time that many whites felt the only good Indian was a dead one. While the Tonto-Lone Ranger relationship is nowhere near as explosive in social terms as Mark Twain's Huck and Jim friendship, this Western liaison is liberal enough to satisfy some of the more open-minded members of the audience while subtly continuing the theme of white supremacy.

With the growth of social consciousness that has occurred in the past decade, it is no longer possible to view the Lone Ranger with the captured innocence of yesterday. But like him or not, the Ranger continues to be a part of our popular American heritage. Recently the Lone Ranger myth has been revived in fiction by John Updike and Ken Kesey. Kesey in *One Flew Over the Cuckoo's Nest* and Updike in *Rabbit Redux* use this American myth as a means to focus on contemporary issues and to suggest alternatives to what they see as the chaos of the present.

Kesey reverses the traditional Lone Ranger story. According to tradition, the Lone Ranger was the last surviving member of a group of Texas Rangers ambushed by a criminal gang. Tonto found the Ranger, saved his life and nursed him back to health. In Kesey's novel, Tonto is saved by the Lone Ranger.

Set in a mental hospital in the Northwest, Kesey's book concerns the struggle of an Indian, Chief Bromden, to regain a sense of self-confidence and identity. Bromden, or Broom as he is called by the inmates, is the narrator. When the novel begins, he is hopelessly lost in what he describes as the "fog." He is not insane as the Big Nurse who dominates the hospital would have him believe, but merely unable to put up with life "outside." Thus the mental ward becomes for Kesey, as for so many modern writers (Gunter Grass in the *Tin Drum*, for example), an ironic comment on the insanity of the outside world as opposed to the sanity of the inmates. Broom's narration is the tale of his recovery once a larger-than-life Irish-American, ex-Korean war hero McMurphy, enters the ward.

McMurphy is a double fisted Dionysian figure. He is variously described as a gambler, a wanderer, a comic book hero and, most importantly, a "T.V. cowboy."[2] It is apparent from the first day that McMurphy arrives that either he or the Big Nurse will eventually be crushed. McMurphy, as it turns out, has worked to get into the mental ward as an alternative to serving time at a work camp. He expected a peaceful vacation but received the tyrannical rule of Miss Ratched, the Big Nurse. Unwilling to buckle under her control as the other inmates, including Broom, have done, McMurphy wages a personal war against impossible odds that can only end in his death.

That Kesey suggests McMurphy may be considered a modern day Lone Ranger has been detailed by Terry Sherwood in his article *"One Flew Over the Cuckoo's Nest* and the Comic Strip," in *Critique* (Vol. XIII, no. 1). Early in the book, as Sherwood points out, Kesey compares and contrasts his story to that of a cartoon world, "...where the figures are flat and outlined in black, jerking through some kind of goofy story that might be real funny if it weren't for the cartoon figures being real guys..." (*Cuckoo,* p. 34). The illusion/reality contrast between the "flat" cartoon world and real life is, however, great. McMurphy seems to be larger than life to the inmates, but as the Nurse knows, and McMurphy comes to admit, "He is simply a man and no more (p. 136)." Like the Lone Ranger, McMurphy rebels against injustice. But unlike the masked rider, McMurphy lives by a personal code in which what he wishes to do is just, and whatever stops him is unjust. McMurphy is, therefore, simultaneously a parallel to and a parody of the Ranger. He is out for himself, but in exerting his individuality, he points a way for others to live their own lives.

Whereas McMurphy has a healthy effect on all the inmates, Chief Broom benefits most. The Tonto-Lone Ranger relationship develops from the start of McMurphy's stay when Broom notes he feels McMurphy knows his secret; that he is only pretending to be a deaf mute. When McMurphy actually corners Broom and calls his bluff, the friendship becomes official. The result of the friendship is that Tonto again believes in himself and his own strength. As the book ends, Broom escapes from the hospital and heads back to his home on the Colombia River where his tribe has been cheated out of land by the government in order to build a dam. We do not know the end of his story but we do know that he is on the road home to self-realization: "Mostly I'd just like to look over the country around the gorge again, just to bring some of it clear in my mind again. I been away a long time (p. 272)."

For Kesey the question today is not how to save society from evil, but how to save oneself from destruction. In Kesey's myth, the Lone Ranger becomes a sacrifice for Tonto. McMurphy is an example of what one man is capable of doing, but he lives too openly and too intensely to survive. Chief Broom as Tonto escapes because he is able to incorporate the Lone Ranger's fierce individualism while preserving his deaf-mute protective mask to those around him. But once he has strangled the masked rider, it is up to Chief to make it on his own in the outside world.

The world itself is a clue to that survival. Unlike McMurphy and the popular Lone Ranger and Tonto, Chief Broom uses a pen to expose corruption. Broom as author and narrator has created the book we read. He succeeds in turning his personal struggle into fiction or art which is "...the truth even if it didn't happen" (p. 13). Thus he transcends the real of self, which McMurphy is unable to do, and provides, by means of his writing, a socially useful tool for the potential cure of the millions of "inmates" who may read it.

Even in the popular Lone Ranger stories the bad guys outnumber the good. But according to Broom, it is the system itself that turns good guys into bad. The Big Nurse's hospital is a metaphor for society. What Broom exposes in his writing, therefore, is not simply the corruption of one institution, but the workings of the entire "Combine" which he explains controls the whole country.

Kesey is not didactic in handling the Lone Ranger parallel. There is in fact only one reference that directly names this American hero; a character comments before McMurphy is supposed to escape (but does not), "I'd like to stand there at the window with a silver bullet in my hand and ask 'Who wawz that'er masked man?' "(p. 258). In general, Kesey hints at the parallel through references to comic book characters and TV cowboy descriptions. The book makes sense by itself without thought of the Lone Ranger or Tonto. But just as one would miss much if he were to read Joyce's *Ulysses* without considering the wanderings of Odysseus, so too a reading of Kesey's highly suggestive novel that does not consider this parallel is that much poorer.

John Updike's *Rabbit Redux* is a complex novel with many threads woven into the narrative of Henry Angstrum's effort to re-relate to himself and others in a rapidly changing society. Set in the fictional Brewer, Pennsylvania in 1969, the action coincides with the first Apollo moon shot, suggesting Rabbit's own "take-off" from life as he has known it. In yet another parallel, Updike carefully introduces and develops the Lone Ranger theme.

Unlike Kesey, Updike makes specific reference to the popular Western hero. As the novel begins, Rabbit, now known to most as Harry, is living as he has lived for the past ten years since he returned to his wife (his brief escape from marriage described in *Rabbit Run*). He works as a linotype setter for the local newspaper, returns home after a drink at the Phoenix Bar, eats, watches TV and falls into bed with his wife Janice. This particular evening, however, Janice claims to be working late for her father, a used car dealer, while she is actually having an affair with a Greek-American salesman who works for her father. Rabbit, at home in front of the TV set, watches Carol Burnett and Gomer Pyle doing a funny skit about the Lone Ranger. According to the skit, Burnett is the Ranger's wife who does not see life as idealistically as her husband does. "You're never home," she says, "you keep disappearing in a cloud of dust with a hearty 'Heigh-ho, Silver'."[3] Rabbit laughs while Burnett complains again. "What do I ever get from you? A silver bullet." She opens a door and a bushel of bullets crashes down and floods the floor (p. 29). Tonto then appears, not as an Indian, but as a "TV Negro" who appears interested in Burnett. The William Tell Overture is played and the two men exit, but when Burnett puts on "Indian Love Call," Tonto returns to claim the Ranger's wife.

Rabbit laughs again, but not heartily. Somehow the skit isn't funny any more. The myth Rabbit had accepted without question in childhood no longer rings true. He realized he knows nothing about Tonto. Why is Tonto riding with the Lone Ranger? What does a red man get out of following a white man's law? Rabbit has no answer. In a sense, however, the whole novel deals with Rabbit's attempt to come to an understanding of the problems raised by this skit. Rabbit's questioning of the Lone Ranger-Tonto relationship foreshadows the more important personal question to which he will be subjected. And the wife-stealing theme in the skit is an ironic parallel to Janice's affair with Charlie Stavros. Furthermore, the similarity between the skit and Rabbit's life, casts Rabbit in the role of the Ranger, for better or worse.

Updike presents the Lone Ranger theme on two levels. On one hand, there are the direct references to the Lone Ranger, Silver (especially the color silver) and Tonto. Indirectly, on the other hand, the opening skit establishes the Lone Ranger parallel which we cannot help but remember even when there are no specific references. On this level other facts begin to relate to Rabbit and the Ranger myth. Of these, the most important is Updike's use of movie titles. Throughout the book we are given flashes of the movie marquee announcing in order of appearance, *2001* (space theme), *True Grit, Butch Cassidy and the Sundance Kid,* and, near the end, *Midnight Cowboy.*

Like the Lone Ranger, Rabbit believes in America. Janice sizes him up as a man who "... wants to live an old-fashioned life, but nobody does that any more, and he feels it (p. 54)." Rabbit's old fashioned beliefs put him in conflict with everyone around him; his son Nelson finds him a square, his wife deserts him in order to be treated like a real woman, and his sister calls him "ridiculous."

Harry's first showdown occurs with Janice's lover, Charlie Stavros, at a Green tavern in town where Rabbit has taken the family for supper. Rabbit is aware that Charlie and Janice are acting too friendly, but he is even more disturbed by Charlie's anti-Vietnam stand. This to Rabbit is treason. The heated debate becomes framed in cowboy and Indian terms when Charlie sums up the Vietnam situation by saying: "We thought it was one more Cherokee uprising. The trouble is, the Cherokees outnumber us now." And Rabbit responds: "Oh those fucking poor Indians,... What were we supposed to do, let 'em have the whole continent for a campfire site? (p. 51)." Charlie is right; the Indians (the non-whites) do outnumber the whites. Cowboy and Indian salutations are no longer feasible. Rabbit cannot accept this verdict though he does add in his mind, "Sorry Tonto." Even Janice appears as the enemy: "dark and tense: an Indian (p. 51)."

Vietnam is an important issue for Rabbit even though he has not had to serve in the war. But a much more immediate problem is that of the Blacks. Harry becomes personally involved with the contemporary American Negro after Janice leaves home. Alone with his son, Rabbit picks up a young, rich, white runaway girl, Jill, who moves into the house as mistress and housekeeper. Soon Skeeter, a young black Viet vet who has jumped bail on a drug charge joins them. This unlikely foursome become friends and fellow searchers after peace of mind.

Skeeter has his theory about the difference between Tonto (Indians) and the American Black. According to Skeeter, the Indians were wiped out because they could not adjust to an agricultural economy. The Black, on the other hand, "was from West Africa, where they had agriculture (p. 212)." Thus the Negroes survived despite exploitation, unlike the Tontos of America who could not. The Lone Ranger is thus attacked from all sides. Rabbit loses Janice to a Greek (who is American but Rabbit refuses to accept him as such), and Jill to Skeeter, who calls himself "the new Black Jesus."

It is paradoxical that Rabbit must lose before he can gain. Because the title is *Rabbit Redux* (with the dictionary meaning of "redux" given on the first page) we realize before starting the novel that Rabbit must come to some kind of healing experience. Ironically enough, although the new Tontos, black and foreign, do not follow the Ranger, the Lone Ranger is nevertheless finally helped by them. Charlie "remakes" Janice so she feels ready to return home, just as Skeeter teaches Rabbit to be forceful; he has Rabbit read from Frederick Douglass, "A man without force...is without the essential dignity of humanity (p. 247)."

Rabbit's growth can be traced more clearly through Updike's use of the silver bullet motif. Carol Burnett complained in the skit that she never received anything from her husband except silver bullets. Harry has treated Janice in much the same way, filling their lives with material objects rather than love and understanding. The night before Janice walks out, for example, Updike places the reader inside her head so that we know that her affair with Charlie is not a wild fling, but a serious reaching out to someone who treats her as a human being. Janice not only wishes to escape temporarily from Rabbit, but from the things their life represents. And of their possessions, one object mentioned a number of times is their silver threaded Lustrex chair. This chair becomes a symbol of their old life as Rabbit and Janice are reunited at the end of the book. As they stand together at the charred ruins of their burnt home (Skeeter's work!), they see among the debris, "the silver threads of the Lustrex chair gleam through an acid mist of fumes (p. 288)." Having viewed the wreckage of their past, they make their first decision since joining together again: to sell the house and all that remains.

Silver is referred to at other moments as well. Before the house burns down, Rabbit watches Skeeter make love to Jill. Instead of feeling jealous that this young Black has taken his partner in his own home, Rabbit is struck by the beauty of the sex act. "A most delicate slipping silvery sound touches up the silence now (p. 260)," writes Updike of the moment. The fact that silver is used to describe the sound is significant for it shows the beginning of a transferral in Rabbit's mind from the notion of silver as object (the bullet, chair), to silver as motion. Rabbit now appreciates the beauty of action.

The next morning Rabbit awakes beside Jill to remember a dream. He recalls:

Pajasek (his boss) and he were in a canoe, paddling upstream, through a dark green country; their destination felt to be a distant mountain striped and folded like a tablecloth. "When can I have my silver bullet?" Rabbit asked him. "You promised." "Fool," Pajasek told him. "Stupid." "You know so much more," Rabbit answered, nonsensically, and his heart opened in a flood of light (p. 263).

Rabbit can make no sense of it, but in relation to the rest of his story, several points are clear. The dream follows the Skeeter-Jill love-making and precedes Rabbit's sacking from his job. Since Rabbit is unaware that he is to be fired, the inclusion of his boss, Pajasek, must be seen as apprehension on Rabbit's part. The fact that the dream occurred after Rabbit's awareness of the beauty of sex helps explain, I feel, why his "heart opened in a flood of light." In regard to Rabbit's growth from an object-oriented existence toward an action and experience-centered life, the old Rabbit worried about his silver bullet (security, job, money) and the new Rabbit is aware of his own folly.

Rabbit has been led back to himself. His return to Janice is not, however, the promise of a re-run of the past ten years. Both partners have grown as human beings. Updike ends this chapter in Rabbit's life with a question ("O.K.?") rather than a statement because their future is not guaranteed. And yet one feels their chance at happiness is much better than it was at first. There is hope because they are beginning to love again. As they bed down in a cheap motel they are still too awkward toward each other to make love. But Rabbit's new concept of "silverness" is present. Janice turns over in bed: "The slither of sheets as she rotates her body is a silver music, sheets of pale noise extending outward unresisted by space (p. 351)." Rabbit's metamorphosis is complete; the Lone Ranger is trying to become a man, not a super hero, a fellow human being rather than a masked rider.

It is interesting that two contemporary writers of the stature of Updike and Kesey should turn to the same popular myth to express their visions of life in America. Updike tried to universalize *The Centaur* by suggesting a parallel to the Greek myths, but he is much more natural and thus successful in *Rabbit Redux* because the Lone Ranger myth is thoroughly American and universal by implication. Kesey is successful in his novel in a similar way. The use of the Lone Ranger in these works is a healthy sign that American writers are turning to popular heroes who used to seem so right, and using them to show us in startling images why they have turned sour. Rabbit comments about the Lone Ranger and Tonto. "It seemed a correct dream then, red and white together, red loving white as naturally as stripes in the flag. Where has 'the side of right' gone (p.30)?"

Notes

[1]David Willson Parker, A Descriptive Analysis of the Lone Ranger as a Form of Popular Art. Ph.D. dissertation, Northwestern University, 1955 (Film), p. 126.

[2]Ken Kesey, *One Flew Over the Cuckoo's Nest* (New York, 1962), p. 73. Subsequent quotes identified in the text.

[3]John Updike, *Rabbit Redux* (Greenwich, Conn.: 1971), p. 29. Subsequent quotes are noted in the text.

The Salinger Story, Or, Have It Your Way

Lawrence Jay Dessner

THIEVES STEAL, the brutal strike and when they are apprehended, confronted with their cache of booty or with their bruised victims, society is vindicated by their shamefacedness, however verbally denied. There are other violators of the public order, whose crimes are less obvious. They may even believe that what they are doing is preventing crime. When these are confronted by their accusers, there is no shame, no outpouring of defensive rhetoric. Yes I did it, they will say, but look what a wonderful thing it was to do. The accusers may be the ones to lower their eyes.

It is with such a culprit that we have now to deal. His act is the writing of a best-selling, widely and loudly acclaimed novel, one that more than twenty-five years later is still in print, still read, still publicly admired by many of those professors of higher learning who ought, at least by now, to know better. J.D. Salinger's *The Catcher in the Rye* has long since been accused of several million counts of impairing the morals of a minor. He has doled out candy which rots more than the victim's teeth; he has thrown us apples in which fragments of razor blades were embedded. And as we became dizzy, as our lips bled, he smiled down at us—a smile that said, Yes, Yes, minds are made to go soft, lips to bleed; blood *is* sweet, and so is the taste and smell of our soul's surrender. So while a few have found Salinger a pernicious influence, the many have gratefully applauded what he did to them. He gave them Holden Caulfield, an idealization of their worst selves, to cherish. While they were doing so, their best selves, their potential to be, in whatever way, better, was ignored, despised, unexercised, indefinitely postponed.

In the ten years after its publication in July of 1951 *The Catcher in the Rye* sold over one and one half million copies. It was adopted as a text in some 300 American colleges and universities, and in countless secondary schools.[1] A great deal of what is called "research" was published on it. In dismay, George Steiner did what he could to stem the flood. He disparaged what he named "The Salinger Industry," called Holden Caulfield "the young lout," and bemoaned comparisons of him with "Alyosha Karamazov, Aeneas, Ulysses, Gatsby, Ishmael, Hans Castorp, and Dostoevsky's Idiot." Steiner added, mischievously but with anger too, that these comparisons "were always rather to [Caulfield's] own advantage." He spoke of the novel's flattery of the ignorant and of ignorance itself, and of its "shoddy...half-culture," and he tried to discover why it is that "literary criticism [is] so determined to get [things] out of proportion." Why, this "gross devaluation of standards."[2]

Steiner's scolding had no apparent influence. This "summer novel," as Harvey Breit called it, a "summer novel" being one which invites us to "relax our...demands on...literature," to suppress our "intelligence,"[3] continues to flourish, to confuse the already confused, to bedevil tenure and promotion committees, to demonstrate the flaccid condition of our culture. The most common critical strategy in the inflating of the Sallinger balloon is to compare it to works of uncontested value and significance. The theme of *The Catcher in the Rye*, one might learn from perusing the *Western Humanities Review,* derives from "ancient and honorable narrative tradition, perhaps the most profound in western fiction,...the Quest.[4] This article, the work of not one but two professors of literature, and clearly the straw that broke George Steiner's back, leaps then to Stephen Dedalus, Eugene Gant and Natty Bumppo. The leap is over elementary logic as well. It should not take two professors to discover that all who share Shakespeare's themes are not his equals. This is the reverse of McCarthyism. Here we have *value* by association, as with McCarthyism, the association need not be more than a flight of the accuser's—or the idolater's—fancy.

The Catcher in the Rye has been most often compared to Mark Twain's *Adventures of Huckleberry Finn,* compared, that is, in terms of form, characters, plot, humor and all this so assiduously that comparison of value, that comparison which would justify making all the others, is ignored, value tacitly assumed. The novels are "akin also in ethical-social import." "Each book," another critic continues, "is a devastating criticism of American society and voices a morality of love and humanity."[5] Steiner grits his teeth; Mark Twain turns over yet again in his grave. And I cannot forbear asking about that "morality of love and humanity." Is there some other kind? Is there a morality of love but not of humanity, or of humanity and not of love? Is this morality "voiced" by Salinger, by Holden? Have we been reading the same book? May one professor turn another one over on his knee and deliver corporal punishment? Is the view of American society which Salinger's novel devastatingly criticizes a fair and accurate view of that society? Is Pencey Prep more than an ill-tempered caricature of some lesser Andover? Is there, in all of *The Catcher in the Rye,* any reference to the historical or political or economic conditions of its moment? Well, I guess there must be, because one of the more eminent commentators on modern literature, after quoting Thoreau and breathlessly wondering "what is the sound of one hand clapping," assures us that "Salinger proves...to be seriously engaged by a current and a traditional aspect of reality in America."[6] Wow! Both a current *and* a traditional aspect of reality. Once upon a time, Robert Browning sent a copy of his famously obscure long poem, *The Ring and the Book,* to a literary friend who had been seriously ill. "It's my mind," his friend cried out from his sickbed. "My strength is coming back but my mind is going. I can't understand the English language any more."

Since the earlier days of Salinger's prominence, criticism has followed the method of praise by association and implication. Some of the more imaginative professors have found it useful, in considering Salinger, to discuss Beckett and Camus,[7] Saul Bellow,[8] and Martin Buber.[9] And no doubt many other giants have been hitched to Salinger's wagon. Nor should we be surprised to learn that *The Catcher in the Rye* "is a masterpiece of symbolist fiction."[10] There are even signs that the period of evaluation, such as it was, is over, and scholars can turn to source studies. One of our colleagues prints his speculations on the possibility of Sherwood Anderson's influence on Salinger.[11] Confirmation of Salinger's place in the pantheon comes from an energetic German scholar who reviews over one hundred critics and concludes that Salinger has made it into the canon of American literature.[12] Here is a fine chance for us to brush up on our German—what a reward for learning the language for our degrees!

Literary judgments of value are usually made tacitly, as assumptions, not logically argued. Merely to write about Salinger, to mention him in the same breath as Mark Twain or, heaven help us Dostoevsky, is to make the claim for his place with the immortals. We must assume that these valuations are made in full sincerity. Many critics, like many readers, enjoyed *The Catcher in the Rye*, felt, in the reading, and in the remembering of the reading, the kind of satisfaction they had come to know as aesthetic pleasure. About their pleasure there is no room for dispute. One does not speculate, nowadays, in public, on one's colleagues' taste. But on the morning after, when mind awakes from its binge or its sleep, and pleasures are re-evaluated, criticism has its opportunity. The present critic leaps, no doubt bruising shins and egos, to seize it.

Beware of the novelists bearing gifts. The more delicious and enthralling the gifts, the more wary we must be. Best of the sweets Salinger has Holden giftwrap and deliver to us is the idea that to the degree that we like Holden Caulfield we were better than anyone who doesn't. The method of Salinger's flamboyant and insidious flattery goes like this: Line up all the people in the world who we, in our weakness, our failures of sympathy, our ignorance, our narrow-mindedness, have ever allowed ourselves to hate. Include in this line-up caricatures of people we know we should not have hated. (Once having hated them, we have a vested interest in seeing them worthy of hatred.) Include persons we hated because we knew they were better than we were. (There is nothing like jealousy to prompt and sustain hate.) Now introduce before that line-up a tortured, bleeding and sublimely "cute" victim of all the insults and injuries all of us have ever imagined ourselves to have suffered. Let this victim be on the edge of insanity, the result, of course, of what others have done to him. Let him ooze the sentimental notion that the doctrine of Original Sin, and all its modern parallels, have been revoked. This is crucial. Not only does it let our victim be perfect, it removes any excuse the evil-doers might otherwise offer on their behalf. Let our victim believe that what the world needs now is not love, not even Coca-Cola, but that fool's gold, Sincerity. He himself has it of course, and some of it rubs off on his admirers, but no one else has it at all. Now the scene is set and the action commences. Blood in his eyes and trickling from his battered little nose, our victim raises a machine-gun and shoots everyone lined up before him. And he cries, weeps, as he does so. You see, utterly guilty as his tormentors are, he forgives them, he likes them!

What super-human magnanimity! What delicious revenge, too! Who could resist enjoying this spectacle? Few have.

We may pause here to examine some of the procedures that make Saliger's trick possible. A student of "The Language of *The Catcher in the Rye*" assures us that "Holden's language is authentic teenage speech." That is surely open to qualification, but those teenagers are now the parents of teenagers. Holden's speech mannerisms, we are told, are "purely arbitrary, with no discernible meaning."[13] With that we may take issue. Holden says: "I *really* did," "He's my brother *and all,* and, "I'm a pacifist, *if you want to know the truth."* Teenagers of today say: "*Y'know,"* "He's my brother *and everything,* and, when asked if they are planning to do something, or if they liked or disliked something, they answer, "Not really." Like today's version of it, Holden's style is a cowering and sentimental yearning to like and be liked. The conveyance of information doesn't matter nearly as much as the expression of goodwill: "You know what I mean, you share with me that knowledge neither of us can or wants to formulate. We are so open, so utterly sincere that we don't need language, but it is warm and cozy to use it this way, to remind ourselves of our special fellowship in the mystical community." And in a different context, with a shift of emphasis, the same words mean this: "*I* know, but you? you couldn't possibly know, and even if I wanted to tell you, which I don't you couldn't understand."

Caulfield's language—he is, of course, the only one in the novel to use it—is highly functional. It is an arrogant weapon of sullen exclusion or a wistfully affectionate means of self-deception. In either mode, it disguises its function of denying communication behind coy, mock innocence. It says, "Who me?" even before anyone asks for clarification. It is a constant reminder and reinforcement of its own solipsism.

The strategy and function of Holden's language can be conveniently noted in the larger structures of individual scenes. When Holden's friend Jane, the checkers player whose father we have just been told is a "booze hound," weeps, "This tear plopped down on the checkerboard. On one of the red squares—boy, I can still see it. She just rubbed it into the board with her finger. I don't know why, but it bothered hell out of me" (ch. 11). (I wonder if those who have made Salinger their hero believe alcoholism is an illness rather than a crime to be condemned with strong language.) I note the repeated denial, by Holden, that he understands the reasons for Jane's tears. Look at his use of "just," a bit of teenage style that persists into our own day. "Just": it is a gesture of refusal to see or allow significance in the action described. It is the habitual insistence on the meaninglessness of events or on the worthlessness of language to convey feeling. Behind this deliberately obvious subterfuge, of course, is the real Holden, who feels things so deeply—much more deeply than those who try to use language— that, for his own survival, he must deny his palpitating heart. He knows why Jane cries, as all know why, but to admit that he knows is to share himself with us. And he won't and he can't, and the "he" in this is Salinger, and Holden is his disguise. We are supposed to see through the disguise, for its message is that we are a good deal less sensitive than they are.

We have no reason to assume that Salinger's attitudes differ from those of Holden Caulfield. It is the author's obligation to unmistakably untangle himself from his hero, or at least to give the reader the means to discover their relationship. But Salinger does neither. It seems absurd that a grown man, and a literate man at that, should hold the jejune opinions of Holden Caulfield. But he does and he lacks the grace or courage to say so outright, in or out of the novel. There isn't a whisper of any other view of life emananting from either quarter. We must take Salinger's silence in the novel to give consent. He is evidently angry that with the exception of himself—and his Holden—sincerity is in very short supply. "Then, after the Rockettes, a guy came out in a tuxedo and roller skates on, and started skating under a bunch of little tables, and telling jokes while he did it. He was a very good skater and all, but I couldn't enjoy it much because I kept picturing him practicing to be a guy that roller-skates on the stage" (ch. 18). Perfect sincerity requires and implies perfect spontaneity. And of course this utterly denies all the arts of life as well as the arts of Art. How does one know, Holden inquires, if the lawyer who has saved his client's life did so because "he really *wanted* to save guys' lives, or because...what [he] *really* wanted to do was to be a terrific lawyer, with everybody slapping [him] on the back and congratulating [him] in court when the goddam trial was over" (ch. 22). This is the question Holden asks of everyone. Its force is rhetorical. Holden wants a guarantee of the purity of human motive. He has been given everything else he wanted, but this complete absolution, of himself and his world, he cannot have. He cries "phoney," and takes up his bat and ball and leaves the game. We are to play by his rules or His Holiness will not play with us.

There is little point in using Salinger's text to show that Holden himself behaves with less than perfect kindness, less than Saintly sincerity. And to take that line against this novel is to accept its premise. *The Catcher in the Rye* urges the young to destroy their own, their only world, and to take refuge in their own soft dream-world peopled by themselves and by shadows of their perfected selves. No adolescent has ever entirely avoided this temptation. All of us had what used to be called "growing pains," fell into what used to be called a "brown study." Among the very rich, in our very rich country, all pleasures, no matter how self-deluding and self-defeating, no matter how selfish, are seized upon, and sold, and admired. Holden is a child of wealth, and most children wish they were too. The richer one is, the longer one may prolong one's adolescence. That is what Holden Caulfield is doing, and what Salinger and his admirers, are praising. Joan Didion comes to my aid here: She said that *Franny and Zooey* was "spurious" because of Salinger's "tendency to flatter the essential triviality within each of his readers." Its "appeal is precisely that it is self-help copy: it emerges finally as *Positive Thinking* for the upper middle classes, as *Double Your Energy and Live Without Fatigue* for Sarah Lawrence girls."[14]

Those of us of a "certain age," brought up in the same streets and schools as Holden Caulfield, may be especially susceptible to Salinger's siren song. The present writer, along with a goodly percentage of our country's literati, shared Holden Caulfield's environment. We wondered about the ducks in Central Park lakes. We enjoyed a good cry about the sadness of life, the disappointments, the rain falling on our tennis courts. We too, in Salinger's most un-mean streets, discovered puberty, the painful way. But we managed to grow up, more or less; to see that it was not true, ever, that everybody was out of step but ourselves, to see that the words "compromise," "compassion," "tact," even "hypocrisy," were not obscenities which desecrated God's creation, but marks of the fact that none of us was, himself, God.

Holden's youthful idealism, his bitterness toward the world he never made might have, had a Holden himself come before us, made for a successful novel. What could be funnier than the confessions of such a one as he? And while we would laugh at Holden, he would be laughing at us. How young we were, how charmingly silly. We could have had some good laughs, shed a tear for auld lang syne, shaken hands all round, and been on our way. But Salinger's Holden Caulfield is made of soggy cardboard. The death of his younger brother Allie hangs over his story forbidding anyone in it more than a momentary laugh. That death, utterly unrelated to the vapid social criticism which is Holden's prime activity, should have made Holden atypical, a special case whose opinions may be regarded only as pointers to his private distress. But Salinger ignores this; evidently he wants Holden's opinions on the general condition of society to be highly regarded, and he wants no one involved, character, author, reader, critic, to see his story as a comedy. We must, out of courtesy, courtesy that has been uncourteously forced upon us, take it all with high seriousness. Salinger needs the dead Allie in his novel so that we may not laugh. Yet the story itself is the quintessential comedy, the story of maturity looking back, with a wince and a smile and a guffaw at its own immaturity.

No character of Holden Caulfield is the only certifiable "phoney" in the novel. No youth, no matter how emotionally shaken, goes so long, so seriously single-mindedly after his real and imagined enemies. When the real Holden Caulfields encounter the terrors, such as they are, of their gilded ghettoes, they stumble every now and then on those insights which will add up to their definition of being grown-up. Not Holden. His larger considerations are bogus. He meanders about as if he were free to find out about things for himself, free to stumble on the other sides of the "phoney" question, to learn why people behave the way they do. But Salinger has put blinders around the boy. He never learns anything; never considers anything antagonistic to his sustaining faith that everything and everybody is wrong. It is as if Holden grew up at the knee of Abbie Hoffman—but even that is more funny than true. No matter how doctrinaire the upbringing, bright boys have a way of seeing around the blinders their elders set in place. But then Holden is not a real boy at all; he is Salinger's dream-boy, the boy who will not grow up. He is immaturity's best defense, a non-stop assault on maturity.[15]

But after all this we really should petition the court to reduce the charge brought against Mr. Salinger. Boys being what we know them to be, despite the example of Holden, the crime is not impairment of the morals of a minor, but only attempted impairment. No real harm will be done by this book, unless professors succeed in making it a classic. *The Catcher in the Rye* is no more than an insult to all boys, to us who have been boys, and to the girls and ex-girls too. It is an insult to childhood and to adulthood. It is an insult to our ideas of civilization, to our ideal land in which ladies and gentlemen try to grow up, try to find and save their dignity.

Notes

[1] Robert Gutwillling, "Everybody's Caught *The Catcher in the Rye*," *New York Times Book Review Paperback Section*, Jan. 15, 1961.

[2] George Steiner, "The Salinger Industry," *Nation*, 189 (Nov. 14, 1959), 360-63.

[3] Quoted from *The Atlantic Monthly* by Marvin Laser and Norman Fruman in *Studies in J.D. Salinger*, ed. Laser and Fruman (New York: Odyssey Press, 1963), p. 13.

[4] Arthur Heiserman and James E. Miller, Jr., "J.D. Salinger: Some Crazy Cliff," *Western Humanities Review*, 10 (Spring, 1956), 129-37.

[5] Edgar Branch, "Mark Twain and J.D. Salinger: A Study in Literary Continuity," *American Quarterly*, 9 (Summer, 1957), 144-58.

[6] Ihab Hassan, "J.D. Salinger: Rare Quixotic Gesture," *Radical Innocence: Studies in the Contemporary American Novel* (Princeton University Press, 1961), pp. 260-89.

[7] Robert Lee Stuart, "The Writer-in-Waiting," *Christian Century*, 82:20 (May 19, 1965), 647-49.

[8] MaxwellGeismar, "J.D. Salinger: The Wise Child and the *New Yorker* School of Fiction," *American Moderns: From Rebellion to Conformity* (New York: Hill and Wang, 1958).

[9] Paul Levine, "J.D. Salinger: The Development of the Misfit Hero," *Twentieth Century Literature* 4 (Oct., 1958), 92-99.

[10] Clinton Trowbridge, "Salinger's Symbolic Use of Character and Detail in *The Catcher in the Rye*," *Cimarron Review*, 4 (June 1968), 5-11.

[11] James Bryan, "Sherwood Anderson and *The Catcher in the Rye*: A Possible Influence," *Notes on Contemporary Literature*, 1:5 (Nov. 1971), 2-6.

[12] Peter Freese, "Jerome David Salinger: *The Catcher in the Rye*," *Literatur in Wissenshaft und Unterricht*, 1:2 (1968), 123-52.

[13] Donald P. Costello, "The Language of *The Catcher in the Rye*," *American Speech*, 34 (Oct. 1959), 172-81.

[14] Joan Didion, "Finally (Fashionably) Spurious," *National Review*, 9 (Nov. 18, 1961) 341-42.

[15] In many respects Philip Roth's *My Life as a Man* may be read as a commentary on *Catcher*. As an antidote to the extravagances of academic criticism, try Saul Bellow, "Deep Readers of the World, Beware!" *New York Times Book Review*, Feb. 15, 1959.

Ludwig Lewisohn: Can He Still Help Us? A Reconsideration of *Expression in America*

Jerrold Hirsch

LUDWIG LEWISOHN. Ludwig *who*? It is a question that contemporary Americans can pose without fear of embarrassment. The Twayne United States Series, now 258 volumes, has a book on Zane Grey and Paddy Chayefsky, but not on Lewisohn. Yet in the 1920s Lewisohn was a widely read and admired literary critic. His work both as translator and critic helped introduce Americans to the work of the French symbolist poets and modern German novelists and dramatists.[1] His books on modern drama and his column in the *Nation* gave critical support to naturalist playwrights and aimed to develop an audience that would regard the theater not as a diversion but as a forum for the exploration of the human dilemma.[2] The various selections Lewisohn put together in *A Book of Modern Criticism* (1919) included the work of foreign writers as well as Americans.[3] It was designed to show rebellious American writers and critics that they were not alone, and to provide them with ammunition in their battle against the literary status-quo.

Criticism, Lewisohn claimed, was a form of *creative expression*. And because he was also a novelist (though he wanted to be remembered for his novels, today they are no better known than his criticism is), his claims did not seem simply the attempt of a critic to gain equal status with poets and novelists.[4] The publication of *Expression in America* (1932), a study of American literature, was greeted as a literary event. It seemed to many the capstone of the work of an influential and illuminating critic. His anthology, *Creative America* (1933), was based on the critical principles he had developed in *Expression in America*. Today, *Expression in America* is out of print. It is forgotten. So, too, is Lewisohn.

Strictly speaking this is not true. There are pieces on Lewisohn's childhood in South Carolina, his role in introducing modern German literature to American audiences, his anti-communism and on his Zionist activities and writings.[5] His work is briefly noted, sometimes only footnoted, in surveys of American literary criticism; it makes a useful exhibit in studies of the impact of Freud on American novelists and critics; it can be used to support a thesis about the end of American innocence, or the impact of ethnicity on American culture.[6]. Unpublished dissertations treat Lewisohn as a Jewish novelist, as an intellectual trying to reconcile his Jewish and American identities, and as a literary critic.[7]

All these writings are helpful and sometimes illuminating, but all also

98

indicate that as a critical force, as someone who influences our view of authors and their works, Lewisohn is dead. And this is the tacit, if not explicit, assumption underlying whatever discussion of Lewisohn there is. Thus the dissertation on Lewisohn's literary criticism is based on a conclusion it never tries to prove: while Lewisohn's fight for free expression and his anti-provincialism were worthy of praise his literary criticism is valuable to us only as a reflection of an exciting and intellectually significant period in American literary history.[8]

Maybe so. And if so the treatment Lewisohn has received is adequate: that is, it might be further developed and given more dimension, but it will remain an aspect of American literary history rather than a part of a living American literature. But the case against Lewisohn needs to be proved, not assumed. It has not even been argued in a long time.

The question is one that Lewisohn himself thought was central to the study of American writing: in *Expression in America* he referred to how Goethe once remarked of a poet: "He can help us no longer." Goethe's comment provided Lewisohn with a principle:

It is the mark of the essential poet that he continues to help us across the ages and across revolutions in morals, religions, economic systems. That a given writer was fashionable in his own day or brilliantly entertained his generation continues to be interesting to the antiquarian study of that day and that generation. In the history of literature conceived of as the ultimate articulateness and intercommunication of man concerning himself and his fate the works of such writers have no place. (p. xxvii)[9]

The fundamental question about Lewisohn, then, is, can he still help us? Has he something to say about literature, about American writing that endures? Do his remarks on individual authors elucidate their particular qualities? Can Lewisohn's voice enrich our appreciation of our literature? My own answer to these questions is a qualified yes. But the first task is to reopen the discussion.

One way to do that is to look at what reviewers wrote about the book and thus have a sense of what they thought noteworthy about *Expression in America*. What qualities did they praise? Which did they find objectionable? Many praised his style and his elevated view of literature. Some attacked Lewisohn's criticism of the Puritans, and his use of Freudian analysis. Marxist critics thought he ignored the class basis of art and did not understand the modern state. And those writers interested in a pure aestheticism, a formalistic criticism and art, found no inspiration in *Expression in America*. Literary historians questioned the validity of Lewisohn's method.

Despite some superficial reviews, some inordinate praise and, much less frequently, inordinate hostility, the initial discussion of *Expression in America* helped define some of the book's qualities. Lewisohn's style won over many reviewers: "[H]e writes in that style of flexible yet weighted beauty which is the best product of the English tradition sharpened by continental clarity." "Who else," another reviewer asked, "has so triumphant a faith that literature is the supreme expression and essential glory of every age; who writes a prose at once so intellectually precise and so emotionally aglow?" And Carl Van Doren thought Lewisohn "touched nothing he did not elevate." However, a minority found Lewisohn's writing merely inflated—that his lofty phrases did not have substantive value.[10]

Reviewers found Lewisohn's discussions of individual authors discerning and illuminating. Joseph Wood Krutch declared: "No matter whom he is discussing he reveals both an ever delightful shrewdness and a fine sensitivity so that almost every page is studded with brilliant *apercus*." Lewisohn, Krutch thought, treated the great writers "as though they were his contemporaries," and was "concerned only with that part of them which is still living in the sense that it still raises living issues." Other critics praised the "freshness," the "scrupulous judicial authority" of Lewisohn's evaluations of writers. Even his controversial opinions were hailed as evidence that "Lewisohn has yet another qualification of the great critic: he is not afraid to stand alone." According to Carl Van Doren, *Expression in America* helped define a new canon of American literature: "He has put down the previously mighty and exalted the previously humble without self-conscious argument." To others Lewisohn's views seemed prejudiced.

Some critics attacked Lewisohn's "Puritanphobia" and his Freudianism: Lewisohn "would lighten his argument and clarify his generally beautiful exposition if he did not see Puritanism written over every kind of stupidity, and intellectual and economic tyranny." Literary historian Ernest Leisy argued that "reducing an author to positive or negative sexuality does not advance much the problem of critical interpretation." One reviewer thought that "Lewisohn's confessedly Freudian analysis is interesting but somehow less necessary than he would lead one to believe."[12]

Even critics who were not impressed by Lewisohn's analysis of the Puritans or use of Freud still found him perceptive on individual writers. They were, however, rejecting that aspect of Lewisohn's work that claimed to be "a portrait of the American spirit," a study of the national character. Such a study, several reviewers pointed out, required attention to history and environment—factors Lewisohn either discounted or ignored. Blaming the Puritans for everything in our cultural history which one does not like, one reviewer argued, is not an historical analysis, but only evidence of Lewisohn's "curious obsession against the Puritans."[13]

Most reviewers took *Expression in America* seriously. Even Granville Hicks (then in his Marxist phase), thought he found more evidence of the breakdown of liberalism and individualism, concluded, "that, if individualism is declining, here is surely one of the glories of the twilight." There were, however, a few reviewers who simply dismissed Lewisohn's work as dated. In a new time and to a new generation, they argued, it was irrelevant. "Sheer weekly journalism," sneered one critic. Another hostile reviewer found the book only "stale novelty," "bastard jargon," and "nonsense, and often offensive nonsense."[14]

Perry Miller, who later became famous for his studies of the depth and intricacies of the Puritan mind, echoed these sentiments. Once, he wrote, he had read Lewisohn with "avidity," but now he found himself "thinking

half-aloud, 'How much a part of *Only Yesterday* does all this now seem?' "
But to Burton Rascoe, a prominent literary journalist of the time,
Lewisohn's views did not seem obsolete. He thought that *Expression in
America* related "the long process of our emancipation from false critical
values which dissociated art and life and made the bulk of our literature for
a long period a shallow performance, varied only by the occasional
appearance of the authentic artist."[15] In contrast, Miller thought
Lewisohn's analysis of American literature not only inadequate, but
boring:

At this point the rules of the game become clear to even the most casual player. Since our revolt is
the best yet, but is still imperfect, the other revolts were more imperfect. Their permanent value is
the extent to which they defied the bogey man [Puritanism].[16]

Lewisohn, H.L. Mencken and Burton Rascoe had participated in a
literary revolution that began before World War I and reached its climax in
the 1920s. They supported and encouraged such naturalist writers as
Theodore Dreiser. Perhaps their very success partly accounted for Miller's
boredom. Younger writers and critics inherited these victories. They could
direct their energies in other directions. The question remained: Could
Expression in America help them, or was it merely a period piece reflecting
the cultural conflicts of the 1920s?

Taken together the reviews of *Expression in America* touched on many
of the critical issues. They did not, however, adequately explore Lewisohn's
view of literature, the role of the artist and the relationship between
experience and expression. Lewisohn's attack on Puritanism, his use of
Freudian analysis and his ahistorical approach need to be examined in the
larger context of his ideas about literature and expression in this country.
Then one can argue about those views and whether Lewisohn's approach
helps us better understand the works of individual authors and the spirit of
American literature.

The reviewer's job, however, was to *introduce* a new work. This they did.
With time more probing studies should have appeared, and *Expression in
America*'s qualities and place in our literature should have become clearer.
The problem was that such studies were not forthcoming. Kazin's view of
Lewisohn in *On Native Ground* (1942) could have marked a beginning, but
it only served to close a discussion that had never really developed.[17]

Though *Expression in America* went through several printings and
was issued in a Modern Library edition in 1937, and in a 1939 edition, with a
new chapter surveying the writings of the '30s, it never had the critical
influence its initial reception promised. Many writers of the '30s were more
interested in Marx than Freud. From this perspective Lewisohn's study
seemed an "escape into the perfumed galleries of religio-freudianism."
Marx not Freud was the true science: "With all his talk of science, it's plain
that Lewisohn's misty and emotional philosophizing reflected a wholly
unscientific, a non-materialist, conception of the history of science."[18] The
Marxist critics of the '30s, who so assuredly dismissed writers whose
viewpoints differed from theirs, now seem as distant, if not more so, than
the writers they tried verbally to guillotine. Yet in the '30s, in the middle of

the Great Depression, one did not have to be a Marxist to be more concerned with a radical than a tragic view of life. Lewisohn claimed to be concerned with the eternal spirit of man. He could seem elevated. He could also seem hopelessly abstract.

During the '30s some writers continued to explore formal aesthetic problems. They denied that the life of the author was of any value in discussing literature. Their "new criticism" eventually had a tremendous vogue. They had no use for Lewisohn's concern with the relationship between life and literature. Therefore he could not help them.

Lewisohn thought his criticism would endure, would make a difference, because it was based on principles that transcended the trends of the moment. He strove for a stance that was Olympian and above the battle.[19] He took sides and offered judgments and interpretations but he no longer saw himself as a partisan in the literary battles of the moment. After all he stood with, or rather tried to stand with, such eminent literary figures as Goethe, Matthew Arnold and Sainte-Beuve. They were as important to him as the Puritans and Freud.

While Lewisohn had joined H.L. Mencken and other critics of the 20s in playing "the liberating game of baiting the Puritans," he finally concluded that this "game" could provide a critic with neither a philosophy nor a method. In *Mid-Channel* (1929), one of his autobiographical works, he wrote:

> Most of my contemporaries and I have a dreadful secret. It is this: Our intellect is the creature of a reaction against something limited and changeable and even perishable. . . . Mencken, Lewis, Anderson, Masters, even Cabell with his escape into romantic irony—how will their work look in a hundred years? The truculent go-getter and the tyrannical Methodist will not last forever. Human types come and go. . . . The human adventure is an eternal thing. Of this overwhelming fact, I find no hint in all our writing.[20]

Although Lewisohn's view of Puritanism was a central aspect of *Expression in America* his aim was not to bait conventional Americans but to interpret and judge the national literature. Lewisohn argued that the function of literature was to offer an expression of life, a creative insight into the nature and meaning of the human adventure. His perspective was cosmopolitan. He intended to assess the contribution of American writers to world literature. In *The Spirit of Modern German Literature* (1916) he had proudly denied that he was a "narrow specialist. Period by period, I know English literature rather better than German, and French reasonably well. Nor have I myself much respect for any criticism that is not intelligently aware of at least two literatures besides the one under discussion."[21] And while he intended *Expression in America* to be cosmopolitan and erudite, he also aimed it, not at specialists but at thoughtful readers: "Whenever thoughtful people gather today in the Western World, their talk, leaving sooner or later the vexing questions of war and peace, or food and oil, drifts toward books" (p. ix). The success of his book offered some evidence to support his thesis.

For Lewisohn acceptance of his cosmopolitan criticism might have seemed a form of personal vindication. The son of German-Jewish immigrants, he had prepared for a career as a professor of English literature. He had studied at Columbia under William P. Trent, a distinguished American literary historian. Because he was a Jew he could not find a position. Yet Lewisohn maintained a confidence in his own erudition that was unshakable: In *Upstream* (1922) he challenged Anglo-America: "What Anglo-American has lived with the poets who are the sources of his great tradition more closely than I?" And he prophesied his own triumph:

Yet I was to be Americanized. I am even now to be assimilated. Suppose I intend rather to assimilate America, to mitigate Puritan barbarism by the influence of my spirit and the example of my life.[22]

Expression in America was offered as fulfillment, as triumph. This partly accounts for a style that was sometimes magisterial, sometimes passionate, sometimes foolish and at times all of these. Whether one found Lewisohn's writing elevated or merely inflated depended to a large extent on whether one shared his views. However, he could seem convincing because he wrote in such an authoritative tone. His style demanded assent. Thus, when Lewisohn was not convincingly authoritative he appeared arrogant, pompous or merely foolish. His style was such that if one disagreed with him one immediately began to wonder if the Emperor really wore any clothes. He could write:

The nineteenth century was the century of easy solutions and the eternal truths that lasted ten years. There is a deep human pathos in this circumstance. . . . It is now clear, tragically clear if one likes, that the nineteenth century succeeded solely in asking the pertinent and crucial questions. (p. 310)

Is this true? Does our century differ? How long will Lewisohn's eternal truths last? And if the nineteenth century succeeded in asking the pertinent and crucial questions, is that not a remarkable accomplishment? Sometimes this authoritative, stately style could sweep the reader along:

Let us disturb once more, if but for a moment, the dust on the work of the New England Puritans. Their flat and crabbed or extravagant seventeenth-century prose has scarcely a moment of expressiveness or warmth. But their long shadow falls upon us to this day. For these dark Calvinists drove God out of the world and intensified unbearably the opposition between a small and artificial realm of grace and the boundless wilderness of sin. By consigning nine-tenths of human life to the devil they withdrew it from cultivation and control. (p. 1)

This is an effective piece of writing. He sounds like he knows. The writing flows. It has a touch of drama. The indictment finds the Calvinist guilt of what they accused others—"driving God out of the world." Phrases that in less skillful writing might seem trite—"long shadow," "dark Calvinists"— here seem convincing. They create a picture. They appeal to liberal sympathies and prejudices: Who would want to consign nine-tenths of human life to the devil? Yet a cautious reader will note that these lines reflect judgments, not evidence. They prove nothing.

Lewisohn could phrase things felicitously. He could sum up an argument in a pithy phrase. The rhythm of his prose supported his meaning. He could be eloquent. He could fire his authoritative style with passionate conviction and if one agreed with him, or if one found oneself agreeing, the prose could be moving.

Lewisohn's style also reflected his rejection of impressionistic criticism. He offered *Expression in America,* not as a personal and evocative record of his impressions of the great writers, but as an assessment of American writing against standards he thought valid. He had definite ideas about the purpose of literature, the role of the artist, the relationship between experience and expression, form and content. While his vision was fundamentally romantic and presupposed an agnostic and relativistic outlook, his attitude toward the forms in which "the poet" could express himself was traditional.[23]

For Lewisohn the purpose of literature was neither aesthetic nor didactic—"an elegant diversion or an illustration of the foreknown and the fixed," (p. ix) but the search for moral values. The modern reader no longer lived in a "fixed and finished world," for

Sometime near the middle of the nineteenth century an old crack in that rigid shell which was supposed to represent the universe suddenly burst, and vistas opened racing into the infinite past and the infinite future. Space joined time in being unimaginable. Authoritative wisdom became dust (p. ix).

In this situation literature was taking over the function of religion. Modern readers sought in literature what they had once found in religion: "*scripture had become literature and literature scripture*"(p. x). In a world in which knowledge could no longer be "assumed to be closed; final and infallible" (p. xi), literature was "moral research, a road to salvation, the bread of life" (p. ix).

A view of literature that did not affirm literature's moral value and its relation to life, Lewisohn argued, ultimately led to nihilistic despair. There could be no literature without values:

Communication implies values, because meaning implies values. Let the value be as new, as revolutionary, even as mad and perverse as you like. The absence of value, the denial that there are values leads to silence or gibberish (p. 407).

Literature was a serious endeavor. It could not be produced by writers who partook in "an age of gin and moral confusion" (p. 337). Rather, Lewisohn thought, "complete moral nihilism...is in its own character crippling and unproductive" (p. 400). He rejected modern writings which, he argued, assumed that "to be civilized was to live by one's passions and one's nerve alone" (p. 406). Such a view ignored an eternal truth: "the strength and glory and terror of passion come from its being implicated with the higher nerve-center, the whole stream of ancestral memories, with pieties, agonies, exaltations old and forever new as the heart of man itself" (pp. 406-407).

Lewisohn, like Sainte-Beuve, believed in the "'passion and the seriousness which consecrate a genuine work of art'" and in the "conviction that the 'study of literature leads naturally to moral inquiry'" (p. xvi). And he echoed Matthew Arnold, when he argued that in an age without traditional faith, literature would substitute for religion, that it could be "both test and tool in the study of perfection" (p. 75). Near the end of *Expression in America* Lewisohn reaffirmed his belief "that art issued from religion and is forever allied thereto and must, in sober truth, again become more and more religion as religion itself loses its hold upon the minds of men" (p. 525).

Lewisohn was not simply describing a new situation. He tought these changes indicated progress: "many an intense small novelist today has more to communicate concerning man and nature and human life than Gottfried von Strasburg or even the great Dante" (p. xxiv), and, "human life, in brief, has made more and more the appearance of the creative spirit" (p. xxiv). Thus he favored modern American writers over their predecessors and of the older writers those who could be seen as moderns. The danger here was neglecting those writers who did not appear to be modern by Lewisohn's standards and misunderstanding significant aspects of those who did.

Creative literature, Lewisohn thought, had a central role to play in modern life. He assumed literature could save the world. Both these assumptions have been denied—often by creative writers. Lewisohn's expectations were boundless. Today we have lowered our expectations. Still, Lewisohn's faith in the ability of the artist to give creative form and meaning to experience is an affirmation of life. At times Lewisohn could express this faith with poetic power.

The role of the true "poet," Lewisohn believed, was to aid modern man in his search for values. The creative spirit addressed himself to that group of readers for "whom the creative words of the human spirit are a new religion" (p. x). The bard, the poetic voice of the tribe, had no place in the modern world. Nor did the artificer who is merely an imitator of stylistic manners, who selects his subject "from without at the dictate of custom or fashion," for whom "expression...has little to do with experience." Lewisohn argued "no sound history of literature can now or hereafter be written that does not recognize and know and exclude him and fix its attention wholly upon the products of the creative spirit" (p. xxii).

Lewisohn wanted to write a study of the true creative spirit, the eternal poet. The poet creates art "out of his experience, out of suffering and vision he rebuilds the world; he needs to wring its secret from it for his own release and for the salvation of his fellows" (pp. xxvi-xxvii). He found in Goethe's life and work a model for the modern poet:

The Divine Comedy is as perfect and complete as a Cathedral, as rounded and seamless as the Christian universe which it illustrates; Faust is like a series of granite boulders strewn on a plain that melts into an infinite horizon. Between the days of Dante and Goethe the great and unparalleled change had come. Tradition and authority had broken down (p. xii).

If expression was based on such personal experience how could it communicate to others? Again Lewisohn found that Goethe, "the first great poet to see the universe as free and becoming" (p. xiv) had the answer—the particular could symbolize the general.

The modern poet, Lewisohn argued, tends to be a rebel, and "all creative spirits are necessarily heretics" (p. 78). Yet he also wrote that an

attitude of either consent or refusal, identification or revolt, could produce great literature!...It is quite open to question whether the greatest works of the human imagination have not been produced when the artist identified himself largely with the collective culture and tradition of his folk (pp. 274-275).

Lewisohn's view of the relationship of the poet to his society is not consistent. While he wrote a history of rebellion, he yearned for an age of affirmation. He supported naturalist writers, but he hoped for something "beyond naturalism."

If, as Lewisohn argued, "great art should be seen in its totality as substance, as life projected and interpreted by a significant personality" (p. ix), the character of the poet becomes a significant consideration. In Emerson's writing he found a title, and a statement of his approach: " 'All men live by truth and stand in need of expression....The man is only half himself, the other half is his expression'." (titlepage). *Expression in America* chronicled the literary fight against those forces in American culture that had led to a divorce between experience and expression. Those writers who advanced the cause were to be celebrated. Some had tried and failed. The reasons for their defeat were to be explained. Others had not tried. They were to be dismissed.

It was the Puritan heritage that kept American writers from integrating experience and expression: "Men wrote not what they thought or believed or experienced but what, according to Puritan business morality, a good and respectable man ought to experience and to believe" (p. xxxi). Lewisohn attributed to the Puritan tradition all that he disliked in American culture, "the roaring crusades against liquor, against vice, against literature, against science....the Volstead Act, the Mann Act, the activities of the Watch and Ward Society, and the Dayton trial..." (p. 3). Puritanism was responsible for "all that is unlovely and cruel and grotesque in the life of the American people" (p. 2). Lewisohn blamed Puritanism for the American search for a scapegoat—the Mormons, the Negroes, the immigrants, the Catholics, the Communists. He and many other writers of his time also participated in this American sin of scapegoating. Their scapegoat was Puritanism. This made it difficult for them to understand the historical Puritans, American culture in later periods and change and continuity in American life. True, Lewisohn acknowledged the moral idealism of isolated groups of Puritan descendants, from Robert Gould Shaw to Roger Baldwin but this could hardly suffice for an awareness of the complexity of the Puritan experience and heritage. Where Lewisohn found only "moral pathology" and "hard depravity," other scholars have found that the Puritans struggled nobly, intelligently and sometimes eloquently, not only with the Puritan problems but with fundamental human dilemmas. Thus, as one critic had noted, in Lewisohn's version of American history the "dramatis personae seem actors on an empty stage haunted by vague luring shadows of Puritanism in the wings."[24]

Lewisohn had no sense of history. He had instead a definition of what constituted literature and a formula to explain why, with a few exceptions, American writers had not produced "literature" until his own time. He claimed that by the pre-world War I period American writers had finally succeeded in reintegrating experience and expression. It was the naturalist writers who "reconquered life for art, reintegrated experience with expression and were the liberators of our cultural life" (p. 465). Lewisohn's view of experience was static and vague. He would no doubt argue that he was interested in those eternally human aspects of individual experience. He had argued like Goethe that the general was rooted in the particular. Yet, he had no feeling for, or interest in, the particular experience of writers; he ignored the impact of public events on private lives. And notwithstanding his own erudition and the value he assigned books, his view of experience was surprisingly anti-intellectual. Part of an author's experience is the ideas of his time, his relationships with his contemporaries, and the books he reads. These aspects of experience Lewisohn minimized or ignored. Some writers succeeded in integrating experience and expression because they were geniuses: "Personalities create cultural changes. Why they are born at certain times to do so is a mystery. That it is the will of God is, properly interpreted, not the least rational of answers to this as to other ultimate questions" (p. 313). Indeed genius is a mystery. and it helps to face such questions humbly. Lewisohn wants to avoid deterministic interpretations—the "mechanistic superstition." Yet, a belief in genius could not substitute for a cultural and historical analysis.

In each period of American history Lewisohn picked out those writers who he thought contributed to a reintegration of experience and expression—Emerson, Thoreau, Whitman, some local color writers, the naturalists—until he could stop and say the revolt had succeeded. Here was the great tradition of which contemporary American writers could claim they were a part. Lewisohn intended his version of the history of American literature to offer creative sustenance to writers and readers. He argued that his goal was not to set the work in its time, determine influences and examine other matters that he thought would concern only literary scholars. Lewisohn claimed his method allowed him to separate the wheat from the chaff. Yet, his method often failed. For example, Lewisohn did not understand that part of what is valuable to us in the writing of Emerson and Thoreau is that they are not our historical contemporaries. One needs to understand what they considered central issues before one can determine whether they continue to have relevance. Lewisohn simply dismissed their talk of oversoul, of Swedenborgianism and related topics. He discussed their work without ever discussing their view of nature. Lewisohn thought that

love, friendship, and so passion and creating being inaccessible to them, Emerson and Thoreau took to nature and metaphysics and morals...because by their very constitutions these were their only possible objects of intense preoccupation, of experience and of expression....They were chilled under-sexed valetudinarians" (p. 112).

Even *if* they were, it is not clear that it matters as much as Lewisohn thought. Certainly it does not offer any insight into key aspects of the experience they sought to express. Lewisohn performed half the critical task. He offered us his judgment of a writer's value. He failed, however, to offer much that would make it easier to understand the writer on his own terms. Thus some of Lewisohn's comments reveal more about him than about the writers he was discussing. Among the German followers of Fichte "there was romantic vagabondage, there were queer marryings and unmarryings and givings in marriage among them. Not so in New England" (p.119).

In place of historical understanding Lewisohn offered Freudian analysis. He assumed, as did others influenced by Freud, that this method was neither culturally not historically bound. Lewisohn used Freudianism as a weapon in the fight for realistic and naturalistic expression. It proved the scientific evidence that Puritan inhibition was unnatural. American writing had suffered too long from "enormous antecedent exclusions" (p. 93). The national literature was not a realistic expression of experience. Individual writers failed to fully reflect their experience because of their Puritan inhibitions and their neuroses. Instead there too often had been a flight into fantasy. Freud, Lewisohn thought, had shown that "sex, contrary to the common uninstructed opinion, is not peripheral and localized, but pervasive" (p. 139). Writers like Howells, who regard the sex instinct as trivial, imposed upon themselves a "crushing handicap."[25] Thus

The realists and naturalists sought. . .to face reality and next to make others face it, to cleanse themselves of childish delusions and then to communicate this process and its findings to their fellowmen. . . .The history of American expressionism, articulateness, literature, is the history of a struggle toward adjustment to the realities of the self and the world, an attempt to restrain flight, to attain balance, to find a center (p. 287).

Lewisohn's use of Freud weakened rather than strengthened the book. He created false dichotomies: "Was it the quality of American life or was it wholly their own natures which drove these three [Poe, Hawthorne, Melville] into expression that has the structure of a neurosis?" (p. 154). His inquiry might have had more productive results, if he had not phrased it in either or terms. Nor is his definition and analysis of these writers' alleged neuroses illuminating or convincing. It is curious that he never used Freudian theory to analyse the work of art itself. His descriptions and conclusions about an author's character were stated with an ease and severity that had not been won from materials: Melville "was disillusioned from the beginning. He adopted all his life the regressive attitude of the neurotic—of the favorite child who wants the world to reconstitute for it the condition of the nursery. Is that not evident even in 'Moby Dick'?" (p. 189). The author's life was discussed to indict the work and vice versa. Finally, one does not believe Lewisohn knew much about either. Melville as a troubled soul, Lewisohn believed. So were Poe and Hawthorne. So are we all. But this hardly proves that "the final image that arises from all of Melville's work is that of a big bearded violently excited man trying to shout down the whimpering, lonely child in his soul" (pp. 188-189). Similar problems occur in Lewisohn's other "Freudian" analyses. It is regrettable, for Lewisohn had eloquently stated the case for the relationship between experience and expression.

In time the conception of American literature as a revolt against Puritan inhibitions was bound to seem a "formula" that had served its purpose. It sustained those writers and critics who fought for a "free modern literature in America." It was inevitable that later scholars, such as Alfred Kazin, would argue "that a kind of historical complacency had settled upon our studies of [modern American] literature, and that while the usual explanation of it as a revolt against gentility and repression had the root of the matter in it, it did not tell us enough and had even become a litany." Kazin argued that modern American literature was rooted in the industrial transformation of America in the post-Civil War years—urbanization, the new immigration, the railroads, the populist revolt, the Progressive movement. While it was exactly these aspects of the American experience that Lewisohn ignored, he did not commit the most serious errors Kazin catalogued. He did not simply tell of freedom won. He did try to answer "whether literature came with the freedom."[26]

Lewisohn cared about expression; he wrote as one who had experienced the power of great literature. Thus, he strove for the "disinterested" assessment that Matthew Arnold had talked about. Occasionally he achieved it. Especially as he came closer to his own time. Always he was concerned with assessing the qualities that made or did not make an author's writing literature. True, his limitations led him to dismiss works that few thoughtful readers would want to neglect. *Moby Dick* is the most notorious example. To mention Edward Bellamy's *Looking Backward* in the same context with the work of E.P. Roe, Lew Wallace, Francis Marion Crawford and Frank R. Stockton and then to dismiss it in a phrase—as "pseudo-idealistic"—deprives us of an important part of our heritage. And a critic who could write of "the mild and easy satiric discourses of Mr. Dooley, disturbing no one, rousing no doubt" (p. 296), had serious limitations as a commentator on the national spirit and literature. Unfortunately not many other critics have tried to define the place of Peter Finley Dunne's Mr. Dooley in our history *and* literature.

Given later critical trends, some of Lewisohn's opinions now appear odd, or possibly refreshing. Henry James' shorter works are held to be superior to his novels, Stephen Crane's *The Red Badge of Courage* is less important that *Maggie, A Girl of the Streets,* Hemingway's *Farewell to Arms* is superior to his *The Sun Also Rises,* F. Scott Fitzgerald's *This Side of Paradise* is discussed, but *The Great Gatsby* is not mentioned. Lewisohn's case for the poets William Ellery Leonard and George Sylvester Viereck is unlikely to convince anyone.

Yet Lewisohn was often at his best in his treatment of poetry. Thus in his discussion of Emerson he quoted lines that he found "harsh, tonic, and veracious," others that were "mystical," or that had "severity," or a "touch of magic." In that way he conveyed a sense of Emerson's poetic qualities. He compared Emerson to the English poet Landor. Emerson, he argued,

had a Landorian taste for lucid serenity and severity. And he had isolated moments when he went beyond Landor in that he treated with that high, cool lucidity the homely scenes and subjects of the New England countryside (p. 133).

In a sense it does not matter whether the reader accepts Lewisohn's conclusions. Such comparisons can only help to define a poet and his poetry. Seemingly Lewisohn addressed himself to a sophisticated reader who had an easy familiarity with both English and American poetry. Thus he asumed that the reader was familiar with Emerson's best known poems, and that he could therefore call his attention to less well known pieces. He assumed that Landor meant something to the reader. But the discussion can also introduce the less knowledgeable reader to Emerson. It suggests the poems he can read, qualities to look for, and poetry to compare Emerson with. Lewisohn used this approach successfully with other poets as well. His comparison of Frost and Sandburg was insightful. Lewisohn concluded in a truly wonderful phrase that the aim of Frost's poetry was to recover "the freshness of the permanent" (p. 497).

Lewisohn made perceptive comments about Vachel Lindsay and Edna St. Vincent Millay, two poets whose reputations have since declined. Lewisohn made a strong case for Lindsay as the mystic poet of American Fundamentalism, "a poet comparable to the best neo-Catholic poets of the Latin countries and in the direct tradition of Blake and Francis Thompson" (p. 573).[27] Turning away from any discussion of "The Congo" he called attention to lines he thought proved that "the man that wrote these lines is an English lyrist of almost Elizabethan sweetness and magic and country charm" (p. 571). Lewisohn argued that while Millay's "sonnets are unthinkable without Shakespeare's, they are equally unthinkable as anyone's save Edna Millay's" (p. 575). It is not, however, the "delightful 'Recuerdo' and 'MacDougal Street'," or the mood of the poet who wrote her "candle burns at both ends," that Lewisohn examined. Rather he called attention to her poems about death.[28] The two types of poems, he argued, are related. Millay "is a pagan with a troubled conscience and peaceless heart" (p. 576). And Lewisohn concluded:

This pagan poet is among the most sorrowful,...of all poets for the simple reason, pointed out by Matthew Arnold long ago, that paganism fails when we are sick and sorry and desolate and afraid of death and dust (p. 576).

Lewisohn's analyses could help reopen discussions that seem closed. Lewisohn sought to discriminate between an author's best work and his inferior pieces. He tried to point out what made their writing effective and moving. He compared Sarah Orne Jewett and Mary Wilkins Freeman and thus defined their respective strengths. O. Henry's faults are obvious; but Lewisohn makes the important point that in "*The Four Million* he saw and for the first time rendered New York....O'Henry discovered the hall bedroom" (p. 329). Lewisohn demanded attention for the now forgotten novelist David Graham Phillips. Phillips, he argued, had not only "rude power of characterization but moments of subtle insight" (p. 328).[29] Lewisohn sought to arrive at a fair critical assessment of Sinclair Lewis. While he acknowledged Lewis's limitations as a novelist he argued that his strength, like Moliere's and Dickens', was as a "delineator of manners." Dreiser is treated respectfully, but not uncritically. Lewisohn was not impressed by Dreiser's philosophical pretensions:

His talk about 'chemism,' his shabby materialism, dotted by flights toward ouija-boards, is nonsense. But it is such sheer and obvious and childish nonsense that one simply passes it by. It is annoying but not disturbing. It is on the level of Victor Hugo's intimacy with God. It does not ripple, [much] less dam the steady stream of life through Dreiser's books (p. 473).

Despite such limitations and "the heavy amorphous verbiage, which will seem duller as time goes on," Dreiser's "power and truth are so great that they will long irradiate their muddy integuments" (p. 482). If rediscovered, Lewisohn's discussion of Dreiser could help balance the contempt with which Lionel Trilling treated Dreiser in his famous essay "Reality in America."[30]

Lewisohn thought there could be no great writers without great criticism. Throughout *Expression in America* he was concerned with examining and defining critical approaches, such as Poe's, Emerson's, the New Humanists', Mencken's and ultimately his own. Critical theories have a fundamental importance. Thus, when first rate critics argue they are fighting about "nothing less than the structure of the universe, the nature of man, the meaning of life, the right goal of all thought and the proper aim of all endeavor" (p. 466). Lewisohn was dismayed to record that while "The Great Critical Debate" between the neo-Humanists and the followers of H.L. Mencken marked the rise of the critical spirit in America, it went no further than opposing "an empty aestheticism...to an empty moralism" (p. 422) a battle between Nihilists and Calvinists. It was a "sham battle."

More hates democracy on account of the exceeding wickedness of men's hearts; Mencken hates it no less on account of the exceeding thickness of their wits;...More wants the populace to be obedient and go to church on Sunday morning; Mencken is willing to let the enslaved "boobs" get drunk on Saturday night (p. 430).

Lewisohn found qualities to admire in Irving Babbitt, Paul Elmer More and H.L. Mencken. He also attacked what he perceived as their weaknesses. The problem was that while the neo-Humanists had correctly answered Mencken "that without values, without guidance man cannot live" (p. 437), they defended traditional values that no longer sufficed.

Lewisohn offered his own alternative to the Calvinists and the nihilists—literature as moral research, as the search for values. Thus "criticism is the disengaging and weighing of these values into which men transmute their experience and from which alone experience derives both its *meaning* and its *form*" (p. 416). From communication come meaning and value. The possibility of creative communication "lies not in the sentiment but in the *fact* that men are brothers, made of one substance and creatures of an equal fate" (p. 455). Expression was rooted in experience: "Experience creates substance and substance creates form" (p. xvi), and form, Lewisohn argued, "is not clothes but flesh" (p. 420). These are all assumptions that have been denied by others, or only meagerly affirmed. Thus, notwithstanding their eloquence, they are debatable. They do, however, speak to central issues. They are thought-provoking ideas. They offer a challenge to those who deny the relationship between art and life, experience and expression, and to those who assume form is neither clothes nor flesh, but message.

Lewisohn was radical in his assertion that there "are no eternal or fixed standards by which either genius may be known from without or a creative activity guided from within" (p. 459). But experimentation in form, he thought, had little to do with the poetic expression of experience:

Writers of high importance have rarely been innovators of style and form of expression but have heightened and made their own an existent tradition. They are almost never of an inventive or ingenious turn and are contented, as Euripides and Shakespeare and Goethe were, to put to their highly personal uses forms, modes and even subject-matter already present in the consciousness of their people (p. 214).

Lewisohn feared that the traditional forms were being destroyed. He continually asserted that they were adequate to our needs, but he was occasionally uncertain. With great eloquence he presented an argument for traditional forms and sought to impugn the validity of those he thought were working to destroy the possibility of communication. Experimentation with form could be liberating, it could help free writers from outdated convention, but it was not the highest creativity. After all, "we do not know who invented the dactylic hexameter; we know that Homer and Hesiod found it ready to their hand..." (p. 377).

Lewisohn claimed that "the innovator is never a master." The master is "too pregnant with meaning...to play with form." He likes existing forms "and pours himself into them" (p. 378). Basic forms endure because they are rooted in the physical and spiritual nature of man. For example, "that eternal mood of narrative which has not changed greatly since the stories of Esther and of Ruth and the tale of the fate and adventure of Odysseus" (p. 401). Therefore, Lewisohn attacked Carl Sandburg for remarking: "'Think what Shakespeare could have done with the emotion behind the sonnets if he had been free, not bound by any verse form'"(p. 494). Lewisohn offered a more traditional and penetrating view:

Shakespeare's emotion is not behind but in the sonnets; the emotion and the form are identical; thus and thus only could that emotion have been born; the antecedent emotion was not this but only its seed or, in another figure, its raw material. The creative process had intervened and transmuted life into art and the temporary and accidental experience into an eternal and universal one (pp. 494-495).

Form, Lewisohn argued, "is in itself always an act of creative faith" (p. 587). To create form is to affirm life. Post-World War I experimenters in form were born of a nihilistic despair that sought to destroy form. This means "a hell of emptiness has been added to the other hells of man's experience..." (p. 383). Lewisohn's principle examples were the work of Ezra Pound and T.S. Eliot. Lewisohn's views of these writers, who have since achieved classic status, do as much to indicate Lewisohn's limits as theirs. Nevertheless, it is challenging to hear someone attack these modernist saints: "Pound's work smells, to use a sound old phrase, ferociously of the lamp." Pound "writes in a musty library; he ransacks the scrolls of the ancients and the mediaevals and writes macaronic free verse, displaying a curious erudition and plentiful lack of anything to say" (p. 381). Pound, Lewisohn concluded, is an example

of the rebel who has nothing but his rebellion, no stock in trade but his resistance and contempt, a just resistance doubtless and a contempt for things contemptible, but who, his liberation accomplished, his irritation projected, has neither meaning nor message nor shaping power, nor new gods nor other altars. He reiterates his hatreds in middle-age as in youth and flees to ever stranger scenes and ever more violent contortions of language in order to hide from himself and others the emptiness in his own breast (p. 382).

This captured one prominent aspect of Pound's career and its expression.

Lewisohn acknowledged and quoted lines from Pound that he described as severe and beautiful: "'Envoi'...is one of the most beautiful of American poems," but "its loveliness is learned and academic and has a touch of bookish dust" (p. 380). It is not simply that Lewisohn cannot understand Pound, or his disciple Eliot, but rather that he cannot appreciate them. In "The Waste Land," he argued, "civilization is disintegrated and meaning is disintegrated and despair and disillusion stalk the waste land of the world....Chaos of the world and the soul is set forth by the learned and calculated chaos of the poem's method" (p. 587). Lewisohn has the heart of the matter. "The Waste Land," however, is about the problem of belief in the modern world, it is not necessarily, as Lewisohn thought, an attempt to destroy faith in life itself. Each reader has to face the problem for himself. Lewisohn concluded that "to a despair so deep that it shatters form and so the world there are two classical issues: suicide or the Catholic Church. Eliot chose the latter" (p. 587). Lewisohn could not foresee that these "minor poets" would receive classic status and the analyses of numerous critics, and that his own commentary would seem not merely wrongheaded but inadequate. In Lewisohn's view Eliot did not represent the poetry of the modern sensibility but only one more example of a temporary defeat in the history of the human spirit. His positions demand thought and consideration:

To the youths who cling to [Eliot] one might say: this is no last word, but one of the oldest. Men not ignoble have gone down before life in other ages and wandered in waste lands and taken refuge in some monastery or hermitage either of the soul or of the body or both....But the creative imagination is at one with life and its procreative processes and withers both in the desert of despair and in the refuge of blank authority...(p. 587).

Lewisohn, like Eliot and Pound, wanted to go beyond naturalism. The problem, he saw, was that there were no generally agreed upon values and symbols; modern art had "no recognized coinage of the spirit in which to pay its self-contracted debts" (p. 524). Though he believed "the individual cannot invent new myths and legends" (p. 525), he thought there was an "urge toward wholeness and coherence and so toward new symbols" (p. 527). Thus he ended on a note of cautious optimism: "the human spirit has not therefore known any long defeat. It will not now. And in any creative rebirth of the future, whether near or far, America will have her appropriate share" (p. 590).

For Lewisohn, then, the story of American literature was neither a record of final triumph nor simply a recounting of successive revolts. Rather, Lewisohn wrote the history of American literature as if it was the story of Goethe's Faust. Goethe wrote the first half of *Faust* when he was a young man and the second part when he was much older. In the first part Goethe removes Faust from a life of scholastic devotion into a world of broader and more varied experience. Faust throws off traditional bounds. It is in the second half of the play that Faust strives to reconcile his newly found freedom with a search for order, for enduring principles. In Lewisohn's version of American literary history the first half of Faust had been written. The question was whether the story of American writing would parallel the story of Faust. Would there be a second act? This is still a relevant question.

Lewisohn offered a noble view of literature's importance to modern man. He had a critical standard. He made it explicit and he defended it eloquently. His weaknesses, however, are glaring. He made no effort to reconcile historical objectivity and private taste. His description of Puritanism lacked any historical depth. His use of Freudianism was seldom helpful. Puritanism and Freudianism could not bear the analytical weight Lewisohn gave to them. And thus his accounts of some writers now appears prejudiced and inadequate. Yet, many of his statements were perceptive and challenging.

Lewisohn expressed his faith in literature to help us live creatively. It seems that our faith in literature has diminished. Is it any longer true that "whenever thoughtful people gather today in the Western World their talk...drifts toward books[?]" (p. ix). Whether expounding on the value of literature, the role of the artist, the relationship between experience and expression, form and content, Lewisohn was affirming the value of literary expression in giving meaning to life.

Our problems are no longer with Puritan inhibition preventing the expression of experience. Only pornographers any longer complain about the repressive force of Puritanism. We have ample avenues of expression. Our problem is determining who and what merits our attention and respect. Lewisohn assumed that literature had a special status; that it could help us meet the future: "I have defined a classic as one whose vision the youth of successive generations can make its own" (p. 148). And he assumed that "youth" or a "saving remnant" of it looked to literature for a vision of life it could through "instinctive and passionate reinterpretation make its own" (p. 136). Today Lewisohn's account of American literature reads best, not as a history of the efforts of successive generations of writers to reintegrate experience and expression, but as a defense of the value of literature itself and a belief in the continuing relevance of our classic American writers.

Lewisohn knew that he would make erroneous judgments, but he thought it was not "grave, since time [was] sure to correct them" (p. viii). He assumed that future readers would correct him, not ignore him and that *Expression in America* would become part of a dialogue. He hoped "that this book [would] cooperate with the corrective forces in American life and that it [would], in the words of Sainte-Beuve, 'advance the question and not leave things hereafter quite as they were before' " (p. viii). *Expression in America,* reconsidered, could make a difference.

Notes

¹Ludwig Lewisohn, *The Poets of Modern France* (New York: 1918); Lewisohn, *The Spirit of Modern German Literature* (New York: 1916).

²Ludwig Lewisohn, *The Dream and The Stage* (New York: 1922); Lewisohn, *The Modern Drama* (New York: 1921).

³Ludwig Lewisohn, *A Book of Modern Criticism* (New York: 1919); Lewisohn's *The Creative Life* (New York: 1924) and *Cities and Men* (New York: 1927) address themselves to the general problem of criticism and creativity.

⁴Ludwig Lewisohn, *Haven* (New York: 1940), p.101. Lewisohn was a prolific novelist and this aspect of his career merits separate examination. *The Case of Mr. Crump* (New York: 1930) and *The Island Within* (New York: 1928) are the best known.

⁵Sidney Cheyet, "Ludwig Lewisohn: The Years of Becoming," *American Jewish Archives,* XI (October, 1959), 125-47; Cheyet, "Ludwig Lewisohn in Charleston, 1982-1903," *American Jewish Historical Quarterly,* LIV (1965), 296-322; Harry Zohn, "In Memorian Ludwig Lewisohn," *Monatshefte,* XLVIII (January, 1956), 43-45; David Singer, "Ludwig Lewisohn: The Making of an anti-Communist," *American Quarterly,* XXIII (December, 1971), 738-748; Morton Mezvinsky, "The Jewish Thought of Ludwig Lewisohn," *Chicago Jewish Forum,* XVI (Winter, 1957-58), 77-82.

⁶Charles I. Glicksberg, ed., *American Literary Criticism, 1900-1950* (New York: 1951), pp.198-200; William Van O'Connor, *An Age of Criticism* (Chicago: 1952), pp.15, 67-68, 87, 139; Floyd Stovall, ed., *The Development of American Literary Criticism* (Chapel Hill, North Carolina: 1955), pp.173, 176, 179, 195, 219; Walter Sutton, *Modern American Criticism* (New Jersey: 1963), pp.21-24; Frederick J. Hoffman, *Freudianism and the Literary Mind* (Baton Ruge, Louisiana: 1952), pp.75-76, 281-286; Louis Fraiberg, *Psychoanalysis and American Literary Criticism* (Detroit: 1960), pp.146-160; Henry May, *The End of American Innocence: A Study of the First Years of Our Own Time, 1912-1917* (New York: 1959), pp.379, 390: Gilman Ostrander, *American Civilization in the First Machine Age, 1890-1940* (New York: 1970), p.332.

⁷Nicholas Karl Gordon, "Jewish and American: A Critical Study of the Fiction of Abraham Cahan, Anzia Yezierska, Waldo Frank, and Ludwig Lewisohn," (unpublished Ph.D. dissertation, Stanford University, 1968); David Singer, "The Acculturation of Ludwig Lewisohn: An Intellectual Portrait," (unpublished Ph.D. dissertation, Brown University, 1968); Richard Charles Hespen, "Ludwig Lewisohn As Literary Critic," (unpublished Ph.D. dissertation, Univrsity of Michigan, 1966).

⁸Hespen, "Ludwig Lewisohn as Literary Critic," *passim.*

⁹Ludwig Lewisohn, *Expression in America* (New York: 1932). The pages from which quotations are drawn are indicated in the text.

¹⁰E.S. Bates, "Through Mr. Lewisohn's Glasses," *Commonweal,* XVI (May 11, 1932), 50; Lewis Gannett, as quoted in "Here is a Book," *Saturday Review of Literature,* VIII (March 26, 1932), 621. Carl Van Doren, *Three Worlds* (New York: 1936), p.148; Dorothea Brande, "Mr. Lewisohn Interprets America," *American Review,* II (December, 1933), 189-98; Perry Miller, Review of *Expression in America, New England Quarterly,* V (July, 1932), 624-629.

¹¹Joseph Wood Krutch, Review of *Expression in America,* New York *Herald Tribune Books,* March 13, 1932, p.1; Gannett, "Here is a Book," p.621; Carl Van Doren, *Nation* CXXXIV (April 13, 1932), 429; Ernest Leisy, *American Literature* V (November, 1933), pp.285-286; Brande, "Lewisohn Interprets America," pp.189-98.

¹²John Macy, Review of *Expression in America, Saturday Review of Literature,* VIII (March 12, 1932), 583; Leisy, Review *American Literature,* p.286; Minnie Hite Moody, Review of *Expression in America, Sewannee Review,* XL (Oct.-Dec., 1932), 508.

¹³See the review of Macy, Leisy, and Moody, cited above; Bates, "Through Mr. Lewisohn's Glasses," p.50. Granville Hicks, Review of *Expression in America, The New Republic,* LXX (April

13, 1932), 240-241; Howard Mumford Jones, Review of *Expression in America, Yale Review,* XXI (Summer, 1932), 836-37; Leisy, Review *American Literature,* and Macy, Review, *Saturday Review,* on various counts criticizes Lewisohn's treatment of historical and environmental factors; Leisy, Review, *American Literature,* p.286.

14Granville Hicks, Review, *The New Republic,* p.241; Gorham Munson, Review of *Expression in America,* Atlantic, CL (August, 1932), p.9; Brande, "Mr. Lewisohn Interprets America," pp.189, 192.

15Perry Miller, Review, *New England Quarterly,* p.625, Rascoe is quoted in Donald Hensley, *Burton Rascoe* (New York: 1970), p.123.

16Perry Miller, Review, *New England Quarterly,* p.626.

17Alfred Kazin, *On Native Grounds, An Interpretation of Modern American Prose Literature,* (New York: 1942), pp.273-81; Adolph Gillis, *Ludwig Lewisohn: The Artist and His Message,* (New York: 1933) is a curious piece of hagiography. As criticism it is thin and puerile.

18C.H. Grattan, "Open Letters to Lewisohn, Krutch, and Mumford," *Modern Monthly,* VII (April, 1933), 175; Bernard Smith, *Forces in American Criticism: A Study in the History of American Literary Thought Horizon: A New Search For Old Truths.* (New York, 1934) in which he defended the bourgeoisie and the acquisitive instinct was viewed as additional evidence of his conservatism, although he strongly supported the New Deal. See the leftist critique, E.S. Bates, "Lewisohn into Crump," *American Mercury,* XXXI (April, 1934), 441-450. David Singer, "The Making of an Anti-Communist," review Lewisohn's political writings and anti-communist novels.

19Grattan, "Open Letter," p.177, dismissed Lewisohn's effort as "a puling attempt to be above the battle.

20Ludwig Lewisohn, *Mid-Channel: An American Chronicle,* (New York: 1929), p.13.

21Ludwig Lewisohn, *The Spirit of Modern German Literature* (New York: 1916), preface not paginated.

22Ludwig Lewisohn, *Upstream, An American Chronicle* (New York: 1922), p.237.

23Lewisohn in a thoughtful and erudite footnote defined:
the term poet as the Elizabethan did and the Germans and Scandinavians (Dichter, digter) have always done as applicable to the creative artist in letters irrespective of external form. The distinction based upon the mere use of prose or verse has always been dangerous and confusing; how much more so is it today when imaginative prose is assuming nearly all the functions of verse and when the boundaries between the two forms are becoming obliterated. The poet-themaker or creator—is such by virtue of his inner character. (p. xviii)

24Leisy, Review, *American Literature,* p.286. The literature on Puritanism is formidable. And while it is true that Lewisohn uses the term in a conventional way for his generation, there were already alternative views that he might have read to temper his own. See for example, Kenneth B. Murdoch, "The Puritan Tradition," in Norman Foerster, ed., *The Reinterpretation of American Literature, Some Contributions Toward the Understanding of its Historical Development* (New York: 1928), pp.83-113. *Expression in America,* however, was written as if nothing else on American literature had been published.

25Lewisohn nevertheless admired Howells: "he and his works,... can never wholly fade from the cultural landscape in America," (p.246).

26Alfred Kazin, *On Native Grounds,* pp.vii-viii.

27Compare with Peter Viereck, "Vachel Lindsay: The Dante of the Fundamentalists," in Louis Filler, ed., *A Question of Quality Popularity and Value in Modern Creative Writing,* (Bowling Green, Ohio: 1976), pp.124-147. Viereck's extraordinary essay compliments rather than supersedes Lewisohn's discussion of Lindsay. Viereck does not cite Lewisohn.

28Compare with Frederick Eckman, "Edna St. Vincent Millay: Notes Toward a Reappraisal," in Filler, ed., *A Question of Quality* pp.193-203. Eckman also emphasizes death and desolation as central aspects of Millay's poetry; however, he does not relate these poems to what Lewisohn called her paganism. Eckman does not refer to Lewisohn.

29Louis Filler, *Voice of the Democracy: A Critical Biography of David Graham Phillips: Journalist, Novelist, Progressive* (Pennsylvania, 1978) is a major effort to reopen discussion and consideration of Phillips and his work.

30Lionel Trilling, "Reality in America," in Lionel Trilling, *The Liberal Imagination, Essays on Literature and Society* (New York: 1930), pp.3-22.

"Cabell" Rhymes with "Rabble"

Maurice Duke

WHEN ONE CONSIDERS the number of books written by James Branch Cabell, along with his dramatic vision and world view, it is hardly less than astonishing that his current critical reputation is at so low a mark. Earlier in this century, his name and the titles of his novels were household words. His photograph, coupled with praise for his books, many of which were translated into foreign languages, appeared as weekly features in the nation's leading newspapers,[1] and his place in American letters seemed permanently secure. Today, however, the situation has reversed and the man who was recognized by his peers—such writers as Hugh Walpole, Sinclair Lewis, H.L. Mencken, F. Scott Fitzgerald and others—as one of the giants of American literature has been relegated to the Ztatus of second rank. The position is, of course, not unique, Zut in this case perhaps the writer who occupies it is.

Descended from a distinguished family that traced its roots to the early days of the Commonwealth of Virginia, Cabell began his career by writing romantic short stories set in the middle ages. His works, lavishly illustrated, began appearing in the national magazines toward the end of the last century, followed in 1904 by his first novel, *The Eagle's Shadow.* As is usually the case with a beginning novelist, the reviewers were lukewarm regarding his early published efforts. However, he soon began to attract notice as a writer who was heading in a direction somewhat different from that of the Realists and Naturalists, who had taken their cue from the critical pronouncements recently made by the influential nineteenth century novelist, editor and critic, William Dean Howells.

With the appearance of his second book, *The Line of Love,* Cabell began to attract more, but still modest, notice of the critics. Perhaps the most representative statement made regarding him and his work during that period was that of a critic, who reported in 1906 that Cabell had "created, as an author, a role for himself that belongs to him individually and exclusively and that has won for him commendation."[2] Cabell was now falteringly on his way in the literary world. He had found his medium in the romantic tale, tinged with more than a hint of irony, and he set to work to perfect his style and to enlarge his world view.

Cabell's third book, *Gallantry,* appeared in 1907, two years after *The Line of Love,* and once again the reviewers passed gentle judgment on his latest effort. The reviewer for *The Nation* liked the book's "cleverness, tact, and invention,"[3] while the Chicago *Record Herald* noted that the stories were "tender and brilliant."[4] At the same time, a reviewer for *The Dial*

117

judged the stories in *Gallantry* as being "studies of temperament, of epochs, of 'precious' stylistic effects; but the story-interest remains strong."[5] Comments on the book were not all positive, however, some reviewers taking Cabell to task for his convoluted prose style. Among these was the reviewer for the New York *Sun,* who objected to the blend of archaic and modern styles, as well as what he thought to be Cabell's neglect to employ a consistent style throughout.[6]

With the appearance of *The Cords of Vanity,* the fourth of Cabell's books, which was published in 1909, a new attitude toward the writer began emerging in the popular press. Although many of the reviewers objected to the moral nature of Robert Townsend,[7] the book's central character, others saw in this new work the qualities of wit, urbanity and sophistication, the attributes which just over a decade later were to make Cabell the literary darling of the 1920s. In the meantime, however, he continued to publish with regularity. *Chivalry* appeared the same year as *The Cords of Vanity,* followed in 1913 by *The Soul of Melicent. The Rivet in Grandfather's Neck* came out in 1915, followed the next year by two titles, *From the Hidden Way* and *The Certain Hour.* The following year saw the arrival of *The Cream of the Jest.*

By now Cabell was in his late 30s, just approaching his prime, and had gained a broadly based, if thinly layered, following. He was becoming known and read, as the Richmond *News Leader,* one of his home town newspapers noted, "in Boston, London, and San Francisco if not," the reporter lamented, "in his own native Richmond."[8]

But it was the next year, 1919, that doubtless contained the most eventful twelve months in Cabell's personal life and literary career as well. That year saw the publication of two books, *Beyond Life,* which attracted the usual critical attention, and *Jurgen,* which rocked the literary world because of its seizure, trial and subsequent exoneration. It was one of the great literary trials of our century, its exact indictment being based on the following:

THE GRAND JURY OF THE COUNTY OF NEW YORK by this indictment, accuse Guy Holt, Robert M. McBride & Co.[9] and Robert M. McBride of the crime of UNLAWFULLY POSSESSING AN INDECENT BOOK, committed as follows:

The said Guy Holt, Robert M. McBride & Co., a corporation at all times herein mentioned existing under the laws of the State of New York, and Robert M. McBride, acting together in concern, in the County of New York aforesaid, on the 14th day of January, 1920, and for a considerable time prior thereto, with intent to sell and show, unlawfully possessed a lewd, lascivious, indecent, obscene and disgusting book entitled JURGEN, a more particular description of which said book would be offensive to this Court and improper to be spread upon the records thereof, wherefore such description is not here given; against the form of the statute in such case made and provided, and against the peace of the people of the State of New York, and their dignity.

Edward Swann
District Attorney[10]

Even though World War I had been triumphantly concluded and a social revolution was beginning to sweep the country, America in the early winter of 1920 still exhibited a marked Victorian sensibility where matters of art and literature were concerned. After all, it was only a mere twenty-nine years since Howells had issued the influential and much-respected *Criticism and Fiction,* in which he inveighed against any author dealing fictionally with what he euphemistically labeled "a guilty love intrigue."[11] Probably only a small segment of America's readers realized in 1920 what Cabell was doing with *Jurgen,* which was actually a witty and sophisticated romance that had far-reaching moral and philosophical implications. On the other hand, however, there were the vocal and vociferous moralists who saw in *Jurgen* only a thinly disguised exploitation of sex, the kind, incidentally, inveighed against by Howells, centering on the fantasized infidelity of the main character. As soon as these public defenders of morality, headed by the articulate but artistically ignorant John S. Sumner, mounted their attack, Cabell found himself with a greatly expanded reading audience coupled with mushrooming media coverage, which spread nationwide in a short time.[12] At the height of the controversy, which was marked by an enormous rekindling of interest in all the author's books, Cabell laconically acknowledged his newly formed following while commenting about the pronunciation of his name. He noted that he continually had to send letters to curious admirers informing them that "Cabell" rhymes with "Rabble."[13] He had obviously, or so he certainly thought, arrived.

As far as selling of books and the boost in his reputation were concerned, Cabell could have suffered no better fate than to have Sumner and his organization, the Society for the Suppression of Vice, seize *Jurgen.* Because of his actions, Sumner became far more effective than any advertising agent could have made him. But there was an inherent danger inextricably interwoven into the fabric of such overnight success. First, there was the danger that the public might forget about both Cabell and *Jurgen* as the matter dragged slowly through the courts. Secondly, if Cabell and McBride lost, there was the likelihood that Sumner's victory might force Cabell to take a different direction with his art. Such was not the case, however. As the months of litigation dragged on, *Jurgen* became more and more the subject of heated interest.

It was not that Cabell was a purveyor of pornography. He most assuredly was not, but many of the episodes in *Jurgen* obviously lent themselves to more than a literal meaning. For example, when Jurgen first meets Guenevere in Chapter 9 of the book he finds her asleep. "In consequence," Cabell writes, "Jurgen kissed the girl. Her lips parted and softened, and they assumed a not unpleasant sort of submissive ardour....She clung a little, and now she shivered a little, but not with cold." Following the kiss, which "was a tolerably lengthy affair," Guenevere and Jurgen converse, the connotation centering on the verb to come:

> "I knew that you would come," the girl said, happily.
> "I am very glad that I came," whispered Jurgen.
> "But time presses."
> "Time sets an admirable example, my dear Princess—"

Again, in Chapter 22, titled suggestively "As to a Veil they Broke,"

Jurgen obviously deflowers a girl named Anaitis. In a mock-ritualistic scene, laden with phallic imagery, he "held his lance erect, shaking it with his right hand, and the tip of it was red with blood." "Then kneeling," Cabell writes of Anitis, "she touched the lance, and began to stroke it lovingly...." "Anaitis placed together the tips of her thumbs and of her fingers, so that her hands made an open triangle; and waited thus." The ritual is completed and the sex act consummated several paragraphs later when Jurgen "found an opening screened by a pink veil. Jurgen thrust with his lance and broke this veil. He heard the sound of one brief wailing cry; it was followed by soft laughter...."

With scenes such as these, which are representative but nowhere near exhaustive, it is no wonder that Sumner squirmed or that, at the height of the controversy *Jurgen* was selling for many times its original price on the black market.[14] It was, as a matter of fact, virtually unobtainable, as witnessed by a letter to Cabell in which Zelda Fitzgerald confessed to having been caught trying to steal one to give to Scott as a present.[15] Finally, Cabell and McBride, as the following acquittal decision by Judge Charles C. Nott, on October 19, 1922, indicates, won their case, bearing legal as well as social testimony to the supposition that they were right all along:

PEOPLE
VS.
HOLT, MCBRIDE & CO. ET AL.
The defendants herein, at the close of the People's case, have moved for a direction of acquittal and the dismissal of the indictment on the ground that the book 'Jurgen' on the possession of which the indictment is based, is not an 'obscene, lewd, lascivious, filthy, indecent or disgusting book' within the meaning and intent of section 1141 of the Penal Law, for the alleged violation of which the indictment has been found.

I have read and examined the book carefully. It is by Mr. James Branch Cabell, an author of repute and distinction. From the literary point of view its style may fairly be called brilliant. It is based on the mediaeval legends of Jurgen and is a highly imaginative and fantastic tale, depicting the adventures of one who has been restored to his first youth but who, being attended by a shadow of his old self, retains the experience and cynicism of age which frustrates a perfect fulfillment of his desire for renewed youth.

The adventures consist in wanderings through mediaeval and mythological countries and a sojourn in Hell and Heaven. He encounters beings of mediaeval folk-lore and from classical mythology. The most that can be said against the book is that certain passages therein may be considered suggestive in a veiled and subtle way of immorality, but such suggestions are delicately conveyed and the whole atmosphere of the story is of such an unreal and supernatural nature that even these suggestions are free from the evils accompanying suggestiveness in more realistic works. In fact, it is doubtful if the book could be read or understood at all by more than a very limited number of readers.

In my opinion the book is one of unusual literary merit and contains nothing 'obscene, lewd, lascivious, filthy, indecent or disgusting' within the meaning of the statute and the decisions of the courts of this state in similar cases. (See Halsey V. New York Society, 234 N.Y.1; People v. Brainard, 192 App. Div. 116; St. Hubert Guild v. Quinn, 64 Misc. 336.)[16]

The motion, therefore, is granted and the jury is advised to acquit the defendants.

There was, of course, jubilation on the part of the *Jurgen* supporters. Robert M. McBride & Co. responded by issuing a statement praising the book and their original decision to publish it.[17] Cabell celebrated the occasion by perpetrating one of the most trenchantly ironic acts in the annals of American literature: With mock praise and gratitude for services rendered, he dedicated his next book to Sumner!

Several important factors, regarding the critics' views of Cabell's works, and more importantly Cabell's view of himself as a conscious myth-maker, emerged from the *Jurgen* controversy. Throughout the legal proceedings, reviewers, critics and readers alike had been choosing sides, each publishing widely in the popular media. Thus Cabell, a meticulous collector and preserver of almost everything written about him,[19] probably began better to understand from the avalanche of published articles the ways that society perceived his contribution to letters. As a result he produced the Storisende Edition, an eighteen-volume edition of his collected works, and one of the most ambitious single undertakings in twentieth century American letters.

The critics who opposed Cabell fell into two distinct camps. First, there were those who objected to him on moral grounds. Writing in the New York World, for example, Robert C. Benchley declared *Jurgen* to be "a frank imitation of old-time pornographers,"[20] while Heywood Broun said in the New York *Times* that it was little more than a "barroom story refurbished for the boudoir."[21] Rarely, if ever, did the moral critics add new meaning to Cabell's books, however, because by its nature moral criticism presupposes on the part of the critic a code to which the artist should adhere. If he neglects to do so he is then dismissed on judgmental grounds that lie completely outside the realm of art.

Those reviewers and critics who favored Cabell took on the aura of a cult regarding the *Jurgen* episode. Chief among them was Burton Rascoe, a popular literary journalist whose name was widely known in newspaper reviewing circles. Although the long span of criticism of Cabell's books is permeated with Rascoe's name, he was by no means alone in his fulsome praise of *Jurgen*. Joseph Hergesheimer wrote in the New York *Sun* describing it with such purple expressions as "fabulous loveliness," "rapture," and "magic."[22] Harry A. Lappin declared in *The Bookman* that "If Mr. Cabell were an Englishman, an Irishman, or a translated Frenchman he would have long before this have been monographed and lectured upon by . . . professors. . . ."[23] Benjamin DeCasseres declared in the New York *Evening Post Literary Review* that Cabell "stands apart in the literature of America to-day. . . . He may be the beginning of a great reaction in our mode of looking at things."[24] Critic Stanley E. Babb declared in the Galveston (Texas) *Daily News* that Cabell "is assuredly a literary artist if America has ever produced one; and he is a man whom posterity will, in all possibility, be very likely to label a genius."[25] And so it went, through scores of newspaper articles and reviews.[26]

Now, more than half a century later, the *Jurgen* controversy may seem quaint. There are no longer either words, actions or innuendo that are not permissible in print, and the hauntingly erotic activities of Jurgen and the ethereal ladies with whom he comes in contact seem but half-remembered visions from a dream. But the reception of *Jurgen* in the 1920s was not as important as Cabell's attitude toward that reception. It changed his view of himself as an artist.

By the time the *Jurgen* affair was over, the name Cabell had become a household word, and there obviously followed a call for more books by this stunningly different American writer. Accordingly, Cabell and his publisher, knowing that the time was propitious, began work toward bringing out the collected edition. Published between September 1927 and March 1930 the eighteen volumes contained the results of what Cabell said was his grand fictional plan as he had envisioned it as early as 1901.[27]

Any astute reader who works his way through the entire Storisende Edition is aware of its artistic flaws and inconsistencies. As Professor Edgar E. MacDonald has noted,[28] the work taken as a whole presents the reader with serious problems, and moreover displays an artist who is working overly hard to make disparate units appear to be finely honed parts of a grand design. This is true. When we read straight through the entire eighteen volumes we are forced to overlook some of the lesser Cabell, which appears right alongside the greater Cabell.[29]

Flaws aside, however, there is a way of viewing the Storisende Edition that will yield from its books a most satisfying meaning, at the same time showing us exactly what the Cabellian plan was, regardless of whether it was conceived in 1901 or, more probably, following the *Jurgen* episode.

Cabell outlined his plan for the Storisende in the second edition of *Beyond Life*. First published the same year as *Jurgen* as was noted earlier, it was used by Cabell eight years later as the first volume of the collected edition as well as the one in which the author defined the ground plan for the entire series:

> Above all does this book attempt to outline the three possible attitudes toward human existence which have been adopted or illustrated, and at times blended by the many descendants of Manuel. I mean, the Chivalric attitude, the Gallant attitude, and what I can only describe as the poetic attitude. The descendants of Manual have at various times variously viewed life as a testing; as a toy; and as raw material. They have variously sought during their existence upon earth to become—even by the one true test, of their private thoughts while lying awake at night— admirable; or to enjoy life; or to create something more durable than life.

Additionally, Cabell maintained that the Storisende, also called Biography of the Life of Dom Manuel, should be read as an all-engrossing work, with the various books forming chapters in that work. Taken together, one soon learns, the books are employed by Cabell to dramatize his ideas of the three ways of perceiving life—the chivalric, the gallant and the poetic. These three ways, according to Cabell, define the gamut of humanity's various philosophical systems.[30]

Their comparative excellence aside, five books treat the theme of chivalry. They are *Figures of Earth, The Silver Stallion, Domnei,* and *The Rivet in Grandfather's Neck.* In the end of these books we find that chivalry is but an illusion. Such a state of being does not exist at all, Cabell argues; we only think it does and thus we delude ourselves. The same is the case regarding the theme of gallantry, the subject of *Gallantry, Jurgen, The High Place* and *The Cords of Vanity.* As the tales unfold, the reader comes to the inescapable conclusion that it is not attainable. Poetry, the subject of *The Certain Hour* and *Something About Eve,* like gallantry and chivalry, is no more than another delusion, something we might seek, but to whose tenets we cannot adhere.

For all its faults, the Storisende Edition is a major undertaking and execution. In conception, it puts Cabell in company with America's major "dark" writers, people such as Poe, Melville, Hawthorne, Emily Dickinson, the early Eliot, Ezra Pound, Hemingway and others. But the fact remains that the Storisende Edition was not a long-term success, nor were the subsequent books that Cabell was to write, and the question as to why must be addressed.

The 1929 Stock Market Crash, a pivotal economic occurrence that also ushered in marked social and moral changes in America, happened less than half a year before the final volume of the Storisende Edition appeared. And Cabell, whose popular reputation to this time, as far as many people were concerned, rested on *Jurgen,* soon found himself with a rapidly dwindling audience. To all except the hard-core Cabell enthusiasts, and a handful of serious thinkers around the country, Cabell's name still evoked popular ideas of the erotic and the exotic, of prankish and wagish Jurgen, whom many associated with the spirit of the '20s rather than with the increasing gloom of the '30s. Although a serious, even pessimistic, world view informed the pages of *Jurgen,* its surface structure could easily cause the casual reader to consider it little more than a period piece. Additionally, fewer people could afford an eighteen volume collected edition of books in 1930 than could have afforded it even a year earlier.

As the decade progressed, moving steadily from the depths of economic, social and moral confusion, through the Civil Conservation Corps, the Works Progress Administration, the ravages of nature in the American Southwest and finally to the return of happy days, as the popular song of the day proclaimed, an entirely new mood gripped the country. By then Cabell as a writer was no more, and his books were mere souvenirs of the dollar decade, a term sometimes applied to the 1920s.

If we would understand more clearly the case of Cabell's sudden decline in popularity, we might do well to consider the differences between his fiction in general with that of *The Grapes of Wrath,* certainly one of the most widely read and accepted novels of the 1930s.

The Grapes of Wrath, narrowly edged out of the 1930 Pulitzer prize for fiction by Marjorie Kennan Rawling's *The Yearling,* is in many ways a literary touchstone for the decade of the '30s. Charting the plight of the Joad family in realistic albeit sometimes idealized fashion, it is a protest novel that seeks to call attention to the plight of America's poor, its displaced and its poverty stricken. Indeed that novel was so influential that it has led one major scholar of America's popular fiction to state that it "became the subject of impassioned discussion as the period's most popular novel representing the search for answers in terms of social values."[31]

Nor was Steinbeck alone in his literature of social protest and social realism. Although he is surely representative, the interested reader might like to read other literary works which, in one way or another, follow in a similar vein, all seemingly different from Cabell's fictional mode, during the 1930s. This partial list, containing both plays and novels, include John Wexley's *The Last Mile, They Shall Not Die;* George Sklar and Paul Peters'

Stevedore; Albert Bein's *Let Freedom Ring;* Reginald Lawrence and John H. Holmes' *If This Be Treason;* Pearl Buck's *The Good Earth;* Sidney Kingsley's *Men in White* and *Dead End;* the plays of Clifford Odets; the 1930s novels of James T. Farrell; John P. Marquand's *The Late George Apley;* Dos Passos' *The 42nd Parallel, 1919,* and *The Big Money;* and Richard Wright's *Uncle Tom's Children.* If we view *Jurgen,* indeed everything in the Storisend Edition for that matter, in light of *The Grapes of Wrath* and all the other socially oriented works of literature, we can see that America in the 1930s was in no mood for what it considered to be the pastiche fantasies, delivered in overly ornate prose, of the aristocratic James Branch Cabell from Richmond-in-Virginia, as he often signed the date-line of his prefaces.

Despite the loss of his audience, however, Cabell did not abandon his career or even, for that matter, slacken his pace. He published twelve volumes in the 1930s, most notably among them the dream trilogy *Smirt, Smith,* and *Smire,* which may have influenced Joyce's *Finnegans Wake,* which appeared in 1939.[32] But Cabell never again captured the imagination of the reviewers, critics and readers, as he had done in the 1920s. Although nearly a score of books were to come from his typewriter from 1930 until his death in 1958, he was always treated as a period piece, never again achieving the position of a major writer. Perhaps this is owing to the fact that the critically depreciated Cabell of the 1930s, '40s and '50s was markedly different from the successful writer of the earlier period. But it is doubtful whether the different reception of Cabell's books actually caused the change. With the Storisende Edition completed, Cabell began signing his books with the name "Branch Cabell," a punning attempt to indicate that the new writer was a branch of the former James Branch Cabell. But the truth of the matter is that Cabell never scaled the heights in his later books—those written after the close of the '20s—that he did in the earlier ones. His style changed little, but, with the exception of *Smith, Smirt* and *Smire* and perhaps some of the autobiographical works, much of the fire was gone.

In addition to seeing Cabell's books of the 1930s in a negative light, the reviewers began planting in their reviews negative asides about the contribution that Cabell had made to literature, while the critics began to wage more general complaints about his entire canon. Such actions do not, of course, represent a clandestine or organized vendetta against Cabell; rather, they are representative of the fact that he had lost his allure to the socially conscious members of the '30s society. In a review of *These Restless Heads,* for example, Newton Arvin, writing in *The New Republic,* found Cabell to be "A grossly over estimated third-rate Anatole France...."[33] Ludwig Lewisohn declared that "The fields of the earth are on fire under our feet and Cabell offers us the day-dreams of a romantic adolescent; there is famine and he goes about hawking expensive and soon cloying sweets,"[34] while Granville Hicks flatly declared that, "He is a fraud,...a sleek smug egoist....Fortunately few writers have followed the example of Cabell...."[35] During this time also, T.S. Matthews, in review of *Smirt,* ventured the opinion that "Mr. Cabell is a snob, and an American snob is almost a traitor to his country."[36]

The closest activity to what could be called a Cabell revival—although it was short-lived—occurred in the 1960s. James Blish, the late science fiction writer who, in addition to his books contributed to television, notably the now-defunct "Star Trek" series, began publishing a fanzine titled *Kalki* that to this day centers on Cabell, his life and work. Because of Blish's reputation among science fiction writers, his colleagues soon, through the pages of *Kalki,* came to recognize in Cabell a forerunner of themselves. Moreover, Cabell began once again to attract the attention of a small group of academics who wrote theses and dissertations about him and who published occasional articles centering on him in scholarly periodicals. Additionally, another journal, this one called *The Cabellian,* was inaugurated by Julius Rothman, a professor in a New York community college. He soon tired of editing, however, allowing the journal, which published some quite good things on Cabell during its short life, to die. Today, Cabell is virtually unknown and unread. He is omitted from all the major anthologies of American literature. His reputation lives in perfect impunity in his native South just as it does elsewhere in the country.

It is of course regrettable that such should be the case regarding Cabell. Whether or not he devised his plan for his grand fictional universe while still a young man of 22, or whether—which is far more likely—he superimposed his philosophy of later years on much of the material that he had formerly written, is really beside the point. Any astute critic will quickly determine that the Storisende Edition is marked by unevenness, even perhaps questionable judgment on the part of the editor if not its writer. The fact remains, however, that it is one of the great intellectual sagas in American letters, some of its individual volumes exhibiting the touch of genius.

Notes

[1]Those interested in the history and development of the popular reception of Cabell's works should consult his personal scrapbooks, the major ones of which are located at the Alderman Library at the University of Virginia in Charlottesville. Additional scrapbooks, dealing with Cabell's early career, are housed in the Special Collections section of the James Branch Cabell Library of Virginia Commonwealth University in Richmond.

[2]Alice M. Tyler, "Lesser Literary Centers of America: V, Richmond, Virginia," *Book News,* 24 (March), 482-88.

[3]"Current Fiction," *The Nation,* 85 (7 November,1907), 423-24.

[4]Anon, "In the Realm of Books," Chicago *Record-Herald,* 30 November, 1907, p. 6.

[5]Anon, Review of *Gallantry, The Dial,* 43 (1 December, 1907), 380-81.

[6]Anon, "New Books," New York *Sun,* 19 October, 1907, p. 6.

[7]Edwin Markham, writing in the 12 June, 1909, issue of the New York *American,* (p. 9), for example, said that Robert Townsend is an "inveterate sensation seeker, the kind of man with whom we do not wish to associate."

[8]Anon, "James Branch Cabell's Vogue Spreads as Critics Praise Merit of His Work," Richmond *News Leader,* 13 December, 1915, p. 10.

[9]Holt was Cabell's editor at the house of Robert M. McBride & Co., Cabell's publisher.

[10]Padriac Colum and Margaret Freman Cabell. *Between Friends: Letters of James Branch Cabell and Others.* New York: Harcourt, Brace & World, Inc., 1962, p. 157.

[11]W.D. Howells, *Criticism and Fiction and Other Essays.* Clara Marburg Kirk and Rudolf Kirk, eds. New York: New York University Press, 1965, p. 71.

[12]Evidence for Cabell's sudden rise in fame was determined by a reading of the scrapbooks, *op. cit.* n. 1.

[13]James Branch Cabell, *Preface to the Past.* New York: Robert M. McBride & Co., 1936, p. 266.

[14]See the scrapbooks. *op. cit.* n. 1.

[15]Colum, p. 211.

[16]Ibid., pp. 268-69.

[17]Ibid., p. 269.

[18]James Branch Cabell, *Taboo.* New York: Robert M. McBride & Co., 1921. pp. 11-13.

[19] See my "James Branch Cabell's Personal Library." *Studies in Bibliography,* 23 (1970), 207-216; also the scrapbooks, *op. cit.,* no. 1.

[20]Robert C. Benchley, "Books and Other Things," New York *Herald,* 14 February, 1920, p. 8.

[21]Heywood Broun, Review of *Jurgen, New York Tribune,* 17 November, 1919, p. 8.

[22]Joseph Hergesheimer, "An Improvization on Themes from 'Jurgen'," *New York Sun,* 26 October, 1919, p. 4.

[23]Henry A. Lappin, "Romance of the Demiurge," *The Bookman,* 49 (April, 1919), 220-22.

[24]Benjamin DeCasseres, "The Romantic Irony of Cabell," *New York Evening Post Literary Review,* 26 June, 1920, p. 3.

[25]Stanley E. Babb, "James Branch Cabell," *Galveston Daily News,* 16 December, 1923, p. 20.

[26]See the scrapbooks, *op cit.,* n. 1.

[27]James Branch Cabell, *Straws and Prayer-Books.* New York: Robert M. McBride & Co., 1924, p. xiv.

[28]For a differing view of the unity in these books see Edgar E. MacDonald, "The Storisende Edition: Some Liabilities," *The Cabellian* 1, No. 2, (1969), 64-67.

[29]Cabell assumed an anticlimactic result. A reader starts with the powerful *Figures of Earth;* the best of the Biography has been covered when one has read Volume VIII, *The High Place.* In store for a persevering reader are more repetitious early short stories, college poetry, a dreadfully dull play, the trivia of *The Lineage of Lichfield,* a final volume entitled *Townsend of Lichfield,* admittedly a grab-bag of left-overs. It is owing to the sterling quality of Cabell's best work that he survived this edition.... Fortunately, it was limited to 1590 sets.

The basic assumption underlying the Storisende Edition, that all Cabell's work is of equal quality, is perhaps its most pernicious liability. Its total lack of discrimination in presenting Cabell's weakest work alongside his masterpieces is a trap for the unwary. The unsuspecting reader who falls first upon the banalities of *The Cords of Vanity* would hardly be encouraged to read the delightful *Silver Stallion.* Had the Storisende Edition been presented as a critical edition of Cabell's work to show his growth as an artist, such an inclusion as *Cords* could have had value for the student; but rewritten and presented as an integral part of the total scheme, it is a literary disaster. And Cabell did not even follow his resolve to make all the material printed in the Storisende Edition conform to his announced purpose. The inclusion of the inept "Concerning David Jogram" in *Townsend of Lichfield* cannot be excused on any literary grounds, and Cabell makes no pretense to relate it to the Biography. In the Storisende Edition, Cabell strangely persisted in confusing the living with the dead. It simply became an attic trunk, full of sentimental souvenirs.

[30]These three themes are more thoroughly discussed in my chapter "The Baroque Waste Land of James Branch Cabell," in *The Twenties: Fiction, Poetry, Drama,* ed. Warren French DeLand, Florida, 1975, pp. 75-86.

[31]James D. Hart, *The Popular Book: A History of America's Literary Taste.* Berkeley and Los Angeles: Univ. of California Press, 1961, p. 250.

[32]Nathan Halper, "Joyce and James Branch Cabell," *A Wake Newsletter* 6, (August, 1969), 51-60.

[33]Newton Arvin, "High in the Brisk Air," *The New Republic,* 120 (2 March, 1932), 78-79.

[34]Ludwig Lewisohn, "James Branch Cabell," in his *Expression in America.* New York: Harper & Bros., 1932, pp. 194, 530-31.

[35]Granville Hicks, "James Branch Cabell," in his *The Great Tradition.* New York: Macmillan, 1933, pp. 220-21 and *passim.*

[36]T.S. Matthews, Review of *Smirt, The New Republic,* 78 (18 April, 1934), 284.

J.S. Pennell's *The History of Rome Hanks:* Contributions Toward Perspectives

Victor Howard

THE HISTORY OF *Rome Hanks and Kindred Matters* was published in 1944 and while it received substantial recognition from the public and reviewers at that time, it has long since settled into obscurity. The author, a Kansan named Joseph Stanley Pennell, did publish a sequel over the next few years, *The History of Nora Beckham* (1948).[1] But it did not create the stir which *Rome Hanks* had engendered.

Pennell was born and raised in Junction City, Kansas, schooled at Kansas University and at his own expense at Pembroke College, Oxford. After working for some years on various newspapers and radio stations, he settled in the late 1930s into a small apartment in Junction City to begin composing a massive autobiographical-family narrative which was to extend across three books, at least. Pennell sent the first volume, *Rome Hanks,* to publishers in 1942, but when it failed to win acceptance, he left the manuscript in the hands of the Junction City Librarian, Thelma Baker, and joined the Army. Miss Baker, a longtime friend and confidante, sent the book to Random House who sent it back. She next packed it off to Scribner's, whose editor, Maxwell Perkins, finally replied after a long silence and indicated his company's interest in this "amazing book." Although Miss Baker acknowledged later that it was "mostly chance" that directed her to Scribner's and Perkins, the task of editing and reorganizing a manuscript over eight hundred pages in length seems, in retrospect and legend, exactly appropriate to Maxwell Perkins' patience and particular genius.[2]

By the end of the winter of 1943, Scribner's had made up its mind to publish *Rome Hanks* though it was evident that much labor had yet to be applied to the shape of the book. I have not seen the original manuscript; I do not know if it exists. But something of its character and quality can be inferred from the correspondence that passed between Pennell and Perkins over the next year.

Rome Hanks is a *bildungsroman* in which a young Kansas named Lee Harrington traces his heritage back to the Civil War and then forward to his birth. His informants are various participants and veterans of that era, all of whom have this in common: they will be ancestors or friends of ancestors of Lee Harrington. The focus of these 'memoirs' is one Romulus Lycurgus Hanks, Harrington's great-grandfather, a man of consummate heroic dimensions, brave, honest, serious, a great Captain to those who know him but one more remarkable American whom the formal histories of that

127

period have overlooked. From his grandfather, Thomas Beckham, from his great uncle, Pinckney Harrington and from a family friend and local legend, Thomas Wagnal, Lee Harrington learns of his origins: of the great battles of the War at Gaines Mill, Shiloh and Gettysburg; of the post-war scenes of peace, livelihood and migration. All of these narratives are conveyed with fine colloquial detail; they bear the marks of careful research and imaginative evocation by Pennell.

There is a plot of sorts which unifies certain of the episodes: the continuing professional and personal conflict between Captain Hanks and General Clint Belton, the latter an unscrupulous soldier-politician who makes his way into Grant's cabinet over the dead bodies of his men and with the careful cultivation and manipulation of comrades and superiors. A decade and a half after the war, Hanks and Belton meet for one last confrontation, Hanks laid waste by war injuries and trauma, barely scraping a living out of the inhospitable Kansas terrain, Belton, ruined by personal scandal. The meeting is a stand-off. Belton disappears from the novel, Hanks dies soon thereafter of consumption. The remainder of the book is given over to the marriage of Hanks' daughter to Beckham, the growth of their family, a move to "Fork City," Kansas, the marriage of their daughter to Robert Harrington, the birth of Lee Harrington. These later sections are given particular credibility by Pennell's careful description of small-town life on the plains in the late nineteenth century.

Pennell explained in an early letter to Perkins that he saw the form of his work as a circular staircase, "a spiral unfolding," whereby events and figures occur and recur in and out of sequence in a freely associated manner. Narratives wheel and turn, dissolve and emerge, shift, distort, inflate, collect, resolve, all of this activity distilled through the sensibility of Lee Harrington. Pennell was quite certain that this was the way the memory worked, impressionistically, haphazardly, imperfectly; this was the way by which History was to be recovered.[3]

The original manuscript, and to a much less degree the published version, contained a contemporary 'overlay' represented by Lee Harrington in which the young man, while seeking to make sense of the several accounts of the old days, also pursues with intense and romantic ardor a young woman he has met while living in St. Louis. Her name is Christa. Bright, blonde, jaded, long-legged, elusive and remarkable, Christa had perversely prompted Lee to his quest after his origins by her sardonic remark: "Yes, I'm sure your Grandfather must have been a fine old Southern gentleman." (p. 3)

From the beginning of their negotiations, Maxwell Perkins made it clear to Pennell that he and his associates at Scribner's viewed that contemporary sequence with great skepticism. Although they agreed

that the Civil War part was magnificent, and that the early America after the war was not less fine or memorable. But we felt that while the contemporary part showed the talent of a true writer, it did not blend with the rest, and was not equal with it,—and that in fact while one was reading those parts, he was impatient to get back to the early America, the war and after the war. The contemporary part is relatively trivial, and causes a let-down whenever one comes upon it, as compared to those so much greater events.[4]

Whatever the specifics of that contemporary part, one thing was clear: language and action were often relayed in obscene manner by Perkins' judgment and so "a great deal of it we think could not be printed *per se.*"[5] Aside from some cursing and a few indelicate but quite understandable and soldierly references to excrement and one late scene in a brothel, nothing remains in the final draft to explain these concerns. The Boston Watch and Ward Society did ban *Rome Hanks* eventually, for what that is worth.

But that pronouncement is nowhere so astounding as the other caution: the characterization of Christa, Perkins proposed, "is unmistakable, unless there has been a most amazing series of coincidences. Anyone who knew the person she appears to be. . . would recognize her instantly. . . . She is she. But nobody could publish what you tell about her without plainly being guilty of libel." How was it that Perkins could recognize the original? "And as for us, we are her publishers and would have no right to do it, whatever the law."[6]

Pennell's heroine happened to be based upon a girl he had known in his youth who had since become a popular writer whose books were handled by Scribners! In response to this incredible coincidence which he had not known, Pennell very naturally asked for time to think it over. He liked what he had written, he confessed to Perkins. Nothing wrong with that. But more important was his plan for a larger, longer work, *Rome Hanks* being the initial section. To cut now in the drastic way argued, to reduce the contemporary sequence to a modest unifying element, to relinquish the Lee-Christa romance was to jeopardize the plan.[7]

For all his misgivings, Pennell must have been persuaded and certainly pleased by the implied analogy betwen Perkins' influence on Thomas Wolfe's materials and a similar responsibility for Pennell's manuscript. Shortly after the crisis broke out, Perkins wrote the distressed author:

You mention Thomas Wolfe: I was simply compelled to work on his book to save him from insanity,—that is, his second book. I remember writing a friend what was going on, and that I would probably later be damned for it, for I had to cut so many good things,—though only with Tom's final consent. . . . I have never done work like that except under compulsion. . . . It is frightfully risky and audacious to try to manipulate a talent,—which is the greatest thing in the world, and mighty rare.[8]

From May, 1943, through December and into 1944, Perkins and his colleagues, prominently Wallace Meyer, conveyed their particular recommendations about deletions and reorganization. As late as November, Perkins was still imposing cuts, ten to twelve pages in length quite often, many falling in the last two-thirds of the manuscript. The effect of these excisions, for the most part, ". . . is to eliminate all contemporary narrative that pulls the reader away from the Civil War narratives."[9] This explanation is not quite precise, since a third or more of the book deals (and perhaps always dealt) with the aftermath of the war.

Christa remains in the final version though her part there is peripheral, to say the least. Her influence on Lee Harrington remains powerful, however. Shall we call her his muse?

Once the deletions had been confirmed in the first galleys, Perkins could turn in December, 1943, to restructuring the balance. Despite his conceit about a "spiral unfolding," Pennell had apparently developed in the original a pair of linear episodes, one of which bore the Hanks-Beckham-Wagnal materials from the battles of the war to the plains of Iowa and Kansas, the other of which then fell back and picked up those passages which dealt with Lee Harrington's southern ancestors and brought these forward from the war. Thus, the North fought its Civil War and came home and then the South fought *its* war and came home. Perkins urged and Pennell agreed to the reordering of the histories so that the war scenes, North and South, were handled in reasonable conjunction, with the post-war materials then placed in similar juxtaposition.[10]

This accomplished and various transitions inserted and touches here and there and the book could move toward its publication in the late spring of 1944. Perkins' finesse as editor (and as a gentleman) is summed up in his letter of March 29, 1943, as he is just starting to think seriously about the unwieldy but remarkable manuscript before him. "Suppose the book began: 'I am sure,' said Christa, 'that your grandfather was a fine old Southern gentleman.' It was that that shocked Lee into remembering. And suppose it ended perhaps just with his birth."[11]

And over a year later, dozens of letters later, after much thought and reflection and negotiation and excision and revision and addition, that is how the book opened and how it closed.

The novel is called *The History of Rome Hanks and Kindred Matters.* One may imagine that it was called a 'history' because it embraces an era and because, though fiction, yet the book was based on verifiable events and figures. The 'matters' referred to in the title were the lives and times and impressions of the several characters who supply Lee with the substance and feel of his past. Now, the Civil War and its aftermath have become the dominant elements. The contemporary overlay (Perkins had once described Pennell's technique as suggesting a palimpsest) was intact but greatly and wisely restricted. A final remark about that controversial section.

One cannot help recalling other novels and authors when he reads *Rome Hanks.* The form of the book, the search into the past, recommend this: Faulkner's *Absolom, Absolom;* Wolfe's *Look Homeward, Angel;* Joyce's *Ulysses.* So far as I can discover, Faulkner's example was never cited by Pennell or Perkins (though it would be by reviewers in 1944). Lee Harrington does remind one of Quentin Compson and his reluctant and then inspired search. Drawn at first in the wake of Rosa Coldfield, Quentin soon voyages alone, illusion and distortion and ambiguity gradually giving way to an appalling perception.

Lee Harrington's expedition never quite matches this intensity nor are his insights during and after the search of such tragic dimensions. Harrington, after all, has been sent on his search by a diffident lady whom he sees as Beatrice Portinari to his Dante. Why go in quest of his ancestors? "It will add to my stature in her eyes?" (p. 4) Lee digresses from his 'research' on occasion in order to brood on his love for Christa who does not apparently brood on Lee and who turns out to be less than willing or capable as a muse. These asides are few and brief enough, although after all is said and done about ancestors and battles and frontier life in old America, Lee (and Pennell) close the book, yes, with the boy's birth but then they add an epilogue of sorts devoted to mooning references to great heroines: Guinevere, Nell Gwynn, Beatrice. Lee recites four sonnets of a decidedly juvenile nature: "If in this impermanence I love you more..." and "Since I am done with pretty compliment...." Lee rightly concludes that he is a "most sterile Dante." (pp. 361-3) The powerful scenes, the compelling figures, the elaborate historical landscape, all that has been told before are put in danger by a meretricious ending.

What moved Perkins and his associates to their initial and to their abiding belief in *Rome Hanks* was "all the Civil War and old America parts—what a wonderful picture the book gives of this country in those days."[12] "A wonderful picture," indeed. Pennell's father had been a professional photographer in Junction City, as Lee's father, Robert, had been in Fork City. The senior Pennell's bequest included thousands of photographs and negatives of prairie life at the turn of the century. The younger Pennell, in the course of his exacting, massive research, inevitably came upon the ten volume *Photographic History of the Civil War,* published early in the second decade of the twentieth century. Steeped in the technique and idiom of photography, Pennell used that medium for its literal and metaphorical values.

Matthew Brady and "his Whatsit" appear suddenly before a group of wounded Union soldiers, among whom is Tom Beckham, Lee's grandfather:

Tom rose up on an elbow and looked at the small Cork Irishman, the great Washington society photographer, the Lincoln-snapper, that preserver of the Senatorial Stare, the Poser of the FFV's. Brady removed the lens-cap and, for a long instant, all was quiet and still: the instant was freezing in the collodion as the light burnt the bromides and iodides of Brady's wetplate. Everyone within the eye of the lens had struck an attitude as if he were a statue in a public square of his home town. Wooden faces grew on the boyfaces, the beards petrified. The dead grew deader before Brady's camera. Tom watched the Irishman's lips silently tell off the seconds of frozen time. Time stretched to the breaking point like a bit of rubber; the buzz of thousands of flies only locked the paralysis of the minutes. Brady returned the velvetlined cap to his shining lens. The camera was blind again. But in 1912 the moment would be there even to the ladder against the house. (p. 75)

Tom Wagnal recalls:

I had a photograph of the regiment once, and in the background—out of focus—there sat a man on a soapbox. You could not see that he had his pants down except by looking carefully.... I don't know who the man in the latrine box was but he was undoubtedly answering the call of nature. Later the same photograph got into the *Photographic History. (p. 41)*

Lee Harrington:

Shiloh is so old...so long ago that even photographs taken at the reunion in 1899...seem now as mysterious as what you see in breathtaking depth...when you look through the eyewindows of a stereoscope at a pair of pictures labelled, Recent Excavations, Pompeii...(pp. 11-12)

Such references are meant, no doubt, to support the historical validity of the narratives. They are infinitely sad. But they also bear witness to the need, in a novel such as *Rome Hanks,* to define as carefully as can be registered through language, the fact and the meaning of the moments. It is this definition of the past that is really the subject of these excerpts and the subject of *The History of Rome Hanks and Kindred Matters.*

Lee Harrington is fortunate in the quality of witnesses whose testimony he solicits. There is Thomas Wagnal, of great antiquity, who sits, like Charlie Marlowe, passing the bottle back and forth to his friend and who is loquacious, sensitive and despairing. Wagnal remembers everything and his singular imagination circulates around, over and through the facts, dates, figures, faces that he summons. His training at Edinburgh as a physician has given him a precision and authority that are all but matchless. Wagnal roams over the roughly drawn anecdotes, their meaning now made clear:

Is it not strange that all over Tennessee, Mississippi, Alabama and Georgia are buried pieces of men that I hacked away from them—arms, legs, fingers, and toes—even a nose or two left ears. Some I shouldn't have cut off. God, there are men even now living in Des Moines or Keokuk or Salina who wake up at night and think: Jesus Christ, it's funny: part of me was buried down on the banks of the Tennessee River in the Spring of 1862. Part of me is already doornail dead, mackerel dead, stone dead—bled like a stuck pig. Maybe, by God, the bones are still down there under the dirt, clean and white. My armbones and my handbones. My meatless hand and arm that used to have such good hard muscles—that I was so proud and vain of. That I figgered ways to get the girls to feel and ways to let them see. God, it's funny: I've got a hand in Tennessee. I can remember how that saw sounded. (pp. 112-13)

Wagnal is the sole source of the Hanks-Belton conflict as it develops during the Shiloh campaign and through the marches into the deep South. Belton falters and hides in mad fear at Pittsburg Landing on the first day of Shiloh, not an encouraging act for the commander of the 117th Iowas. Rome Hanks, a company officer, finds Belton and brings him back into the action. Belton repays Hanks by treating him with great condescension and by promoting his own career at the expense of others.

As Wagnal develops his memoir, Hanks recedes into the background and Belton and Wagnal move forward in importance. There ensues a remarkable interlude that takes place as the regiment pushes its way into Mississippi. Belton and Wagnal chance upon an estate occupied by two wondrous sisters, Katherine and Una Theron. Their father is a smuggler; their grandfather, a Confederate general who has just died in a duel. We are now suddenly thrust into what one can only call a Gothic Romance.

The brilliance of the sisters is only scarcely surpassed by the grandeur of their home. Never mind the cutglass chandelier, the French windows, the piazza, the Gobelin tapestries, the Amontillado. Never mind the huge servant named Rasselas. Here is the watercloset that Wagnal finds in his rooms:

The stoolbowl was made of figured pottery with the griffin, lion and crocodile device on it. [The Theron family seal] The seat was shaped like an English saddle and covered with well-seasoned padded cordovan leather. Along the wall within easy reaching distance was a shelf of books and above the stool hung a bracket of glass-shaded candles. On top of the bookshelf sat the ewer attributed to Cellini, holding matches and an old flintlock powdertester. [Nearby] the obscene little statue of Cloacina sitting in a wall niche. (p. 93)

Belton and Wagnal succumb to such charms. Wagnal, at least, is happy in his arrangement. Though she is young, haughty, vain, outrageous, Katherine Theron is also spirited, brave, witty and loving. They will marry and move to Iowa where they will continue Wagnal's friendship with Hanks after the war.

Clint Belton marries the other sister, Una, whose range of emotion, love and fidelity is as brief as her name. They live in Iowa for a time but give it short shrift and move to Washington where Belton joins Grant's cabinet as Secretary of War. They are soon ruined by the revelation that Una Belton has used her position to secure an appointment in the West for a trader who pays her several thousand a year. Belton resigns; Una dies shortly, having caught cold in a "topless Worth gown."

Whereas the flavor, not to say the credibility, of *Rome Hanks* is secured in the vivid chronicles of war and of life and times on the plains, the chronicles of 'old America,' the Belton-Wagnal-Hanks plot is not particularly convincing. Hanks and Wagnal suggest mythic dimensions. To borrow Hamlin Garland's phrase about the return of a private from the war: they "rise into magnificent types." Belton, loosely based on one W.W. Belknap, leader of an Iowa regiment and later, Grant's secretary of war, is too villainous, too singular in his meanness.

Lee Harrington's maternal grandfather, Thomas Beckham, migrates to Kansas after the war. As a boy in the 97th Pennsylvania, Drakes Zouaves, he had suffered a terrible leg wound at Gaines Mill, a struggle that is set alongside the Shiloh days at the beginning of the novel. Beckham marries Rome Hanks' daughter, Myra, and their child, Nora, will marry Robert Harrington of North Carolina, likewise a recent arrival in Kansas. Beckham is a narrator of sorts, better call him a source, for his life and war saga have been absorbed by Lee Harrington over many years of affectionate association. In fact, Beckham dominates the later scenes of the book before and after Hanks' death. Wagnal steps back as an eyewitness; Lee, himself, is not yet born or else too young to understand. The Harrington grandfather, Judson, and his son, Robert, Lee's father, are scarcely mentioned in those years. The narrative voice all but disappears.

Because he knows his ancestor best of all, Lee Harrington holds Beckham in special and tender regard:

...he walked (perhaps it would be better to say he tramped, for there was always a certain marching aspect in his carriage—and he would sometimes turn to me and say, Take care don't tramp on the toad, he eats potato bugs, or don't tramp on your Grandma's clean floor with those muddy shoes, or don't let the horse tramp on your toe) with a firm upright carriage, his head held high still, as if he had never heard those saws which every Polonius is eager to tell us all....I rarely saw his face when its expression was tired, or cynical or in despair, but I conjecture that weariness, cynicism, defeat and despair must have eaten at the edges of him as they eat at the edges of all. (p. 55)

It is a measure of Lee's growing involvement in the recovery of the past that he goes to North Carolina to talk with his Great Uncle Pinckney Harrington, Pink, who, like Wagnal, is garrulous, except in his recall. His fund of anecdote, local history, folklore, comic opera, is rich. But it is his account of Pickett's Charge at Gettysburg on July 3, 1863, that confirms his genius.

That battle is set almost exactly half-way through *Rome Hanks* and effectively brings to a close the Civil War era. For good reason, probably, Perkins had urged Pennell to take it out of its place near the end of the original manuscript. Even so, the description of the charge is so powerful that the second half of the book is placed in some jeopardy: nothing so exciting will occur again.

Uncle Pink's account of those minutes on July 3 is distinguished by the colloquial idiom; the homely perspective of the rank and file soldier; the meticulous detail. Here is the advance:

Keep close up, Wagg hollered. An' remembah what the Lawd Gahd said to Jeremiah! After a little way you could look around, Uncle Pink said, because it was such a long walk in the hot sun to the Yankee lines—you could look around and wish for a drink of water and wondah what was goin' to happen. You could look up and down the line and wondah if that part oveh there had hit the Yankees yet. For a while I thought the bayonets looked like a tall steel picketfence in the sun. You could walk along and figgah: I got me a Yank in front of me comin' at me with his bayonet! I can't shoot him, because I just fired. Shall I jump outa his way and come in and stick him from the side, or shall I knock his bayonet to one side and stick him from the front, or shall I mash in his head with a clubmusket? Supposin' he gets me fust? Supposin' I tuhn and run—and he sticks me in the back? And I kept thinkin', if it wasn't so damn hot and I had a drink, I wouldn't really mind gittin' kilt. (p. 197)

The withdrawal:

It was a strange part of Seminary Ridge—not where we started from—Uncle Pink said. Men were comin' back just like we were. They all looked bewildered.

There were some officahs on hawses—one with a red jacket and a queer hat. One of 'em in a plain shabby gray uniform rode out to us. He had a Vandyke beard like yore grandfather use' to wear. I knew him in a minute, even if I't never seen him before. It was Lee. Nobody could mistake him. By Gahd! You could feel him. It was all my fault he said. We must all stand together now, to save the rest.

I didn't say anything, but Lacey came up hollering: Look Gen'l Lee! he hollered, and ripped the flag out of his jacket. I saved the Old Eighty-Six flag.

Lacy began to cry—and the Old Man took off his hat. That was what they called Pickett's charge, Uncle Pink said. (pp. 203-304)

Uncle Pink now relates the story of the return home of his brother, Judson, and himself, their brief time in college, Judson's marriage and departure for the west. Pink is like Wagnal in his easy grasp of storytelling, but there is one noteworthy difference: Wagnal brings to his histories a certain quality of self-importance while Uncle Pink is unassuming and amusing. Wagnal broods over his long-dead Katherine, lives in isolation, drinks. Uncle Pink has married late in life, has a young family, laughs.

Once Uncle Pink loses track of the Judson Harrington branch, his account ends. The migration of Judson and his son, Robert, who will become Lee's father, is not described here, nor is there any effort made to provide a chronicle of the Harringtons in Kansas prior to Lee's birth. One can only speculate, at this point, about the absence of this history: whether it was present in the original manuscript and subsequently cut or whether it was to be reserved for a later novel.

The narrators accounted for, it remains to say something of Rome Hanks himself. Much is made of him by Wagnal in the first chapters and, indirectly, by Beckham, in the later ones. But though we understand that these men revere Hanks and with good reason, yet the man remains essentially a mystery. This may well be because the novel depends so much on narrators, on voices, at times on what might be described as interior monologues. Hanks is seldom heard from directly.

I have noted the prominence of the Wagnal-Belton scenes in Mississippi and the consequent retirement of Hanks as a major figure in that period. Hanks is eventually wounded and captured. He survives Andersonville to stagger home to his family in Iowa. In time Belton persuades Hanks to co-sign a loan for ten thousand dollars. When Belton defaults, Hanks must sell his business and home and take his family to Kansas for a fresh start. Beckham wanders by, marries Myra Hanks and across the next decade, the two families live drearily on the prairies.

The single protracted view we have of the interior shape and sensibility of Rome Hanks comes some fourteen years after the war and *coincidentally* on the very evening when Belton turns up, Una now dead, his career in ashes. Belton wants to kill Hanks for supposedly having gossiped about Belton's failure at Pittsburg Landing.

Hanks sits at home alone, Darwin's *Origin* opened before him to the great passage which contemplates "a tangled bank, clothed with many plants. . . with birds singing. . . with various insects flitting about, and with worms crawling through the damp earth. . ." (p.286). Hanks wishes he had been able to sit and write, as Darwin had, "some work of penetration and discovery." But Hanks had become a man of action instead until, late in his life, he is too tired to take up a new calling, to concentrate.

But Mr. Darwin's pen moved in tranquility and content: he had never viewed such a segment of the process of Natural Selection. . .as occurred on the banks of the Tennessee River, April sixth and seventh, Eighteen Hundred and Sixty Two, among the higher animals. (p.287).

Hank's younger brother, Remus, died there and Rome and Wagnal buried him near a big tree, their tools a bayonet and a tin cup.

Belton walks in out of the darkening prairie, proposing to kill Hanks who replies that Belton was not more a coward than anyone else. If that is cowardice, then he himself was regularly a coward. As this assurance spills out, Belton turns and leaves.

Since it is just possible that heroism is inexplicable and that heroes are always mysteries, Pennell may have been right in keeping Rome Hanks vaguely drawn as a character. Wagnal, Beckham and the others have not exaggerated his qualities; Belton's iniquity certainly illuminates them by contrast. It is hard to accept Hanks' admission to Belton that he did not risk his life in the war for any principle: ". . .I wanted the distinction and the spoils which come to a conquering hero just as you did. No, I was not humanity's hero. . . ." (p.295). This could explain Hanks' refusal or inability to challenge Belton when that officer resorts to brutal punishment of errant soldiers under his command or his reluctance to believe the stories that

Belton has been seen in battle shooting at one or another of the men who saw him cringe before Pittsburg Landing. But there is no other real evidence of Hanks' ambition to be "a conquering hero". Presumably his own men, Wagnal among them, would have grasped such a motive and not have been so adoring.

Hanks dies of consumption caught when he goes out on a chill evening to bring lambs in out of the weather. He has had an intuition that he will not live out his life and perhaps it is just as well: ". . .in his house at the edge of the Kansas prairie, with his family around him, he was as a man marooned in an icy waste of solitude" (p.300). That "solitude" is not just physical though it is that to a degree; the prairies in those days were fearfully desolate. The "icy waste of solitude" is emotional, as well, and intellectual. The old warrior who sits reconciling Darwin's theory of evolution with his own experiences finds horrors there that cannot be relayed to others. What then, of your hero?

****

What then of your hero? What then of humanity and its vaunted progress if the slaughter at Shiloh can be allowed to take place, can be celebrated years later in pageant and song?

Rome Hanks' greatness lay in his physical and moral courage and in his decency. Although his friends extolled his performance in the war, the real test of his capacities comes in the next dozen years when he must live a paltry anonymous existence on the prairies. It is Hanks' anonymity that is paradoxically so compelling. On the one hand, we can be reassured that such a man might be found in every village in America: the incarnation of the American virtues of simplicity, humility, industry, devotion. But on the other hand, one wants to inscribe the name of Rome Hanks in public places. It is sweet and sad that this cannot be.

****

The History of Rome Hanks and Kindred Matters appeared in bookstores in July, 1944. The following January, Scribners contracted for the sale of the book through the Doubleday Dollar Book Club and as a selection of the Literary Guild. Doubleday also received permission to issue a reprint edition in September, 1945. Metro-Goldwyn-Mayer purchased film rights during this same period. Finally, so far as this writer has been able to determine, Avon brought out the last edition of the novel in paperback in 1956 under the title: *Dishonoured Flesh: The History of Rome Hanks.*

The Scribner publication followed by a month or so the Allied invasion of France. Burdened by a series of lacklustre assignments as an Army officer, at forty, too old to be sent to combat training, Pennell wrote Perkins of his chagrin and despair at missing the great adventure.

Pennell could take satisfaction in the acclaim his novel received that summer and autumn. Given the ferocity of the battles on the continent it may well have been that American audiences seized on *Rome Hanks* because they could read there of victory and sacrifice and dedication, purge themselves of anxiety and take vicarious comfort in the description of another war which was safely in the past, though yet remaining a singular event in the history of the nation.

The reviews were numerous and thorough. The form of the book gave cause for concern although the portrait of Hanks was appreciated: R.E. Danielson in the October, 1944, *Atlantic:* "Obscure as it can be, this is yet a book of real power and promise." George Mayberry in August 13, 1944, *New Republic:* "And when the noise of Pennell's language and the confusion of his method die down a little, the figure of Romulus Lycurgus Hanks, soldier and citizen, remains to remind us that all the giants in the land didn't get into the history books." Harrison Smith in July 22, 1944, *Saturday Review of Literature:* "...he has added in this book a solid and memorable volume to the fictional history of America...."

Not a few reviewers sensed a resemblance between Pennell's style and subject and those of Thomas Wolfe, but they were not inclined to be mischievous in pointing out that detail. Perkins and Pennell do not seem to have discussed this matter in their correspondence, though Pennell had read Wolfe. The reader can detect the similarities hopefully with the help of the synopsis provided here and the inclusion of representative passages cited: the autobiographical motive, the experiments with technique, the exploration and dramatization of Self, the profound sense of the Past, the epic design intended to embrace the substance and shape of America. In these respects, the two authors seem to have anticipated that other saga of the nineteenth century, Ross Lockridge's *Raintree County,* published in 1948.

The Civil War is the central and unifying subject of *Rome Hanks.* The achievement of that book derives from Pennell's vision and art, but it also springs from the author's powerful instinct for the details of battle and soldiering. Pennell may have examined a thousand books on that era before setting out to write, as he had claimed. But in the end, it all came down to an act of the imagination. Maxwell Perkins understood this when he responded to Pennell's chagrin and despair at having missed the invasion of Europe in the summer of 1944:

You needn't tell me what you felt, I know all about it. I know it was a tragic disappointment. But I agree with you that it is probably someone who was not present who will do the thing. There is a consolation for missing great events and spectacles. One man can see in experience very little, actually, but the imagination is boundless. This is commonplace, I guess, but it is consoling.

Perkins was talking about Normandy, but he was also talking about the historical novel and about *Rome Hanks.* The first edition of that book had its dust cover framed in sculpted garlands, Johnny Reb and Billy Yank poised stiffly in the upper corners, a series of scenes, photographs perhaps? running down the sides and across the bottom. Perched on a stone bench in the middle there sits a man, dressed in a business suit of the 1940s, his head resting on one hand. It is Lee Harrington and, who can say otherwise? Joseph Stanley Pennell, recreating their "wonderful picture...of this country in those days."[14]

Notes

[1] All quotations from *Rome Hanks* are taken from the one edition published by Scribners in 1944.

[2] The Kansas City Star, September 10, 1944.

[3] Correspondence of Joseph Stanley Pennell to Maxwell Perkins, March 19, 1943 in the Scribners Archives, Princeton University. I am indebted to Charles Scribner III for permission to examine the Pennell-Perkins letters and to quote from the Perkins materials. I am also indebted to Ann Farr of the Princeton University Manuscript Collection for her generous assistance.

[4] Correspondence of Maxwell Perkins to Joseph Stanley Pennell, March 29, 1943.

[5] *Ibid.*

[6] *Ibid.*

[7] Pennell to Perkins, undated letter but undoubtedly falling sometime after March 29, 1943 and before April 8, 1943.

[8] Perkins to Pennell, April 8, 1943.

[9] Perkins to Pennell, December 30, 1943. The comment actually is enclosed in a summary note prepared by Wallace Meyer and forwarded by Perkins.

[10] *Ibid.*

[11] Perkins to Pennell, March 29, 1943.

[12] *Ibid.*

[13] Perkins to Pennell, June 13, 1944.

[14] Pennell published *The History of Nora Beckham* in 1948, in which he represented the youth and young manhood of Lee Harrington. Subtitled, *A Museum of Home Life,* the novel is distinguished by its powerful evocation of Harrington's powerful relationship with his mother. Pennell died in 1963.

Lolita:
A Modern Classic in Spite of Its Readers

Phillip F. O'Connor

LOLITA STAYS like a deep tattoo. Critics tumble over one another racing to publish articles on its twists, myths and artifices. Paperback houses have reprinted it again and again. It is the second most often cited title in *Book Week*'s Poll of Distinguished Fiction, 1945-65. It has been made into a movie, a successful one at that. Sales and critical attention have opened the way for the appearance of many of Nabokov's other novels, particularly his early or Russian novels. Without *Lolita,* Nabokov's rise to literary sainthood might have been delayed beyond his natural years. Indeed, it might never have occurred.

Nabokov's twelfth novel was brought out in 1955 by Maurice Girodias' Olympia Press in Paris when the author was fifty-six years old. It had been rejected by four American publishers on a variety of grounds, all, according to Andrew Field, stemming from "a compound of fright and incomprehension" (*Nabokov, His Life in Art,* Boston, 1967, p. 335). Though Girodias had now and then published the works of distinguished writers such as Durrell, Beckett and Genet, he was known mainly for an output of "dirty books." He saw in *Lolita,* some of whose literary values he recognized, mainly a weapon in the fight against moral censorship. Nabokov was soon forced to insist that he would be hurt if his work became a *succes de scandale (Ibid.,* pp. 335-36). The author needn't have worried; during the year following its publication, *Lolita* was given not a single review and soon became just another book on the Olympia list, not even sufficiently pornographic to compete with some of Girodias' other titles, such as *White Thighs* and *The Sex Life of Robinson Crusoe.*

An early sign of the lastingness of *Lolita* seems to be the unanimity of contempt it aroused in snobs and slobs alike after it did find a public of sorts. Orville Prescott in the daily *New York Times* (August 18, 1958) declared:

Lolita, then, is undeniably news in the world of books. Unfortunately it is bad news. There are two equally serious reasons why it isn't worthy any adult reader's attention. The first is that it is dull, dull, dull in a pretentious, florid and archly fatuous fashion. The second is that it is repulsive.

Prescott shared contempt with "Stockade Clyde" Carr, a barracks-mate of Nabokov's former student and, later, editor, Alfred Appel, Jr. Appel found and purchased the Oympia edition in Paris in 1955 and brought it back to his Army post, where Clyde, recognizing the publisher said, "Hey, lemme read your dirty book, man!" Urged to read it aloud himself, Clyde stumbled through the opening paragraph: "Lo...lita, light...of my life. Fire of my...loins. My sin, my soul. Lo...lee...ta" then tossed down the book and complained, "It's goddam littachure!" (Alfred Appel, Jr., in *The Annotated Lolita,* by Vladimir Nabokov, New York, 1970, pp. xxxiv-xxxv). Nabokov seems to have anticipated some of the fads, fashions and contempts of both schools. In the foreword to the novel, Nabokov's alter-ego, or mask, the scholar John Ray, Jr., says "...those very scenes one might ineptly accuse of a sensuous existence of their own, are the most strictly functional ones in the development of a tragic tale, tending unswervingly to nothing less than moral apotheosis." Nabokov's works are full of such clues and warnings, but only sensitive readers pick them up. In fact, *Lolita* remained an underground novel until 1956 when Graham Greene in *The London Times* placed it on his list of the ten best novels published during the previous year (*Ibid.,* pp 6-7). As Field points out:

> Greene's pronouncement aroused great controversy, but also stimulated the interest of many important and respected critics and writers, who, with few exceptions, were quick to recognize the enormous importance and non-pornographic nature of the novel (p. 336).

By 1959 many literary people had taken and followed Greene's signal (I might say, *"Not until* 1959..."). V.S. Pritchett in *The New Statesman* (Jan. 10) appreciated the novel and addressed the problem of the so-called pornographic content, no doubt aware that the U.S. Customs Bureau had for a time confiscated copies of *Lolita:*

> I can imagine no book less likely to incite the corruptible reader; the already corrupted would surely be devastated by the author's power of projecting himself into their fantasy-addled minds. As for minors, the nymphets and schoolboys, one hardly sees them toiling through a book written in a difficult style, filled on every page with literary allusions, linguistic experiment and fits of idiosyncrasy (p. 38).

Such praise seems mild, given what we now know of the general richness of the novel. To one degree or another, for example, critics have demonstrated that *Lolita* is a full-blown psychological novel with roots deep in nineteenth century models; a detective novel with conventions that date back to Poe, perhaps beyond; a confessional novel; a Doppleganger Tale; an extended allegory for the artistic process; a sexual myth more complicated and mysterious than comparable Freudian stereotypes; even a fable with correspondences to the Little Red Riding Hood story. And of course it to some degree parodies these types.

In his final confrontation with Quilty, "the kidnapper," Humbert, "the detective," comically plays his role to the extreme. Then, as if to remind us that popular genres often share both conventions and cliches, Nabokov mixes matters; that is, for moments at least, a scene from a detective novel becomes, as well, a scene from a Western, "detective" becoming "cowboy," etc. Quilty has just knocked Humbert's pistol ("Chum") under a chest of drawers:

> Fussily, busibodily, cunningly, he had risen again while he talked. I groped under the chest

trying at the same time to keep an eye on him. All of a sudden I noticed that he had noticed that I did not seem to have noticed Chum protruding from beneath the other corner of the chest. We fell to wrestling again. We rolled all over the floor, in each other's arms, like two huge helpless children. He was naked and goatish under his robe, and I felt suffocated as he rolled over me. I rolled over him. We rolled over me. They rolled over him. We rolled over us (Appel, pp. 300-301).

The final sentences signal exhaustion, not only in the narrator and his opponent but, as importantly, in the author who lurks behind them and the reader who waits ahead. Yet Nabokov still isn't satisfied; as parodist he has recognized and used the possibilities for exhaustion in the detective/Western, pushing the scene to its sterile limits; now he provides the rewarding twist, presented in Humbert's comment:

> In its published form, this book is being read, I assume in the first years of 2000 A.D. (1935 plus eighty or ninety, live long, my love); and elderly readers will surely recall at this point the obligatory scene in the Westerns of their childhood. Our tussle, however, lacked the ox-stunning fisticuffs, the flying furniture.... It was a silent, soft, formless tussle on the part of two literati, one of whom was utterly disorganized by a drug while the other was handicapped by a heart condition with too much gin. When at last I had possessed myself of my precious weapon,—both of us were panting as the cowman and the sheepman never do after their battles (Appel, p. 301).

Heretofore in the scene we've been presented with a mocking of roles and literary genres; but now we find connections between poor detective writing and poor Western film making, specifically in the fight-scene cliche. Not only do genres share cliches; so do modes (fiction and film).

Here, as in many of Nabokov's novels, parody is close to essence. Literature is not the only object of Nabokov's playful pen. Material as unrelated as the author himself (anagramatically called Vivian Darkbloom) and artifacts of the American culture, such as motels, come under the writer's amused eye. That Nabokov's work and its parts are at the same time themselves and imitations of themselves is no surprise to readers of *The Real Life of Sebastian Knight, Laughter in the Dark,* and other of the author's subversive fictions. As L.S. Denbo says, parody is what reminds "the reader of the novelist's presence in and above his book as a puppeteer in charge of everything, establishes the fiction as total artifice." It is certainly that which most separates *Lolita* and other of Nabokov's works from the conventions of the traditional or realistic novel (*The Man and His Work,* Madison, 1967, p. 117).

Characters imitate literary or historical figures outside the work (Humbert Humbert as Edgar Allan Poe), they imitate characters within the work (Humbert as Claire Quilty) and they imitate themselves (Humbert, the lecherous father and Humbert, the dutiful father). They constantly confront mirrors, adopt disguises or masks, and become, at least in terms of *motif,* butterflies, hunters and chess pieces. Word-games abound, particularly those that involve repetitions (Humbert Humbert or John Ray, Jr. ——J—R, J—R) and connotative resonances (like the surname Haze). Punning and similar games which allow a kind of verbal playback appear frequently. Clues, false clues, symbols and allusions are bounced against each other like the white dot in an electronic tennis game, though the author's hand remains steadily, constantly on the controls. And beneath all the trickery and games, as if in concession to realists like Flaubert and Saul Bellow, there lies a more or less traditional, a tragic, love story.

Humbert's comment on the fight, quoted above, also reveals a quality that readers attending Nabokov's parodic vision may easily overlook: a depth of characterization. There are dimensions to Lolita, Quilty, Charlotte and others in the novel. Humbert is extraordinarily complicated: a lover, criminal, detective, cowboy, mocker, serious in each endeavor, even the most foolish. After noting "this mixture in my Lolita of tender dreamy childishness and a kind of eerie vulgarity," Humbert shares the depths of his feelings for her, saying:

...all this gets mixed up with the exquisite stainless tenderness seeping through the musk and the mud, through the dirt and the death, Oh God, oh God. And what is most singular is that she, *this* Lolita, *my* Lolita, has individualized the writer's ancient lust, so that above and over everything there is—Lolita (Appel, pp. 46-47).

The subject here, however, is the novel and its readers: what happened and what might have happened. Consider. Because Lolita survived, as literature, as a popular novel, it prepared the way for subsequent Nabokov works, especially *Pale Fire* and *Ada,* which might otherwise have found no audience of notable size, might not even have been published by a commercial press. In sustaining a reasonably healthy life for itself, *Lolita* also made possible the translation and publication of Nabokov's important early novels, including *Mary, King, Queen, Knave, The Defense* and *The Eye.* Further, it brought invitations for Nabokov's short stories from editors of good-paying magazines who previously had ignored his work. (True, *The New Yorker* published some short stories prior to *Lolita,* but Nabokov seems to have been unknown to the editors at places like *Playboy* and *Esquire.*) Finally, it provided for the author that glowing credential of a writer's popular success, a movie, which came about largely because of solid paperback sales. A work, then, which at the beginning was completely ignored, then existed as a controversial under-the-counter pornographic novel was finally published by a respectable house (The first Putnam edition appeared in August, 1958, and there were seventeen printings in the following thirteen months.) seemed to catapult its author into daylight. Yet this was decades after he had begun writing. How strange, especially when one recalls that *Lolita* was not discovered by an informed critic making a studied response *or* by an enterprising editor at a commercial publishing house but as the result of the bare mention of it made by another practitioner of Nabokov's lonely craft, a mention that itself might have gone unnoticed had the novel lacked the power to stir and sustain controversy. The oddness of it all might appeal to no one more than to Nabokov himself.

And so it did.

In "An Afterword to Lolita" (Capricorn Edition, New York, 1972) he recalls his experiences with the four American publishers who'd rejected his novel before he sent it to Girodias: He found some of the reactions "very amusing." One reader thought the book would be all right if Lolita were turned into a twelve-year-boy and he was seduced by Humbert, "a farmer, in a barn, amidst gaunt and arid surroundings, all this set forth in short, strong, 'realistic' sentences." Nabokov insists that everybody knows that he detests symbols and allegories,

...an otherwise intelligent reader who flipped through the first part described *Lolita* as "Old Europe debauching young America," while another flipper saw in it "Young American debauching old Europe." Publisher X, whose advisers got so bored with Humbert that they never got beyond page 188, had the naiveté to write me that Part Two was too long. Publisher Y, on the other hand, regretted that there were no good people in the book. Publisher Z said if he printed *Lolita,* he and I would go to jail (p. 316).

The author, after years of absurd neglect, had developed a shell of protection; any response now would amuse him. In jail or an asylum he would surely have laughed, perhaps scribbled out the folly of his fate on the walls of his cell.

I've intended my remarks to be informative and stimulating, not conclusive, and therefore I must warn myself away from the temptation to make something definite of all of this. The best closing is to be found in some of the words Nabokov himself wrote about *Lolita.* They seem to be a gentle phosphorescent light by which trailing fish—critics, teachers, writers, students, publishers and the like—might be guided. When he thinks of the novel, he says:

...I seem always to pick out for special delectation such images as Mr. Taxovich, or that class list of Ramsdale School, or Charlotte saying "waterproof," or Lolita in slow motion advancing toward Humbert's gifts, or the pictures decorating the stylized garret of Gaston Godin, or the Kasbeam barber (who cost me a lot of work), or Lolita playing tennis, or the hospital at Elphinstone, or pale, pregnant, beloved, irretrievable Dolly Schiller dying in the Gray Star (the capital town of the book), or the tinkling sounds of the valley town coming up the mountain trail (on which I caught the first known female of *Lycaeides sublivens* Nabokov).

These parts he calls "the nerves of the novel." They are the "secret points, the subliminal co-ordinates by means of which the book is plotted" (*Ibid.,* p. 318).

And surely, I dare add, some of the reasons the novel has survived even its own audiences.

The Writer and His Middle Class Audience: Frank Norris: A Case in Point

Robert A. Morace

WHAT AN AUTHOR is in large measure is shaped by the nature of the audience he writes for and the extent to which is aware of that audience.[1] For the American Realist, the author's problem of defining his audience was necessarily difficult. One part of the problem derives from the broad democratic thrust of the Realist movement itself,[2] and another stems from the incredible expansion and changing character of the American reading public that occurred during the late nineteenth century and that was caused in part by various advances in printing technology and in the distribution of printed matter.[3] There were more literate Americans buying more books, magazines and newspapers than ever before. For the Realist this meant a larger market, but too it often meant having to write for an audience that was either dangerously vague, as is evident in DeForest's *Miss Ravenal's Conversion,* or unfortunately reductive, as Boyesen's "Iron Madonna" and Howells' "Young Girl" make all too clear. However, there was one way in which some of the Realists were able to avoid these extremes, at least this is what the career of Frank Norris suggests. In 1896 and 1897 Norris served as a staff writer and then the assistant editor of the San Francisco weekly *The Wave. The Wave*'s readership was small and homogeneous. It was one which Norris knew intimately and to which he quickly learned to adapt his writings. Moreover, after he left *The Wave* and began to write for a national audience, he continued to write with a specific type of reader in mind—a type that was usually, though not always, identical with his earlier *Wave* audience.

The Wave was founded in 1888 by Ben C. Truman, a member of the publicity staff of the Southern Pacific Railroad.[4] The Del Monte *Wave,* as it was then called, served as the advertising organ for the Southern Pacific's new resort, the Hotel Del Monte, located just outside Monterey, California. In 1890 *The Wave* was moved north to San Francisco where it was purchased by two enterprising local journalists, Hugh Hume and John O'Hara Cosgrave. Although Hume soon lost interest in the venture *The Wave* steadily developed under Cosgrave's direction into a magazine of considerable, if entirely local, significance.

By mid-1895 the sub-title "A Weekly For Those in the Swim" was no longer appropriate to its new character as "A Society, Literary, and Political Journal" and so was dropped. Although its character had changed from advertising organ and society sheet, one aspect of *The Wave* remained the same: it continued to direct itself to the same upper middle class readers who frequented resorts such as the Hotel Del Monte. It made no attempt to appeal to the entire range of middle class readers, as, for example, Hearst's newspaper the *San Francisco Examiner* did. Nor did it make any pretense about being the journal of the city's upper crust whose activities were reported in gossipy paragraphs in the "Things and People" section rather than the regular society column which was reserved for its own class of readers, such as Norris's mother, founder of the city's Browning Society. During its twelve-year life, *The Wave* never did become "the *Collier's* or *Harper's Weekly* of the Pacific Coast" as Cosgrove hoped it would, nor did it ever become financially stable for more than very brief periods. It did, however, publish the early work of such notable American writers as Gelett Burgess, Will Irwin, Jack London and Frank Norris. Moreover, it served its own class of readers rather well—so well, in fact, that it even had a small circulation among vacationing and expatriated San Franciscans in Chicago, Washington, New York and Paris.

The relationship which existed between Norris and his *Wave* audience consists of four distinct aspects. One is generic. *The Wave* was a weekly magazine, not, as some have thought, a newspaper.[5] As a result, its writers could not simply fill up the sixteen pages of each issue with news stories, these having been already covered by the city's numerous dailies. Weekly journalism forced the writer to find new material, or, if he did choose to cover week-old news, to find some new angle that would interest his readers. Norris recognized that magazinists faced other difficulties too. Since the modern magazine had to cover a wide variety of subjects, space was often in short supply. The writer, especially the short story writer, had to resort to the use of various literary "tricks" which seasoned magazine readers learned to recognize and even look for. Then there was also the problem of taste to be considered. As Norris pointed out, the standard of taste varied according to the magazine and the audience it served. *Scribner's, Harper's* and *The Century* were governed by the tastes of the "Young Girl." *McClure's,* on the other hand, was noticeably less restrained, and *The Wave* had an even less priggish editorial policy as a result of its audience's demand for a more truthful presentation of life, or so Norris believed.

Another aspect of the relationship between Norris and his audience is its having been a relationship in time. However obvious this point may seem, the specific historical context of Norris' *Wave* writings has usually been entirely overlooked. Consider the case of the rather slight story "The Puppets and the Puppy." One critic called it Norris's "most cynical work,"[6] and another thought it his most complete denial of the will.[7] Norris's readers, however, would have seen it in a far different light. They would have known that the story's sub-title, "Disrespectfully Dedicated to Annie Besant," linked the story to the lecture by Mrs. Besant, a Theosophist leader, at San Francisco's Metropolitan Hall on May 9—just thirteen days before the story appeared in *The Wave;* as a result they would have read the story for what it was and is—a satirical take-off on Mrs. Besant's lecture on reincarnation. One of these same critics made the same kind of mistake with another story, " 'Boom'," seeing in it evidence of what he called Norris's "almost hysterical hatred of a decadent civilization."[8] Given this critic's overall interpretation of Norris as a transcendental populist, the reading is plausible, but that interpretation has nothing to do with the story's actual historical context. *The Wave's* readers would have known that the story's setting, the city of San Diego, was, as Norris described it, the victim of real estate speculation, and, moreover, they would have read " 'Boom' " chiefly as a warning to San Franciscans then being caught up in the excitement and reckless speculation of the Alaskan gold rush.

This brings us to the geographical aspect of the relationship, for Norris was specifically and consciously addressing a San Francisco audience. His readers understood that a parenthetical mention of "private rooms" in an article about the California oyster industry was an allusion to improprieties in certain San Francisco saloons.[9] And they would have known the three beggars who figure prominently in the story "The Associated Un-Charities" not just as fictional characters but as three of the city's most familiar street people. Norris also shared with his readers certain biases, such as the sense of urban superiority which lies behind his ridicule of Monterey's flag-raising ceremony and a Santa Cruz Venetian Carnival. This division between city and country Norris put to a more serious use on several occasions, as in his article "Man-Hunting" where he was able to effectively jar his readers' sense of security simply by pointing out the proximity of an outlaw refuge to their own city homes.

But as I noted earlier, Norris's audience can be defined even more closely. Specifically they were members of Norris's own social sphere, the upper middle class. When, for example, he mentioned "a summer resort down the coast," he was drawing on a personal experience that he knew was also a class-wide experience shared by his readers. Knowing that there existed a common store of experiences and a common background, he could be reasonably sure that what struck him as new and unusual would strike his readers in the same way. Thus he was often able to clarify his point by citing a shared experience and then contrasting it with whatever new experience he had just had.

Just how fully aware Norris was of the specific character of his audience is evident in his report on the funeral of the notorious "Little Pete," a Chinese shoe manufacturer who had been murdered on January 23, 1897. Both the murder and the funeral had been amply covered in the newspapers during the week before Norris's article appeared on January 30. That meant that Norris had to find a new angle, and the one he chose was to point out the incredible vulgarity of the white mob of onlookers who eventually plundered the funeral altar. This aspect had been barely mentioned—when it had been mentioned at all—by the city's newspapers. Given the anti-Chinese sentiment then so pervasive among San Franciscans in general—among, that is, the newspapers' general readership—the reticence is understandable. Norris and the readers of *The Wave* were not as a class any less prejudiced and, of course, were in fact part of that same general readership. Yet Norris could make copy of something the newspapers were reluctant to even mention because he knew that his readers stood as far removed from the vulgar white mob as they were from the city's Chinese population, and that an attack on one or on both would not have challenged their own sense of superiority.

This finding of a unique angle of vision parallels the chief point in Norris's literary creed: the writer must break through the surface realism of middle-class respectability in order to expose the naturalistic truth below. In his novels and in much of the short fiction published in *The Wave,* he accomplished this goal by limiting the action to periods of crisis. Most of his contributions to *The Wave* were non-fiction, however, and for these he had to devise a new method. The one he chose seems simple enough: he would present some value, idea or viewpoint common to his readers and then contrast it with another based on first-hand observation rather than mere convention. The problem with this method is that to use it on a weekly basis, and in Norris's case often in more than one article each week, is to risk alienating the readers whose views are being repeatedly deflated. In order to obviate the risk, Norris developed a repertoire of three narrative poses, each of which differs from the other two both in tone and in character.

In one Norris cast himself in the role of discoverer. This pose was adopted chiefly for reports about places he had visited and was often signalled by means of a formulaic opening sentence, such as this one from an article about a trip to a nearby navy yard:

> To fit out a cruiser for sea service implies an amount of labor and expense that the lay landsman can have but little idea of until he has visited the docks (dry and otherwise) or Mare Island and seen the great war engines laid up there for repairs.

Norris employed the discoverer pose in a more imaginative way and for a more critical purpose in a number of other *Wave* writings. In "How It Strikes an Observer," for example, he used it to prick the bubble of middle-class respectability within which his readers had enclosed themselves a few nights earlier while attending a fashionable horse show. The women who were, as Norris says, "rigidly decorous and reserved" at the show, had "shouted [themselves] hoarse and split [their] gloves in [their] excitement" at a recent football game. And the men who had suppressed "all emotion" at the horse show were "not decorous, nor reserved, nor choice in their language" at a boxing match just one week before. And at the end of his article "Latin Quarter Christmas," he made a similar point by means of a fine use of second and third person pronouns. After having described some children gaping at a gimcrack nativity scene at one of the city's poorest churches, Norris wrote:

> Can't you imagine the effect of positive awe upon some of the little Italian children of the quarter—some of those, for instance, who have never seen Kearny street? Looking at it, with the tiny red lamps burning about it, there can be but little doubt that they feel much the same as you do—at moments—for instance, the other day when Mr. Eddy was playing the "Twelfth Mass" on the great organ at St. Ignatius. You who "have seen Kearny street" and "the world outside" must have a sixty thousand dollar organ and the greatest organist between the oceans before you can rise to the sensation. But a few cheap toys, the manikins of statuette vendors, and crumpled cloth suffice for those little Italians of Dupont and Filbert streets.
>
> And after all, is there so much difference between you?

In his second pose Norris acts the part of a bumbling naif. As the discoverer his tone is serious and his reader is asked to personally involve himself in the act of discovery. Here, however, the tone is comic, and the reader is allowed to remain detached; he is able to learn Norris's point without having to undergo the same indignities suffered by the narrator. This pose Norris adopted most often in his pieces about the theater, especially his interviews with actresses and vaudeville performers. The naif stumbles around backstage, or is struck dumb by the beauty or volubility of some visiting starlet, or nearly suffers nervous prostration while interviewing a professional actor "waiting for his cue," all to show the reader the reality that lies behind the scenes.

At the opposite pole from the naif is the third pose, the authority. Although related to the discoverer in that both confront the reader directly with the errors of his views, the two differ in tone: the authority is hypercritical and even condescending rather than explanatory. Here the risk of alienating the reader is greatest, and not surprisingly, Norris was quite sparing in its use, reserving it for just a few editorials, some of his literary criticism, and, most conspicuously, the series of football reports he wrote in the Fall of 1896. Throughout these reports Norris repeatedly criticized the local teams for what he considered inferior and uninspired play and reproved the spectators who he felt did not perceive these faults and therefore failed to demand more of their teams. Since football matches were as much society functions as athletic contests in the San Francisco of the 1890s, to attack the spectators as Norris did was also to attack a large portion of his *Wave* audience. By adopting his third pose Norris was able to make his points and to make them seem justified. He buttressed his position with a consistent and well-defined theory of football strategy and interlarded his reports with an imposing array of facts drawn from his careful observation of games he had witnessed as a student at Berkeley and Harvard. In addition, Norris further strengthened his case by touching on various responsive chords in his readers. He based his appeal on the strenuous life philosophy then coming very much into vogue among the city's upper middle class, and he also mentioned the rivalry between the East and West Coasts that was certain to elicit a response from chauvinistic San Franciscans. Moreover, he focused his criticism on the University of California, his own alma mater and the favorite team among his local readers. And finally he appealed to one of the chief concerns of the middle classes—getting their money's worth. Each week his reports became more forceful and more critical. And at the end of the football season he used many of the same tactics in one of his best known pieces of literary criticism, his attack on "The 'English Courses' at the University of California."

Norris's intimate knowledge of his audience was the chief factor that affected the relationship between himself and his reader, but it was not the only one. Another was his changing attitude toward his position on *The Wave*.[10] When he first joined *The Wave* as a staff writer in April 1896, he apparently thought of himself as an author, not as a journalist. His position enabled him to at least partially free himself from his financial dependence on his mother and, while he slowly recovered from the fever he had caught in South Africa, to practice the craft of fiction. During the first three months he contributed mostly short stories and book reviews, and only rarely showed even the slightest awareness that he was addressing a clearly defined audience. Following a three-month break, Norris returned to *The Wave* in October and worked steadily and prolifically until March. He virtually abandoned the writing of fiction as he immersed himself into what he later called "the hammer and tongs work" of weekly journalism. The would-be novelist had transformed himself into the professional journalist, and his awareness of his audience became a significantly noticeable characteristic of his writing. During this same period Norris became a much more visible presence in San Francisco society, chiefly as a result of his starring role in a well publicized charity performance of the Tom Robertson play *Caste* in January. At the beginning of his third *Wave* period in May, Norris suddenly realized that the careers of journalist and fiction writer need not be incompatible, that the one could, in fact, be turned to the other's advantage. His excitement over this possibility is most enthusiastically expressed in his article "An Opening for Novelists: Great Opportunities for Fiction Writers in San Francisco." "The tales are here," he wrote. "The public is here. A hundred clashing presses are hungry for you, future young story-writers of San Francisco, whoever you may be. Strike but the right note, and strike it with all your might, strike it with iron instead of velvet, and the clang of it shall go the round of the nations. A qui le tour, who shall be our Kipling?

The question was, of course, merely rhetorical, but in his excitement Norris had unfortunately mistaken his limited success on *The Wave* as a sure sign of imminent success among a larger local and even national audience. Despite his best efforts to become the California Kipling, he was not able to find a publisher for the short story collection he had just prepared, and as a result he began to see the limitations rather than the "great opportunities" for the writer working in San Francisco. Parallelling this disenchantment with his local chances for success was Norris's growing critical attitudes toward his own society that resulted from his courtship of Jeannette Black, a social non-conformist who had refused to "come out" in society. This attitude manifests itself in the sudden spate of social fiction written during this period, especially the Leander-Justin Sturgis dialogues that appeared in July and August. After spending several months away from San Francisco revising *McTeague* he returned to *The Wave* with little interest in his *Wave* work and even less concern for his readers' pleasure. From late November through January he offered them perfunctory articles and reworkings of fiction he had written at Harvard three years earlier. Even his most important work of this period, the serialized *Moran of the Lady Letty,* was written not for the local readers but in hopes of attracting the attention of an Eastern publisher. It did, and in February, while in St. Louis visiting Jeannette Black on yet another of his breaks from *The Wave,* Norris accepted an offer from S.S. McClure to join his staff in New York.

What Norris learned on *The Wave* about the relationship between an author and his audience affected his career in several significant ways. For one thing, as he made clear in his essay "The Novel with a Purpose," he continued to think of his readers as members of the upper middle class. This definition of his audience may in turn have been at least partly responsible for his decision not to publish his earliest novel, *Vandover and the Brute*; perhaps he realized that his readers would have found its naturalistic portrayal of a well-to-do young man's degeneration both shocking (as they did find *McTeague)* and too close to home. Norris's revision of *McTeague*, it should be remembered, occurred at the end of his *Wave* tenure and involved the re-casting of his characters on a lower social plane than they had at first occupied in the original draft composed at Harvard in 1895. In his post-*Wave* literary criticism, too, there is clear evidence that Norris continued to write with a specific audience in mind.[11] The seventeen pieces he wrote for the Chicago *American* from May to August 1901 have a breezy style and are often anecdotal—just the right combination for this Hearst newspaper. His contributions to a much more staid newspaper, the *Boston Evening Transcript,* are much more formal in tone and in structure. At the same time he was writing these pieces for the *Transcript,* he was also writing essays for syndication.[12] Although the subjects for both are frequently identical, again there are important differences: the tone and style of the syndicated pieces are less constrained and more like the earlier weekly letters published in the Chicago *American;* furthermore in the syndicated essays he twice made disparaging remarks about New England's contributions to American literature that he did not include in his *Transcript* essays. Perhaps more interesting are the articles he wrote for *World's Work,* an offshoot of Doubleday, Page & Co., Norris's publisher and the firm for which he was then working as a reader. The twin ideals of the success ethic and beneficent capitalism emphasized in *World's Work* were also prominent themes in Norris's essays for this magazine—specifically, he stressed the moral responsibilities of the novelist and the formula for literary success. Norris's last—and longest—literary essays appeared in *The Critic.* Founded in 1881 by Jeanette and Joseph Gilder as a high-toned literary review, *The Critic* became less elitist after it was purchased by the Putnams in 1898. Although most of what Norris said in his "Salt and Sincerity" column was a rehash of points he had developed earlier, one new element was his espousal of a Whitmanic faith in the American public—a reading public that he was talking *about,* not *to;* a reading public that formed his subject, not his audience.

   In summary, we can say that among the several benefits Norris received as a result of his tenure on the San Francisco *Wave* was the opportunity to write for a clearly defined audience and to learn to adapt his writing so as to accommodate his own artistic purposes as well as the values of his readers. Late in his career, Norris defiantly claimed that he had "never truckled"; he didn't mention that he had, however, rewritten passages in two novels—*McTeague* and *A Man's Woman*—that reviewers of the earliest printings had found objectionable. This is not to say that Norris did indeed truckle, merely that he didn't really have to. His relationship with his readers was not antagonistic, as, for example, Stephen Crane's seems to have been at the beginning of his career; nor was it one of compromise, as Hamlin Garland's certainly was at the end of his.

Rather, it was one of accommodation that derives chiefly from his *Wave* experience. In an age in which the reading public was expanding and the author was in danger of thinking of his reader—if at all—as an amorphous archetype of the American middle classes, Norris, and perhaps other Realists who shared a similar experience, was able to adapt to the possibilities of a growing mass market without losing sight of the specific character of his "Dear Reader."

Notes

Although the theory of the author-audience relationship is itself of great significance, most of the subtle distinctions that have been made concerning it apply chiefly to contemporary writers like Barth (and to a lesser extent earlier writers, especially Poe) but very little to the Realists (Henry James excepted) for what seem to me to be obvious philosophical implications of Realism. The theory has been variously discussed, in books by Wayne C. Booth and Norman Holland, for example, and in three especially important articles: Walker Gibson, "Authors, Speakers, Readers, and Mock Readers," *College English* XI, 5 (Feb. 1950), 265-69; Walter J. Ong, S.J., "The Writer's Audience is Always a Fiction," *PMLA*, 90, no. 1 (Jan. 1975), 9-21; Peter J. Rabinowitz, "Truth in Fiction: A Reexamination of Audience," *Critical Inquiry*, 4 (Autumn 1977), 121-41. For a provocative though often far-fetched discussion of how the knowledge of one's audience can be used for manipulative purposes, see Wilson Bryan Key, *Media Sexploitation* (1976; rpt. New York: New American Library, 1977).

[2]See especially the first chapter of Edwin H. Cady, *The Light of Common Day: Realism in American Fiction* (Bloomington: Univ. of Indiana Press, 1971).

[3]Joseph Katz, "Bibliography and the Rise of American Literary Realism," *Studies in American Fiction,* II, 1 (Spring 1974), 75-88.

[4]The following sketch of *The Wave* is drawn from Robert A. Morace, "A Critical and Textual Study of Frank Norris's Writings from the San Francisco *Wave,"* Diss. Univ. of South Carolina, 1976).

[5]Joseph J. Kwiat, "The Newspaper Experience: Crane, Norris and Dreiser," *Nineteenth-Century Fiction,* 8 (Sept. 1953), 99-117; Joseph J. Kwiat, "Stephen Crane and Frank Norris: The Magazine and the 'Revolt' in American Literature in the 1890s." *Western Humanities Review,* XXX (Winter 1976), 309-22.

[6]Warren French, *Frank Norris* (New Haven: College and University Press, 1962), pp. 26, 121.

[7]Arnold L. Goldsmith, "Charles and Frank Norris," *Western American Literature,* II (Spring 1967), 45.

[8]French, p. 122.

[9]See Norris's description of the Imperial in *Vandover and the Brute.*

[10]The bibliographical history of Norris's *Wave* tenure can be found in Morace, "A Critical and Textual Study of Frank Norris's Writings from the San Francisco *Wave"*; a corrected bibliography, Joseph Katz and Robert A. Morace, *Frank Norris: A Bibliographical Checklist* (Columbia, S.C.: J. Faust & Co.), will be published in 1978.

[11]I am indebted to Paul Werstein for first pointing out to me the relationship between Norris's later literary criticism and the newspapers and magazines in which they appeared.

[12]These syndicated pieces were published in early 1902, not 1903 (as was reported in *The Responsibilities of the Novelist);* see Joseph Katz, "The Elusive Criticisms Syndicated by Frank Norris," *Proof 3* (Columbia, S.C.: Univ. of South Carolina Press, 1973), pp. 221-51.

On Our Own: Trilling vs. Dreiser

Charles Shapiro

IN HIS FREE-SWINGING, peppy introduction to the first volume of *A Question of Quality: Popularity and Value in Modern Creative Writing,* the editor notes how changing times inevitably bring forth changing attitudes toward literature. Assorted teachers and critics alter their judgments, and patient readers, students and sycophants are treated to the prejudices of their smug mentors.

Our problem, then, is somehow to establish guidelines for ourselves, and, if professors, explain them to our students. Just how do we go about answering the lad in the third row who persistently inquires how you can ascertain if a novel is of any aesthetic value? This inevitable and honest query becomes worse when, due to television, open enrollment and God knows what else, the young man in question has been treated to literature in high school and has honed his reading skills on *Silas Marner, The Mill on the Floss,* and perhaps as an added attraction, *Ivanhoe.* If unpopular among his peers, he has also glanced at Bible I and Bible II.

I usually reply by citing Edmund Wilson to the effect that art gives meaning to experience and obviously the more fiction he reads the easier it is to spot those authors who appeal to him. I also relate to him and his classmates the probably apocryphal tale of the artist who charged a lady a huge sum after spending only two hours working on her portrait. After hearing her complaints, the painter pointed out that she was being billed not for the 120 minutes but for the forty years of experience that resulted in the moment he could produce such a masterpiece.

But this flip reply, of course, begs the question, and most of the more mature students will take their cues as to the value of a novel from the teacher, critics, and Monarch or Cliff notebooks. There must be a way to judge a collection of words, but to attempt an individual poetics of fiction is both a noble and almost impossible task. As Mark Spilka has put it in *Towards a Poetics of Fiction:*

The New Critical shift of attention then from poetry to fiction has brought with it an avalanche of image and point-of-view studies of uneven merit, and a penchant for treating novels as poems which proves more suitable to the poetic and hermetic strain in modern fiction than to novels of the past.

No more puzzling test for critics exists than in evaluating Theodore Dreiser's finer novels. As I once mentioned in a study of that writer, there is an underlying theme to each novel, and he was not simply a polemicist but, at his best, an artist as well. It is patently idiotic to believe that he created powerful fiction but was a perpetually inept technician. Early critiques by such worthies as Stuart P. Sherman and his cronies concentrated on Dreiser's immorality and are easily dismissed by anyone who can count to ten; but the problem of evaluating Dreiser becomes complicated when his work is devasted by one of our most important critics, a man I never met but whose writings have taught me a good deal, Lionel Trilling in his essay in *The Liberal Imagination* with the challenging title "Reality in America." Trilling manages to set up Dreiser as a straw man to further the doctrinaire premise that permeates the critic's book and gives it form.

Before examining Trilling's famous indictment, it is necessary to realize how powerful this Ivy League critic was. Alfred Kazin, in his gossipy *New York Jew,*[1] notes that during the heyday of Marxist criticism "I had been grateful to him for writing against the spirit of the age.... He still believed in culture as a guide to society." Kazin claims that "society" was a term utilized by ex-radicals like Trilling to mean "manners." No other writer "was now so much an influence on the 'liberal imagination' in America, so much a metropolitan figure and yet one of the purest prestige to the derivative critics who could find an intellectual home, wanted an intellectual home, nowhere but in an English Department." Kazin continues the barrage of praise:

No other distinguished professor of literature was so much a man of letters as Trilling, so much interested in Freud, Babel, the Kinsey Report,the E.M. Forster he made a part of our "intellectual baggage." The galley slaves of criticism in the universities were chained to eighteen sacred poems, to Brooks and Warren, to tension, to ambiguity, and paradox. Trilling, with his strong sense of history and his exquisite sense of accommodation, was the most successful leader of deradicalization—which was conducted in the name of the liberal "imagination" against those who lacked it or had the wrong kind. "Radical" was not mentioned. "Communist" could be applied only to those who would not confess their past, like Alger Hiss; or those anti-Communists who had turned all the way around, like Trilling's old college acquaintance Whittaker Chambers, and could talk of nothing other than Communism.

Kazin puts it that just as Trilling admired Matthew Arnold for smiting the philistines, so Trilling took it upon himself to smite the "liberals." Perhaps his forays against the liberal "mind" were not an evasion but a form of "middle-class claustrophobia."

In retrospect it appears that Trilling's approach to Dreiser was part of an inevitable changing of the literary guards. Malcolm Cowley, in *And I Worked at the Writer's Trade,* refers to these changes as "clusters," noting that today "much of our fiction, much of our poetry, and a substantial body of our criticism have become more and more unpeopled, unliving, and even unhuman. But fashions will change, as they always do."

Trilling's essay under discussion is bifurcated. The first part, published in 1940, goes to town on V.L. Parrington's often controversial volumes, *Main Currents in American Thought.* Trilling felt that Parrington's writings were as bibles to liberal historians, for

Parrington formulated in a classic way the suppositions about our culture which are held by the American middle class so far as that class is at all liberal in its social thought and so far as it begins to understand that literature has anything to do with society.

Trilling, after some lukewarm praise for Parrington, goes on to say that the man was hopeless when faced with literature that was "complex, personal, and not literal." For Parrington, 'reality' is always the critical key to evaluating literature.

Parrington's characteristic weakness as a historian is suggested by his title, for the culture of a nation is not truly figured in the image of the current. A culture is not a flow, not even a confluence; the form of its existence is struggle, or at least debate—it is nothing if not a dialectic. And in any culture there are likely to be certain artists who contain a large part of the dialectic within themselves, their meaning and power lying in their contradictions; they contain within themselves, it may be said, the very essence of the culture, and the sign of this is that they do not submit to serve the ends of any ideological group or tendency.

In his most telling indictment, Trilling asserts that although Parrington "lies twenty years behind us," he still remains at the center of American thought about American culture because "he expresses the chronic American belief that there exists an opposition between reality and mind and that one must enlist oneself in the party of reality."

In a sense Trilling's notions persist. The "twenty years" mentioned have turned to sixty (time's winged chariot being what it is) and his prejudices are still held by many despite the strange intellectual journeys his "liberals" have taken on their way to face such gut matters as black liberation, an immoral way, and the fight for the Equal Rights Amendment.

The second part of "Reality in America" was first published in *The Nation* in 1946 and is specifically aimed at Dreiser, using him as an example of Parrington's belief in the incompatibility of mind and reality. Dreiser is juxtaposed against Henry James "at the dark and bloody crossroads where literature and politics meet." Trilling feels that these two novelists both addressed themselves to virtually the same social and moral fact. The question, then, is one of quality. I doubt this Trilling concept; but even if absurdity is true, who cares? I love to read both men and, in fact, prefer James, who meticulously and carefully staked out his own turf, the international and national machinations of the rich and useless. Dreiser, often unwisely, attempted a more Tolstoyan approach, trying somehow to capture all American life. And, alas, he often had a tin ear when trying to reproduce the speech of the upper-class. He was a writer who wrote best about what he knew best; and he was more than capable of producing some indefensible work: his plays, his poetry, his philosophical treatises are awful. Dreiser was at his best in *Sister Carrie, Jennie Gerhardt, The Financier* (the first novel in a trilogy), portions of *The "Genius,"* portions of *The Bulwark,* some autobiographical works, and, best of all, in his masterpiece, *An American Tragedy.* In this ambitious novel, Dreiser is in almost complete control of his material. This work involved all the themes of previous works (*An American Tragedy* was published in 1925), the forces that accounted for the failures of the American family, religion, business and art. He dwelt, as in other novels, on the hopelessness of the individual in America, his sadness as well as his striving. Dreiser's perceptions came together in the long novel about the short life of an American boy; and in a curious way it remains contemporary. A recent brilliant film, *Saturday Night Fever,* dealt with some of these same ideas, and John Travolta could very well have been an updated Clyde Griffiths.

But back to Trilling's buckshots. The critic feels that we regard Dreiser as a "peasant" and thus excuse his deficiencies. According to Trilling, Dreiser's fans are attracted only to his social and political beliefs; Trilling fails to realize here that Dreiser, like most of us, had different philosophical beliefs during different stages of his career.

Trilling points out that Dreiser's admirers tolerate his "doctrinaire Anti-Semitism." I readily admit that Dreiser was often a bigot and a fool; but so, at times, were my two favorite writers, Dickens and Dostoevsky.

Trilling plunges on. Dreiser lacks the true Middle Western diction, he is bookish in a pejorative sense, he is a vulgar philosopher, he indulges every current idea, and is anti-intellectual. Unfortunately Trilling then focuses on one of Dreiser's uneven works, *The Bulwark,* noting its strange mysticism and mood of acceptance. It is a novel, Trilling feels, that displays a failure of mind and heart. Certainly *The Bulwark* is not Dreiser's finest novel, but it is far from being a failure for the reasons Trilling gives. It is a work that is a study not simply of religion but of the values and inadequate family relationships in the career of Solon Barnes, a protagonist who represents an older generation, a man who is constantly baffled by the changing America around him. He is brave but unseeing, honest but not perceptive. What we today blithely term "a generation gap" becomes, for Dreiser, a tragedy.

We are reminded that Dreiser, in his dotage, joined the Communist Party and Trilling quotes Robert H. Elias who once wrote that the logic of Dreiser's life was seen in the fact that the novelist made this bubbleheaded political decision while writing *The Bulwark.* A careful reading of the Dreiser canon, however, proves that he was never, in his works, a slave to any of the many brands of Marxism that were popular during his lifetime.

In summing up, Trilling has it that the scope of reality being what it is, ideas are "held to be mere 'details' and, what is more, to be details which, if attended to, have the effect of diminishing reality." For liberals cannot separate ideas from ideals, and ideals "consort happily with reality" and urge us to "deal impatiently with ideas." The only trouble with this indictment is that very few major American novelists of our century are guilty of Trilling's charge, and Dreiser certainly was not one of them. Our problem, as critics, is to see just *how* the author of *An American Tragedy* successfully incorporated his ideals into his realistic architectonics. How his much attacked use of details are not idly tossed into a novel but are very much a part of a perceptive design.

In the past I have attempted to give a close reading to some of Dreiser's paragraphs, not indulging in a New Critical workout but trying, to quote Cowley again, to utilize some details of explication "in order to demonstrate...the validity of Dreiser's prose in many instances." But this is just one possible methodology.[2]

For one example: Paul Orlov, in a penetrating essay, "The Subversion of the Self: Anti-Naturalistic Crux in *An American Tragedy*" (*Modern*

Fiction Studies [Autumn 1977]) sees the development toward a humanistic approach to this novel and cites Robert Penn Warren and Richard Lehan as but two critics viewing Dreiser's concern with the artistic treatment of the idea of individual identity. Orlov further sees *An American Tragedy* as not being naturalistic at all. Orlov effectively kicks Dreiser out of the convenient cubbyhold labeled "NATURALISM." As a result of this attitudinal switch, college specialists in American Literature can no longer (if they are honest women and men) give the usually dull lecture on "NATURALISM" and drag in Dreiser to justify their preformulated prejudices. Worst of all, they will have to read *An American Tragedy* for the second time, or perhaps for the first.

Orlov contends that Dreiser sees man, for example Clyde Griffiths, as having a genuine individuality, "a true selfhood."

The emphasis upon looks and money implicitly suggests that the world in which Clyde absorbs beliefs and goals subscribes to a way of seeing that discovers meaning only in the surfaces of things and people. Identity consists of the external and extrinsic—that is, of people viewed empirically as bearers of appearances, literal as well as figurative possessions, and approved behavior forms.

Clyde, as Dreiser describes him, "had a soul that was not destined to grow up." A growing irony develops in *An American Tragedy* as Clyde attempts in numerous ways to falsify his identity.

We do care about Clyde, about Sister Carrie, about Jennie Gerhardt and Frank Cowperwood. A mediocre novelist could never have accomplished this.

Dreiser was not his own best press agent. It is easy to fall into the much heralded "intentional fallacy." We must read his books, not his inane comments to reporters, fans and enemies. Two American novelists, both honored with the Nobel Prize for literature, understood this. Sinclair Lewis (in 1930) praised Dreiser for his "honesty, boldness, and passion of life." And years later Saul Bellow viewed Dreiser's history as "that of a man convinced by his experience of 'unpoetic reality' of the need to become an artist." Our job, now, is to look, once more, at the great gifts Dreiser has given us, the suffering heroes and heroines, the artful and stupendous portrayal of our America.

Notes

[1]There is, at this moment (summer of 1978) a literary brawl concerning what Alfred Kazin revealed about Lionel Trilling in *New York Jew*. I am deliberately avoiding this nonsense, and am only concerned with what Dreiser, Kazin and Trilling wrote, not about how they lived their lives.

[2]For one obvious example see the famous example of the lobster and squid sequence in *The Financier,* and for another, Hurstwood's fall, as reproduced here.

Sister Carrie [Excerpt]

Theodore Dreiser

It was when he returned from his disturbed stroll about the streets, after receiving the decisive note from McGregor, James and Jay, that Hurstwood found the letter Carrie had written him that morning. He thrilled intensely as he noted the handwriting, and rapidly tore it open.

"Then," he thought, "she loves me or she would not have written me at all."

He was slightly depressed at the tenor of the note for the first few minutes, but soon recovered. "She wouldn't write at all if she didn't care for me."

This was his one resource against the depression which held him. He could extract little from the wording of the letter, but the spirit he thought he knew.

There was really something exceedingly human—if not pathetic—in his being thus relieved by a clearly worded reproof. He who had for so long remained satisfied with himself now looked outside of himself for comfort—and to such a source. The mystic cords of affection! How they bind us all.

The colour came to his cheeks. For the moment he forgot the letter from McGregor, James and Hay. If he could only have Carrie, perhaps he could get out of the whole entanglement—perhaps it would not matter. He wouldn't care what his wife did with herself if only he might not lose Carrie. He stood up and walked about, dreaming his delightful dream of a life continued with this lovely possessor of his heart.

It was not long, however, before the old worry was back for reconsideration, and with it what weariness! He thought of the morrow and the suit. He had done nothing, and here was the afternoon slipping away. It was now a quarter of four. At five the attorneys would have gone home. He still had the morrow until noon. Even as he thought, the last fifteen minutes passed away and it was five. Then he abandoned the thought of seeing them any more that day and turned to Carrie.

It is to be observed that the man did not justify himself to himself. He was not troubling about that. His whole thought was the possibility of persuading Carrie. Nothing was wrong in that. He loved her dearly. Their mutual happiness depended upon it. Would that Drouet were only away!

While he was thinking thus elatedly, he remembered that he wanted some clean linen in the morning.

This he purchased, together with a half-dozen ties, and went to the Palmer House. As he entered he thought he saw Drouet ascending the stairs with a key. Surely not Drouet! Then he thought, perhaps they had changed their abode temporarily. He went straight up to the desk.

"Is Mr. Drouet stopping here?" he asked of the clerk.

"I think he is," said the latter, consulting his private registry list. "Yes."

"Is that so?" exclaimed Hurstwood, otherwise concealing his astonishment. "Alone?" he added.

"Yes," said the clerk.

157

Hurstwood turned away and set his lips so as best to express and conceal his feelings.

"How's that?" he thought. "They've had a row." He hastened to his room with rising spirits and changed his linen. As he did so, he made up his mind that if Carrie was alone, or if she had gone to another place, it behooved him to find out. He decided to call at once.

"I know what I'll do," he thought. "I'll go to the door and ask if Mr. Drouet is at home. That will bring out whether he is there or not and where Carrie is."

He was almost moved to some muscular display as he thought of it. He decided to go immediately after supper.

On coming down from his room at six, he looked carefully about to see if Drouet was present and then went out to lunch. He could scarcely eat, however, he was so anxious to be about his errand. Before starting he thought it well to discover where Drouet would be, and returned to his hotel.

"Has Mr. Drouet gone out?" he asked of the clerk.

"No," answered the latter, "he's in his room. Do you wish to send up a card?"

"No, I'll call around later," answered Hurstwood, and strolled out.

He took a Madison car and went direct to Ogden Place, this time walking boldly up to the door. The chambermaid answered his knock.

"Is Mr. Drouet in?" said Hurstwood blandly.

"He's out of the city," said the girl, who had heard Carrie tell this to Mrs. Hale.

"Is Mrs. Drouet in?"

"No, she has gone to the theatre."

"Is that so?" said Hurstwood, considerably taken aback; then, as if burdened with something important, "You don't know to which theatre?"

The girl really had no idea where she had gone, but not liking Hurstwood, and wishing to cause him trouble, answered: "Yes, Hooley's."

"Thank you," returned the manager, and, tipping his hat slightly, went away.

"I'll look in at Hooley's," thought he, but as a matter of fact he did not. Before he had reached the central portion of the city he thought the whole matter over and decided it would be useless. As much as he longed to see Carrie, he knew she would be with some one and did not wish to intrude with his pleas there. A little later he might do so—in the morning. Only in the morning he had the lawyer question before him.

This little pilgrimage threw quite a wet blanket upon his rising spirits. He was soon down again to his old worry, and reached the resort anxious to find relief. Quite a company of gentlemen were making the place lively with their conversation. A group of Cook County politicians were conferring about a round cherry-wood table in the rear portion of the room. Several young merrymakers were chattering at the bar before making a belated visit to the theatre. A shabby-genteel individual, with a red nose and an old high hat, was sipping a quiet glass of ale alone at one end of the bar. Hurstwood nodded to the politicians and went into his office.

About ten o'clock a friend of his, Mr. Frank L. Taintor, a local sport and racing man, dropped in, and seeing Hurstwood alone in his office came to the door.

"Hello, George!" he exclaimed.

"How are you, Frank?" said Hurstwood, somewhat relieved by the sight of him. "Sit down," and he motioned him to one of the chairs in the little room.

"What's the matter, George?" asked Taintor. "You look a little glum. Haven't lost at the track, have you?"

"I'm not feeling very well to-night. I had a slight cold the other day."

"Take whiskey, George," said Taintor. "You ought to know that."

Hurstwood smiled.

While they were still conferring there, several other of Hurstwood's friends entered, and not long after eleven, the theatres being out, some actors began to drop in—among them some notabilities.

Then began one of those pointless social conversations so common in American resorts where would-be *gilded* attempt to rub off gilt from those who have it in abundance. If Hurstwood had one leaning, it was toward notabilities. He considered that, if anywhere, he belonged among them. He was too proud to toady, too keen not to strictly observe the plane he occupied when there were those present who did not appreciate him, but, in situations like the present, where he could shine as a gentleman and be received without equivocation as a friend and equal among men of known ability, he was most delighted. It was on such occasions, if ever, that he would "take something." When the social flavour was strong enough he would even unbend to the extent of drinking glass for glass with his associates, punctiliously observing his turn to pay as if he were an outsider like the others. If he ever approached intoxication—or rather that ruddy warmth and comfortableness which precedes the sloven state—it was when individuals such as these were gathered about hem, when he was one of a circle of chatting celebrities. To-night, disturbed as was his state, he was rather relieved to find company, and now that notabilities were gathered, he laid aside his troubles for the nonce, and joined in right heartily.

It was not long before the imbibing began to tell. Stories began to crop up—those ever-enduring, droll stories which form the major portion of the conversation among American men under such circumstances.

Twelve o'clock arrived, the hour for closing, and with it the company took leave. Hurstwood shook hands with them most cordially. He was very roseate physically. He had arrived at that state where his mind, though clear, was nevertheless, warm in its fancies. He felt as if his troubles were not very serious. Going into his office, he began to turn over certain accounts, awaiting the departure of the bartenders and the cashier, who soon left.

It was the manager's duty, as well as his custom, after all were gone to see that everything was safely closed up for the night. As a rule, no money except the cash taken in after banking hours was kept about the place, and that was locked in the safe by the cashier, who, with the owners, was joint keeper of the secret combination, but, nevertheless, Hurstwood nightly took the precaution to try the cash drawers and the safe in order to see that they were tightly closed. Then he would lock his own little office and set the proper light burning near the safe, after which he would take his departure.

Never in his experience had he found anything out of order, but to-night, after shutting down his desk, he came out and tried the safe. His way was to give a sharp pull. This time the door responded. He was slightly surprised at that, and looking in found the money cases as left for the day, apparently unprotected. His first thought was, of course, to inspect the drawers and shut the door.

"I'll speak to Mayhew about this to-morrow," he thought.

The latter had certainly imagined upon going out a half-hour before that he had turned the knob on the door so as to spring the lock. He had never failed to do so before. But to-night Mayhew had other thoughts. He had been revolving the problem of a business of his own.

"I'll look in here," thought the manager, pulling out the money drawers. He did not know why he wished to look in there. It was quite a superfluous action, which another time might not have happened at all.

As he did so, a layer of bills, in parcels of a thousand, such as banks issue, caught his eye. He could not tell how much they represented, but paused to view them. Then he pulled out the second of the cash drawers. In that were the receipts of the day.

"I didn't know Fitzgerald and Moy ever left any money this way," his mind said to himself. "They must have forgotten it."

He looked at the other drawer and paused again.

"Count them," said a voice in his ear.

He put his hand into the first of the boxes and lifted the sack, letting the separate parcels fall. They were bills of fifty and one hundred dollars done in packages of a thousand. He thought he counted ten such.

"Why don't I shut the safe?" his mind said to itself, lingering. What makes me pause here?"

For answer there came the strangest words:

"Did you ever have ten thousand dollars in ready money?"

Lo, the manager remembered that he had never had so much. All his property had been slowly accumulated, and now his wife owned that. He was worth more than forty thousand, all told—but she would get that.

He puzzled as he thought of these things, then pushed in the drawers and closed the door, pausing with his hand upon the knob, which might so easily lock it all beyond temptation. Still he paused. Finally he went to the windows and pulled down the curtains. Then he tried the door, which he had previously locked. What was this thing, making him suspicious? Why did he wish to move about so quietly. He came back to the end of the counter as if to rest his arm and think. Then he went and unlocked his little office door and turned on the light. He also opened his desk, sitting down before it, only to think strange thoughts.

"The safe is open," said a voice. "There is just the least little crack in it. The lock has not been sprung."

The manager floundered among a jumble of thoughts. Now all the entanglement of the day came back. Also the thought that here was a solution. That money would do it. If he had that and Carrie. He rose up and stood stock-still, looking at the floor.

"What about it?" his mind asked, and for answer he put his hand slowly up and scratched his head.

The manager was no fool to be led blindly away by such an errant proposition as this, but his situation was peculiar. Wine was in his veins. It had crept up into his head and given him a warm view of the situation. It also coloured the possibilities of ten thousand for him. He could see great opportunities with that. He could get Carrie. Oh, yes, he could! He could get rid of his wife. That letter, too, was waiting discussion to-morrow morning. He would not need answer that. He went back to the safe and put his hand on the knob. Then he pulled the door open and took the drawer with the money quite out.

With it once out and before him, it seemed a foolish thing to think about leaving it. Certainly it would. Why, he could live quietly with Carrie for years.

Lord! what was that? For the first time he was tense, as if a stern hand had been laid upon his shoulder. He looked fearfully around. Not a soul was present. Not a sound. Some one was shuffling by on the sidewalk. He took the box and the money and put it back in the safe. Then he partly closed the door again.

To those who have never wavered in conscience, the predicament of the individual whose mind is less strongly constituted and who trembles in the balance between duty and desire is scarcely appreciable, unless graphically portrayed. Those who have never heard that solemn voice of the ghostly clock which ticks with awful distinctness, "thou shalt," "thou shalt not," "thou shalt," "thou shalt not," are in no position to judge.

Not alone in sensitive, highly organised natures is such a mental conflict possible. The dullest specimen of humanity, when drawn by desire toward evil, is recalled by a sense of right, which is proportionate in power and strength to his evil tendency. We must remember that it may not be a knowledge of right, for no knowledge of right is predicated on the animal's instinctive recoil at evil. Men are still led by instinct before they are regulated by knowledge. It is instinct which recalls the criminal—it is instinct (where highly organised reasoning is absent) which gives the criminal his feeling of danger, his fear of wrong.

At every first adventure, then, into some untried evil, the mind wavers. The clock of thought ticks out its wish and its denial. To those who have never experienced such a mental dilemma, the following will appeal on the simple ground of revelation.

When Hurstwood put the money back, his nature again resumed its ease and daring. No one had observed him. He was quite alone. No one could tell what he wished to do. He could work this thing out for himself.

The imbibation of the evening had not yet worn off. Moist as was his brow, tremble as did his hand once after the nameless fright, he was still flushed with the fumes of liquor. He scarcely noticed that the time was passing. He went over his situation once again, his eye always seeing the money in a lump, his mind always seeing what it would do. He strolled into his little room, then to the door, then to the safe again. He put his hand on the knob and opened it. There was the money! Surely no harm could come from looking at it!

He took out the drawer again and lifted the bills. They were so smooth, so compact, so portable. How little they made, after all. He decided he would take them. Yes, he would. He would put them in his pocket. Then he looked and saw they would not go there. His hand satchel! To be sure, his hand satchel. They would go in that—all of it would. No one would think anything of it either. He went into the little office and took it from the shelf in the corner. Now he set it upon his desk and went out toward the safe. For some reason he did not want to fill it out in the big room.

First he brought the bills and then the loose receipts of the day. He would take it all. He put the empty drawers back and pushed the iron door almost to, then stood beside it meditating.

The wavering of a mind under such circumstances is an almost inexplicable thing, and yet it is absolutely true. Hurstwood could not bring himself to act definitely. He wanted to think about it—to ponder over it, to decide whether it were best. He was drawn by such a keen desire for Carrie, driven by such a state of turmoil in his own affairs that he thought constantly it would be best, and yet he wavered. He did not know what evil might result from it to him—how soon he might come to grief. The true ethics of the situation never once occurred to him, and never would have, under any circumstances.

After he had all the money in the hand bag, a revulsion of feeling seized him. He would not do it—no! Think of what a scandal it would make. The police! They would be after him. He would have to fly, and where? Oh, the terror of being a fugitive from justice! He took out the two boxes and put all the money back. In his excitement he forgot what he was doing, and put the sums in the wrong boxes. As he pushed the door to, he thought he remembered doing it wrong and opened the door again. There were the two boxes mixed.

He took them out and straightened the matter, but now the terror had gone. Why be afraid?

While the money was in his hand the lock clicked. It had sprung! Did he do it? He grabbed at the knob and pulled vigorously. It had closed. Heavens! he was in for it now, sure enough.

The moment he realised that the safe was locked for a surety, the sweat burst out upon his brow and he trembled violently. He looked about him and decided instantly. There was no delaying now.

"Suppose I do lay it on the top," he said, "and go away, they'll know who took it. I'm the last to close up. Besides, other things will happen."

At once he became a man of action.

"I must get out of this," he thought.

He hurried into his little room, took down his light overcoat and hat, locked his desk, and grabbed the satchel. Then he turned out all but one light and opened the door. He tried to put on his old assured air, but it was almost gone. He was repenting rapidly.

"I wish I hadn't done that," he said. "That was a mistake."

He walked steadily down the street, greeting a night watchman whom he knew who was trying doors. He must get out of the city, and that quickly.

"I wonder how the trains run?" he thought.

Instantly he pulled out his watch and looked. It was nearly half-past one.

At the first drug store he stopped, seeing a long-distance telephone booth inside. It was a famous drug store, and contained one of the first private telephone booths ever erected.

"I want to use your 'phone a minute," he said to the night clerk.

The latter nodded.

"Give me 1643," he called to Central, after looking up the Michigan Central depot number. Soon he got the ticket agent.

"How do the trains leave here for Detroit?" he asked.

The man explained the hours.

"No more to-night?"

"Nothing but the sleeper. Yes, there is, too," he added. "There is a mail train out of here at three o'clock."

"All right," said Hurstwood. "What time does that get to Detroit?"

He was thinking if he could only get there and cross the river into Canada, he could take his time getting to Montreal. He was relieved to learn that it would reach there by noon.

"Mayhew won't open the safe till nine," he thought. "They can't get on my track before noon."

Then he thought of Carrie. With what speed must he get her, if he got her at all. She would have to come along. He jumped into the nearest cab standing by.

"To Ogden Place," he said sharply. "I'll give you a dollar more if you make good time."

The cabby beat his horse into a sort of imitation gallop, which was fairly fast, however. On the way Hurstwood thought what to do. Reaching the number, he hurried up the steps and did not spare the bell in waking the servant.

"Is Mrs. Drouet in?" he asked.

"Yes," said the astonished girl.

"Tell her to dress and come to the door at once. Her husband is in the hospital, injured, and wants to see her."

"The servant girl hurried upstairs, convinced by the man's strained and emphatic manner.

"What!" said Carrie, lighting the gas and searching for her clothes.

"Mr. Douet is hurt and in the hospital. He wants to see you. The cab's downstairs."

Carrie dressed very rapidly, and soon appeared below, forgetting everything but the necessities.

"Drouet is hurt," said Hurstwood quickly. "He wants to see you. Come quickly."

Carrie was so bewildered that she swallowed the whole story.

"Get in," said Hurstwood, helping her and jumping after.

The cabby began to turn the horse around.

"Michigan Central depot," he said, standing up and speaking so low that Carrie could not hear, "as fast as you can go."

Ross Macdonald
as Canadian Mystery Writer

Russell Brown

KENNETH MILLAR, writing under the pen name of Ross Macdonald, has achieved considerable success and esteem in the United States—where he is perceived as the heir apparent of the American detective writers Dashiell Hammett and Raymond Chandler and the writer who has done the most to revivify their genre of hardboiled stories. Millar's mysteries, most of which are set in California and feature a private eye from there named Lew Archer, were described in 1969 on the front cover of *The New York Times Book Review* as "The finest series of detective novels ever written by an American."

However—even as Millar once attributed Raymond Chandler's special feeling for the American language to his having spent his developmental years in England—the fact that Kenneth Millar's parents were Canadians coupled with the fact that, although born in the United States, Millar himself grew up in Canada, has surely left him profoundly shaped by that country and its culture in a way that affects his own fiction. Viewing his novels in a Canadian tradition, one discovers that even while they draw on a literary tradition that has its roots in pulp magazines of the American twenties and thirties, his books also have many qualities about them which are demonstrably Canadian, that in fact the very qualities which have distinguished Millar's novels from other American mysteries turn out to link him with many contemporary Canadian novelists.

His Canadian background is something about which Millar has remained somewhat reticent until recently, but lately he has himself been publicly reflecting on its effects. In an interview published in a 1973 issue of the *Journal of Popular Culture* he referred to it:

I have certain advantages from having been brought up in two cultures, Canadian and American. They're closely related but, nevertheless, they're different...having not only studied literature and history, but taught them in Canada before I became an American writer, I can see American life in relation to another culture which I know equally well. I really know the Anglo-Canadian culture more deeply and thoroughly than I do the American culture. The things you know best are what you learn between the ages of five and twenty-five....That Canadian background is really an essential differentia of my books. It would be hard to point out how. For me to point it out. But I know that's the difference. (JPC, 7 (1), 1973, p. 215)

In the following year, Millar contributed to a symposium on "The Writer's Sense of Place," in which—observing that "We writers never leave the places where our first lasting memories begin and have names put to them"—he returned to this topic:

I am both literally and imaginatively a biped, resting one uneasy foot in California where I was born and have spent the best part of my adult life, and the other foot in Canada where I was raised and partly educated. This geographical range and stretch accounts for some of the peculiarities of my work.... The main stories generally begin and end in the open self-inviting society of California, but their outcomes are determined, predetermined, by an ethical and psychological causality which I associate with my forebears in the north.... Canada seems to hang like a glacier slowly moving down on me from its notch. I expect it to overtake me before I die, reminding me with its chill and weight that I belong to the north after all. (*South Dakota Review,* 13, no. 3 1975, pp. 83-84)

Even though Millar says he would find it hard to point out exactly how he has been affected by his Canadian experience, the evidence of the novels is that he shares many concerns with writers in the Canadian literary mainstream. Less obvious, perhaps, than some of the aspects of his fiction I wish to consider, I would argue that the first of these Canadian characteristics inheres in his use of landscape: the way in which Southern California becomes a kind of presence of which we are always aware and which has to be taken into account because it has as much importance as any of the people with whom Lew Archer interacts. This is quite similar to the prominence of landscape in much of Canadian writing, from its presence as a shaping force of great consequence in the prairie fiction of F.P. Grove and Martha Ostenso earlier in the century, through the powerful animate quality of the physical world in the poetry of E.J. Pratt, to the concern for terrain and territory that continues to be important in contemporary fiction, poetry and even criticism. It is true that Chandler had, well before Millar began writing, made his intensely vivid descriptions of Los Angeles a familiar feature of his Marlowe novels, but the attention paid to landscape in the Lew Archer novels seems to belong to a different mode. In Millar's writing landscape become surreal and symbolic to the point that its literal fidelity or even its ability to evoke "mood" are concerns that become secondary at best: in a Macdonald detective story, space is—as it often is in Canadian fiction—first of all mythic.

The creation of a symbolic or mythic landscape in Millar's mysteries is accomplished in several ways. First of all, the world is frequently described in terms that emphasize its illusory quality—sometimes, for example, settings are given a shifting "watery" appearance, spoken of as belonging to the sea floor or associated with something like the "drowning pool" of an early title (imagery which, as we will see, is consonant with other important features of this fiction: the probing of psychic depths and of the unseen depths of the past). Secondly, the reader is constantly reminded of the subjective nature of the landscape that he does see and of the primacy of the interior worlds we all contain over the external ones we hardly move among. ("Her eyes looked through me into the complex inner world that was growing like a city in her mind" *Sleeping Beauty).* Moreover, geographical place in these novels is given such consistent associations that the very map becomes mythic for Archer: California is a kind of purgatory or limbo occupied by lost souls trapped in a meaningless and poorly-understood present, Nevada as the inferno which serves as a source of corruption to these California lost, and the mid-west and Canada the repository of those forgotten pasts, or the locus of search for the obscured sources of the present, or else the Eden which exists no more—the place of now-lost innocence and unattainable sanctuary.

This tendency to move from real space to the dimensions which belong to the unconscious or to the mythic mind is an often-discussed feature of Canadian writing—one that can readily be documented, from Grove's depiction of a stark and awesome land that invites men of epic proportions into heroic contests, to the way the prairie is utilized in Robert Kroetsch's recent fiction in such a way that it becomes a place where Indian and classical myth can be comically reenacted, or from the way that the natural landscape in Ostenso's *Wild Geese* becomes an embracing demon-lover to the way the north is depicted, in a book like Margaret Atwood's *Surfacing,* as a kind of mental landscape, a subconscious world in which one can lose and find oneself, a land which, as Jeremy Sadness puts it in Kroetsch's *Gone Indian,* is "rife with illusion."

Not only does Millar's fiction create the sort of space that characterizes Canadian more than American writing, but the dramas played out within his landscape take on a distinctively Canadian flavor. To begin with, when Millar wrote of himself, "We writers never leave the places where our first lasting memories begin and have names put to them," he was making an observation much more true of Canadians than of the more mobile and less obviously rooted American society; he was also, of course, making a statement that repeatedly applies to the characters who inhabit his books. The most striking innovation that Millar has made as a mystery author has been his location of the solutions, the keys to all his mysteries, in the times and places of the distant past. He has done this so that the discovery of truth in his detective stories can stand as an indication of the way in which events and deeds which lie hidden in each man's personal history may prove to be the unexamined causes of his present condition. Again and again, we are reminded that anyone may be, like Archer's client in *Sleeping Beauty,* "hit by a long shot fired from below the curve of time."

This sense of a past which, if understood, would explain the present, and the need, which therefore arises to reconstruct that past—is not only the controlling pattern of all of Millar's Lew Archer novels, it is that of much contemporary Canadian literature as well. Margaret Laurence's *Stone Angel,* for example, recounts the slow reassembly of a fragmented past, a recovery of lost memory that enables the narrator to understand her present petrification and eventually leads her to comprehend and accept the truth about events surrounding the death of her son. All three of the novels in Robertson Davies' Deptford trilogy similarly involve reconstructions of the past and investigations of long accomplished acts as sources of the present: *Fifth Business* details Dunstan Ramsay's attempt to understand why he has spent his life searching for saints (and the careful reader can discover enough clues to realize that a single incident in his childhood interactions with his mother is the cause); *The Manticore* is David Staunton's account of a psychotherapeutic reconsideration of his childhood which becomes an impassioned attempt to solve the (apparent) murder of his father; *World of Wonders* is the piecing together of the mysterious life of Paul Dempster so that the reader can finally learn the truth about the crucial role he played in the elder Staunton's death. Robert Harlow's *Scann* details the laborious attempts of a small-town editor to discover and chronicle—if necessary by willing into existence—the origins and meaning of the town. All of Kroetsch's novels are repeatedly built on the process of gathering together events from the past that explain the brutal or mysterious ends of various central characters. In fact, the search in the past for clues to the present and future is so often a topic in the modern Canadian novel that its heroes and major secondary characters are frequently drawn from the ranks of men whose roles are those such as historian, paleontologist and occasionally detective. (One thinks of Davies' Ramsay, of the narrator in Leonard Cohen's *Beautiful Losers,* of Mark Lerner in Henry Kreisel's *The Betrayal,* of William Dawe in Kroetsch's *Badlands,* of Webb in Michael Ondaatje's *Coming Through Slaughter.)*

There is something indigenously Canadian about this desire for an explanatory past. In general newly-established cultures, such as the U.S. and Canada, will, because of their separation from the European sources of tradition, inevitably feel a loss of history. However the founding and the subsequent development, the politics and the values of the two countries have resulted in opposed responses to this condition. Americans in their popular mythologies and in their fiction have celebrated their freedom from the past and the way a radical break with history allowed them to aspire to be "self-made" men—what R.W.B. Lewis has called the American Adam. Canadians, on the other hand, (and I include Millar here) have responded to their sense of disruption with stories that attempt to account for discontinuities in history, that make known the crucial but forgotten acts that have shaped us all, and that thus restore the flow of historical time.

Closely related to this tendency to locate his mystery solutions in a single event in the distant past is the way Millar treats the topic of responsibility. In the more conventional examples of the genre, the murderer has acted freely, even gratuitously, to commit a violent deed (often only one) which, once revealed, will end his career. In the Archer novels, however, the revelation of the details of a single act of violence is never enough. Instead, Millar's tales are calculated to show how the question of responsibility reveals that the act is both crucial and very complex and shows how the actions of an individual conform to some larger pattern and how the acts of many individuals are interrelated and contingent. Thus balanced against the complexity of his plots is a sense of inevitability that runs through this fiction, the feeling that certain large actions, once put into motion, will lead through almost unalterable sequences of causality down to our present circumstances. This same concern over the issue of individual responsibility, often even given similar statement, is one that informs a surprising number of important contemporary Canadian novels: Mordecai Richler's *St. Urbain's Horseman,* Kreisel's *The Betrayal,* Leo Simpson's *Peacock Papers,* Matt Cohen's *The Disinherited,* and Davies' trilogy are but a few Canadian books that trace the consequences of a single act, a single moral choice, or that show the way a single individual may set into motion a complex pattern of cause and event, or which ask how we are to go about setting things right again. Perhaps a single quotation from Davies will suffice to indicate the importance of this to such Canadian novelists. In an essay about his own fiction he wrote:

> How early in life does the responsibility begin? I concluded, not without long debate, that it began with life itself, and that a child was as responsible as anyone else if it chose a course of action knowingly.
> In *Fifth Business*...a boy makes a choice: he wants to hurt his companion so he throws a snowball at him, and in the snowball is a stone.... The consequences of the snowball with the stone in it continue for sixty years, and do much to shape the lives of three men.... (*One Half of Robertson Davies* Toronto: Macmillan, 1977 p. 16)

A final aspect of Kenneth Millar's mystery fiction that is also worth noting here is—like the topic of responsibility—also associated with concern for the past: the preoccupation with fathers and father-figures. As the authors of the *Encyclopedia of Mystery and Detection* have observed: "Since *The Galton Case* (1959) the dominant theme in the Macdonald mysteries has been the search by children for their 'lost' fathers." As they go on to point out this search has personal relevance for the author: "Millar admitted that this book, written after a period of psychotherapy, marked 'a personal and, especially, a professional, watershed.' There is much autobiography in this book, in which Archer travels to Canada to trace a father missing more than twenty years."

There are, however, many ways Millar might have chosen to deal with his loss of father, and the one he did choose seems to have cultural relevance as well as personal because, in a way that symbolizes the sense of the missing past, lost fathers are a recurrent motif in Canadian fiction. While American fiction, with its revolutionary roots, is father-denying, frequently patricidal, a contrasting search for the father is a repeated subject in Canadian writing. To name a few of the most important examples, much of Hugh MacLennan's fiction, as well as Kroetsch's *Badlands,* Davies' *The Manticore* and Atwood's *Surfacing* all take the form of quests for a father. The heroine of *Surfacing* and the hero of *The Manticore* are no less preoccupied with the discovery of the truth about their own fathers than are John Galton of *The Galton Case* or Fred Johnson in *The Blue Hammer.* Indeed, and interestingly, the decision to build their plots around a search for the facts about a vanished father or a murdered one leads both Atwood and Davies to engage in some self-conscious play with the form of the mystery in their novels. Indeed the underlying resemblance between *The Manticore* and the fiction of Kenneth Millar is sufficient that one book reviewer was led to observe, apparently without any awareness of a cultural link between the two men: "Davies is a Jungian Ross Macdonald" (Roger Sale, *New York Review,* 8 Feb. 1973, p. 21).

There are other connections to be made between Millar and his Canadian contemporaries, and I might in passing suggest just one more: Millar has broken with the American dualism that was so much a part of the tough guy mystery story and that gave it a moral universe of clearly defined good and evil. In replacing this vision with one of a world not so much of moral ambiguities as a world where a single deed may turn out to be both good and evil and in which guilt and innocence are virtually indistinguishable, Millar's perspectives are linked in one more way with those of Davies, Kroetsch, Kreisel and especially with that of Sheila Watson in *The Double Hook*. Seeing Kenneth Millar in the context of these Canadian writers indicates the way in which he was shaped by and responded to Canadian culture. Because of this we might conclude that Millar has done more than merely reinvigorate the American mystery. He has also Canadianized it.

John D. MacDonald:
The Liabilities of Professionalism

Thomas Doulis

MOST STUDENTS of mass culture have ignored the technical aspects of literary works and have concentrated, instead, on the values for which these works are vehicles. By dismissing the technical considerations of mass fiction as "formulaic," however, they have ignored the critical issue of how the formula inhibits the writer when it no longer serves his aesthetic purposes. John D. MacDonald, whose readership can be numbered in the hundreds of thousands has produced approximately six hundred short stories and more than sixty novels, provides an interesting example of the formulas as aesthetic aid that has turned into handicap. The already developed framework superimposed on his characters and their milieu has helped him considerably in the structuring of his fiction, but it has also become a structural liability when he has attempted to shape the meaningful fiction that at times he has wanted to write.

If he had never varied from his craftman's attitudes, his successes and failures would be accepted for what they are. Obviously potboilers like *Judge Me Not* (1951), *Murder for the Bride* (1951) or *The Neon Jungle* (1953) have ceased to interest him beyond a certain point. Clearly something about the locale, the characters or the story-line had attracted him at first. But the content, somehow, could not withstand further development. He finished them off quickly, almost disdainfully, but with commendable shrewdness—the way a master cabinetmaker has patched up a bad job for which his apprentice was responsible, disguising the mistakes from everyone's eyes but those of another carpenter—and went on to something else.

Scattered throughout this large body of work, however, are novels of such a personal nature, fiction so genuinely and deeply felt, that MacDonald had clearly lost the craftsman's distance toward his theme and found himself inside the book. Despite the fact that these deeply felt works are flawed, they provide the reader with more valuable aesthetic experiences than the potboilers in which he has successfully used the formulaic plot. That they are failures because of MacDonald's professionalism will be the burden of this essay to prove. Before we undertake this, though, we must look at his successes, since it would be absurd to study a popular writer only to ignore what has brought him to our attention in the first place.

The Travis McGee adventures, a series that by now has reached a dozen books, is MacDonald's foremost achievement as a craftsman. But even a professional like himself had to evolve by trial and error the framework that supports these stories. Anyone who has read a Travis McGee (identified by a "color" in the title: *The Deep Blue Good-Bye, Nightmare in Pink,* etc.) will realize when studying one of the early, pre-Travis thrillers that MacDonald's crucial technical problem—among others—was located in the person of his antagonist. Briefly stated, many of MacDonald's potboilers, before the McGee series, suffered from the novelist's need to invent a new hero, with new attributes and abilities, for every adventure.

A study of his early work shows a technical development of structure that eventually becomes the elegant formula of the McGee series. In most novels we find—albeit in rudimentary terms—the beginning of his awareness of the technical problems of the genre and the demands of the audience that MacDonald will ultimately need to confront and solve.

Perhaps a brief checklist of the readership demands and technical problems of the craft is in order before we can see how Travis McGee rescued MacDonald from the bumbling heroes that populated his earlier fiction.

1. The "Bonus." Frequently dependent upon the protagonist's job, the "bonus" is a glance at an ordinarily obscure facet of contemporary society and often a commentary on American life. The "bonus" is convincing because of its accurate though surface realism. In *The Brass Cupcake* (1950), for example, the hero is an insurance agent whose job involves meeting jewel thieves before they have recourse to "fences," since the company he represents can save the substantial difference between what the thieves would be willing to sell the gems for and their market value. The process by which he performs his duty and maintains his reputation for fairness comes under the category of "bonus." In *Judge Me Not,* the "bonus" is an illustration of good government issues in a vice-ridden town; in *Area of Suspicion* (1954, revised 1961), it involves the running of a defense factory which, under the control of foreign agents, turns out defective ICBMs. In *The Only Girl in the Game* (1960) by far the most impressive of these pre-Travis novels, the "bonus" is a commendable analysis of the interplay between the rackets and the casino-hotel complex in Las Vegas. In this novel the "bonus" becomes a significant factor in the formula, fulfilling the role of milieu, plot base and trigger to the finale.

2. Romantic interest. There can certainly not be a strong element of escape in fiction without some love interest.[1] This serves a number of purposes: sexual titillation for the males, reader identification for the females, and the preparation for the all-important buttressing of middle-class values at the novel's conclusion.[2]

But as MacDonald has discovered many times, there is a problem here. Male readers might tend to be rather indiscriminate in their acceptance of sexual adventures and female readers might allow themselves to identify briefly with a tramp, but no amount of adventure will allow them to accept a finale that would have the hero and the tramp setting up house together in bourgeois stability. For all their delight in surface glitter and derring-do, mass readers appear to be rather conservative in the moral sphere and subscribe to Goldsmith's attitudes: when lovely ladies like Mary Olan in *You Kill Me* (1955, 1961), Toni Rasselle in *On the Make* (1955), and Felice Carboy in *Judge Me Not* stoop to folly, only death can wipe their guilt away.

Sexually promiscuous women might supply the necessary erotic adventure for the novel, but merely by being what they are they are unable to provide the requisite terminal reassurance. They must either die, to leave the hero free for a young lady with a relatively unblemished past, a girl like the suitable Toni MacRae in *You Kill Me* or Ruth Stamm in *On the Make,* or, if their reputation is tarnished by being call-girls (a great possibility in MacDonald's fiction), to undergo a physical beating, possibly even disfigurement, an experience that presumably will make them better people.

For example, Barbara Heddon, the hero's inamorata in *Judge Me Not,* is at best a disquieting choice for his wife, for though she is beautiful and intelligent, her years as a girl on call would make for an inadequate terminal reassurance. But she falls in love[3] with the hero on the strength of a few pleasurable couplings, and not only wants to leave the profession for him but takes great risks for a girl who means very little to him. Facially disfigured by beatings received while trying to save this girl, Barbara wins our sympathy and forgiveness. We approve of the hero's marriage to her and hope she recovers her beauty through plastic surgery because, as far as we are concerned, her heroism has cleared her record.

For the Fatal Woman, however, there is no future. Though she need not necessarily die or be imprisoned, her presence must be removed from the hero's existence. Fatal Women have the exceptional talent of being able to turn men into helpless love slaves willing to do anything to please them. Mary Olan of *You Kill Me* was one, but the reader must meet the title character of *Clemmie* (1958), Niki of *Area of Suspicion,* Crissy Harkinson of *The Last One Left* (1967) and Jerrana of *Slam the Big Door* (1960, an uncharacteristic novel in which MacDonald forgets himself and begins sounding downright evangelical, (like some of his fat women who have found God in the rural backlands of Florida) to see a Fatal Woman of major dimensions in her native habitat.

But technically there is more involved than this: the female lead must also provide the hero with information he would ordinarily be unable to gather on his own. It is obvious to determine that novels like *You Kill Me* are badly conceived since MacDonald is compelled to employ three female characters—one for sex, one for technical information and the last for terminal reassurance—to do what one character should be able to do. *Where is Janice Gantry?* (1961) is also flawed in that the title character, killed and forgotten after the initial narrative hook, is replaced by someone who acts—down to the last passionate gasp—very much like her and can provide the hero, in Janice's stead, with all the love and factual information MacDonald needs to tell the story. But this is annoying since it only emphasizes the interchangeability of all characters in formulaic fiction.

What MacDonald is obviously searching for is a formula that would provide him with an attractive woman, with an interesting but not too lurid past, who will bring to his story, besides the necessary reams of information, an abundant sexuality that is unmarred by any hint of wickedness. In this case, the final resolution of the plot will find the eligible hero embarking on a marriage that can be considered suitable by

MacDonald's paperback audience.

3. The Threatening Force. Particularly evident in the earlier and more melodramatic novels, the Threatening Force is usually a man (less often a Fatal Woman) who possesses great physical energy and power, a diabolical craft and occasionally a disturbing attraction for women. Ultimately, however, he is vulnerable. He is the villain, of course, at times in league with a Fatal Woman of lesser proportions (like the sinister Mottling-Niki duo in *Area of Suspicion*), or at times a relative solitary like Fitzmartin in *On the Make* or Willy Prior in *You Kill Me,* the last a brutally powerful, physical exercise addict whose religio-mystical certitudes are an immediate tip-off to this criminal bent.

4. The Trump Card. At times, no matter how cleverly MacDonald has solved his technical problems, there are still several strings left hanging at the end of the novel. In cases of this sort, the Trump Card is a structural solution that permits him to escape from the tangle. Willy Prior in *You Kill Me* and the eventually zombie-like Mayor Carboy in *Judge Me Not* are Trump Cards in that they make a point of killing off whoever seems to be giving MacDonald trouble in the execution of the plot. The Communist menace in *Area of Suspicion* is also a Trump Card since the bumbling hero feels he must lecture his skeptical and morally correct, though certifiedly lusty, bride-to-be on the threat of godless bolshevism in order to extricate MacDonald out of the impossible structural mess he had backed himself into.

5. Terminal Reassurance. The villain's defeat, which illustrates the eventual superiority of the decent people, usually precedes the culmination of the novel: most often the reader is tastefully preserved from witnessing the wedding of the hero and heroine. But if MacDonald's people were only decent, his readers would not be as interested in them as they are. They are beautiful people as well, and their pasts do not show on them.[4] Though his women have been shot, stabbed and beaten, their wounds—physical and psychological—are not at all visible. Forever young and attractive, renewed and refreshed by good conversation, food and sex (unlike the corrupt ones whose voices become hoarse from decades of drink and their skins, from too much sun, become dry and brown as saddles) they are apt to want a certain dignity without these 'wounds,' which give them a sadness and a mature sensitivity to people who would ordinarily be as blank as pretty mannikins. This is obviously for reader identification, as is the mawkish treatment of romantic love, from which MacDonald was rescued by Travis McGee.

In *The Deep Blue Good-Bye* (1964), the first of the Travis McGee series, MacDonald found the hero he had been searching for, an articulate, witty strong man who operates in the morally gray area of the law. In the past, most of his characters (with the rare exceptions of Paul Stanial in *The Drowner* (1963) and Cliff Bartells in *The Brass Cupcake*) were relatively incompetent, vulnerable physically to Threatening Forces and sexually to Fatal Women, unable ultimately to defeat their opponents without help. The entrapment of the evil forces in most of the early potboilers had to be made by official guardians of the peace and security, the police or the F.B.I., toward whom MacDonald has, besides the sensitive man's ambivalence, the mystery writer's competitiveness.

The modus operandi of the McGee series is this: a person, usually a woman, has had something of value taken from her. There is no recourse to the law, however, since the law in these situations is either unwritten or is written in such a way that it protects the criminal. McGee's function is to use his brawn, ingenuity and knowledge of contemporary life to defeat the Threatening Force in this area unaccountably left unsystematized and untaxed (or untaxed because unsystematized) by the overpowering state, and to return whatever was taken to the innocent client, keeping half of its value as his commission. McGee operates out of a barge-like houseboat. This boat, "The Busted Flush," which he won in a poker game, becomes the shrine for the defenseless, whom the highly touted public servants of a computerized America are unable to protect. For them, Travis McGee is the unconventional hero, the mouthpiece for the writer's humanist jeremiads, Super-MacDonald.

But there is a problem here. Travis suspects most of the devices of modern finance that offer profit, security and comfort to man:

...And I am wary of a lot of other things, such as plastic credit cards, payroll deductions, insurance programs, retirement benefits, savings accounts, Green Stamps, time clocks, newspapers, mortgages, sermons, miracle fabrics, deodorants, check lists, time payments, political parties, lending libraries, television, actresses, junior chambersof commerce, pageants, progressed, and manifest destiny....I am also wary of earnestness.[5]

Yet one of the dilemmas MacDonald finds himself plagued with in this series is his need to express his own genuine commitments to man's search for honesty and permanence through an honest man whose attraction for the reader rests on the impermanence of his relationships, particularly with women. McGee is not a gigolo. He is a forthright man whose superb physical condition and marital status [6] allow him to be constantly with and pleasing to sexually attractive women. But, since he is sensitive, too, MacDonald has the usual problem of escape fiction, the necessity to teeter on the edge of middle-class reassurance after the adventure.

These are the playmate years, and they are demonstrably fraudulent. The scene is reputed to be acrawl with adorably amoral bunnies to whom sex is a pleasant social favor. The new culture. And they are indeed present and available, in exhausting quantity, but there is a curious tastelessness about them. A woman who does not guard and treasure herself cannot be of much value to anyone else. They become a pretty little convenience, like a guest towel. And the cute little things they say, and their dainty little squeals of pleasure and release are as contrived as the embroidered initials on the guest towels. Only a woman of pride, complexity, and emotional tension is genuinely worth the act of love, and there are only two ways to get yourself one of them. Either you lie, and stain the relationship with your own sense of guile, or you accept the involvement, the emotional responsibility, the permanence she must by nature crave. I love you can be said in only two ways.[7]

Put bluntly the problem is this: McGee, to remain maritally free, is condemned to the bunnies, since we would lose our interest in him if he settled down with a "woman of pride." But his seriousness and honesty as a man compel him to be contemptuous toward promiscuous sex. What is to be done?

The solution to this problem is MacDonald's discovery of a category of love between that which the bunnies offer and the total commitment expected by the woman of pride. This middle category might be termed "therapeutic sex," a McGee speciality. One partner heals the other for a period of several weeks or months—a nice compromise between the grubby and the grating—until the young lady, who had earlier verged on the brink of alienation and angst, finds her way back to emotional stability, to the point, that is, where she no longer needs the ministrations of McGee—who she knows is unsuitable for marriage—and then leaves him free for another adventure against the odds.

Frankly, though, only a matter of time seems to distinguish promiscuous from therapeutic sex. Toward the former he is harsh; toward the latter, as in *A Purple Place for Dying* (1964), the third in the series, MacDonald is permissive. Isabel Webb, the repressed sister of the murdered Humanities Prof at State Western, provides the love interest, and Travis' introducing her to the mysteries of therapeutic sex acts as the concluding palliative.

Seeing a little more of Travis in *A Deadly Shade of Gold* (1965) we realize that he is not as fresh as we had first thought him. That he is invincible is clear. His attractiveness for women is attested to by the numerous grapplings. But we do not believe him when he rejects the easy sex of the bunnies because he shows us that he is also guilty of promiscuity: he too can use sex as a weapon, as when he seduces the widow Betty Borlicks to gain information abou the gold Aztec statuettes that are the goal of the adventure. His attacks on modern society also become rather suspect: he uses a gasoline credit card when he needs the slender tautness of plastic to force the lock on a door; he has an elaborate telephone system rigged up on the Busted Flush; his way of life is the ultimate in mobility; and his adventures are compelling because he has cut his period of mourning for his friends (Travis seems to be without relatives) down to the minimum. Nora Guardino, the woman whom Travis rushed to help initially, is providentially killed when an explosion on a yacht sends a mahogany splinter flying to lodge in her throat, which does not sadden us since it frees Travis for Constancia Melgar and the second caper.

The discovery of the ideal hero in McGee and the subsequent perfection of his formula has liberated MacDonald in the writing of his potboilers. We need not create a new point of view character, nor call on the police or the F.B.I., nor pull out a Trump Card, nor marry the hero off. As long as the other elements of the equation are ready—attractive women in need of help, the promise of an interesting "bonus," an exotic locale, a worthy opponent—Travis McGee is able to perform with formulaic perfection. In fact, the only problem here may be that perfection may bore the seeker in MacDonald, and it seems that this is close to happening in the most recent McGee novel, *The Turquoise Lament*.

This may be the perfect time to sell the idea to Kingsley Amis or to program the necessary information into a computer and let the series write itself.

As indicated earlier, formulaic fiction requires characters who can be manipulated without undue violence. For this to be avoided, they must not be so specific as to be unique, not so real as to demand a freedom of action consistent with their humanity. In fiction of lesser seriousness, MacDonald has little trouble in creating characters who allow themselves to be orchestrated within his work as novelist too well. By creating characters whose humanity threatened to overwhelm the formula he had devised for them, MacDonald had to crush the intractable human material and tack on an ending that made little structural sense.

Essentially he tells four stories in this novel. Betty Dawson, a beautiful entertainer at the Cameroon, finds herself trapped by the "Mob" into a whore's life: without her knowledge, films had been taken of an affair she had had at the Playland Motel. Boss Al Marta, threatening to show them to her father, forces Betty to accept what turns out to be her real job; whenever there is a big winner ($400,000 or more) at the casino, she is to try to delay his leaving Las Vegas in the only way a young, attractive woman can.

Hugh Darren, the assistant hotel manager, has originally come to Las Vegas to put the Cameroon on a paying basis. Darren is out of his element; he is in town only to make enough money to finance an island resort in the Bahamas. In the long tradition of MacDonald heroes who realize that promiscuous sex is a waste of energy, clean-cut Darren knows that the dynamism that drives him must be channeled to more productive ends. Little by little his position at the Cameroon is disturbing to Marta who, by temperament and profession, needs to have a hold over his subordinates.

Darren and Betty are the major characters, but, without the sub-plots that elaborate their development, their story would be a conventional one between a fallen woman and a man with goals. One minor character, old Homer Gallowell, who energizes a sub-plot, has returned to Las Vegas to retaliate against the Cameroon for having taken $100,000 from him at the tables the previous year. Prepared by his company mathematician with a fool-proof system to break the casino, the Texas millionaire does so only because, aside from the revenge motive, he is a man devoted to reason and prudence. It is through the informed points of view of Gallowell and Marta that MacDonald, in his "bonus," illustrates the scope of his research into the workings of the casinos.

Temple and Vicki Shannard provide the final component of the story. Temple is an old friend of Hugh and a possible partner with him in the Bahamas venture. A number of poor investments, however, have overcommitted his resources, and he finds himself in Las Vegas hoping to borrow money from the Mob. But Marta and his associates do not want to be anyone's partners; they want to buy Shannard out completely and invest directly into the highly lucrative Caribbean area. Since no financial support can be expected from the Syndicate, Shannard decides to win what he needs at the tables. By this time the reader knows, through the technically admirable preparation given us by Gallowell and Marta, the mathematical impossibility of anyone's winning on impulse or luck. The moral of Gallowell's story, which in turn is a foreshadowing of Shannard's disastrous end, is that a man who needs money will never win it.

This recapitulation has now pointed the way that the novel is to develop. Homer wins $400,000 from the Casino, which decides Marta to order Betty to try to seduce the old man into delaying his return home. Since Gallowell knows Hugh and Betty and likes the young couple, the story has taken a significant turn. There is no retreat; once Hugh learns of Betty's visit to Homer, he will know what her position at the Cameroon has actually been. Darren has entered his own time of crisis because Vicki Shannard, disgusted with what she interprets as her husband's inadequacy, rebuffs him and tries to seduce Hugh in order to guarantee her security. Shannard's expected failure at the tables and Vicki's scorn ultimately lead him to suicide.

Then MacDonald sabotages his beautifully functioning machine. Before going to her meeting with Homer in the Playland Motel, in a room equipped with cameras, Betty learns of her father's death. The Mob's hold on her is broken. She need not attempt Homer's seduction. Yet, because Marta knows something about her that Darren does not, she is still vulnerable. She is morally tainted. If she survives the violent conclusion that MacDonald is brewing, her lurid past will be disturbing to the reader and will provide Darren with the unpleasant dilemma of either marrying her or breaking off their relationship. Though not a Fatal Woman, she is sister to Barbara Heddon of *Judge Me Not* and Toni Rasselle of *On the Make* and, like the former must be beaten and disfigured, or, like the latter, must be killed so as not to entangle Hugh Darren in an unfortunate marriage.

When she meets Homer, therefore, Betty confesses all; Gallowell insults Marta over the phone; Marta orders his henchmen to beat some sense into Betty; inadvertently she is killed, and MacDonald and we find ourselves back in the comfortable formula plot. Darren must vindicate her death, which he does by implicating the men responsible in a robbery of Casino property. This results in their being murdered by Marta, a Trump Card like Major Carboy and Willy Pryor.But we had grown to like and respect Betty Dawson. Why did MacDonald treat her like an old shoe, like a puppet who had to say certain words at a certain time so the novel could end on page 224?

The problems, when they occur, seem to come in the area of values. Escape novels must choose for their subject matter realms that are neither threatening nor controversial to the individual reader and must deal with issues about which everyone wants to read yet about which there is unanimity. Presumably issues like crime, murder, blackmail, narcotics rings, graft, although everyday matters in our society, can be made interesting and by definition not immediately threatening to a reader as long as he can be convinced that there is some distance between him and the actual criminality. If this distance is violated, however, we are no longer discussing escape fiction.

Paradoxically, MacDonald's trouble areas seem to be those which he has exploited for his lesser yet consistently more successful fiction: sexual morality, particularly as it relates to middle class values, and the ethics of business society seen through the viewpoint of a sensitive and thoughtful man. *The Only Girl in the Game* carried within it both these issues, compounded by the fact that his characters were attractive people who could have uncovered enough conflicts between their ideals and their personal histories to have given MacDonald the option of concluding the novel with the inevitability of tragedy (which itself is formulaic) rather than the terminal violence of the commercial formula. Instead, their humanity was demeaned by their being compelled to act out the myth of the clean-cut hero and his call-girl sweetheart.

Much the same thing happens in *A Man of Affairs* (1957) except that Sam Glidden's preoccupations and his position as Vice President of Harrison Corporation bring us more into the sphere of business ethics than of sexual morality. Glidden is alienated from every stratum of the business world: he comes from worker stock, but "the eight hours' pay for three hours' work" philosophy of the unions has severed any loyalty Sam might have had toward them; the managerial class, of which he is a part, are pale, frightened functionaries who exist to manipulate and increase the fortunes of people like the McGanns and the Dodges, the pleasure class. Sam Glidden's concern about his integrity leads him to question the confused loyalties he has managed to retain over the years because he has never considered them carefully.

Mike Dean, a raider of companies and a 'Threatening Force,' has been buying into Harrison and can either control its executive decisions or be represented on the Board of Directors. He plans a weekend at the Bahamas hideout to get the McGanns and Dodges, children of the founders and major shareholders, to sign over their proxy votes to him. Glidden gets himself invited along so that he can watch over the interests of the working people of Portston, with whom he still identifies somewhat.

The major tension of the novel occurs when Glidden has his loyalties tested by Dean and finally decides that the offer of a three year contract at $40,000 a year and a stock option agreement is too good to resist. He capitulates.

So far so good. The problem enters not when Sam begins having second thoughts, but when the mechanics of melodrama begin operating as efficiently as they must in order to take the reader's mind off the significant contemporary issues MacDonald has raised. It is as though he deliberately seeks to calm the troubling questions he has asked.

"You were bought and you won't stay bought," Dean shouts at Glidden.

What kind of ethics is that? What kind of morality is that?....You pollyanna boys want to go around thinking the business world is honorable and reasonably decent....Listen to me. There's no more morality or ethics in industry than there is in...barracuda....You want to live in a dream world. I tell you that the only limitation is the law. And everything goes. Oh, how I love to run into Christers on a deal. (8)

What possibilities are open for MacDonald at this point? Glidden can triumph by walking out on Dean; his character would thus have been extended to an impressive point of renunciation. In a corrupt, self-seeking world, one man of executive ability is strong enough (a Christer) to turn down the many attractive rewards our society offers the talented. Or, he can capitulate again, which would be a more believable and interesting solution: his first refusal would have attested to his exceptional moral strength, while his final acceptance would have won both our credence in his reality and our sardonic and possibly masochistic pleasure at viewing the pitfalls of our society. In either case, the options are memorable and intellectually disquieting.

MacDonald, though, chooses a violent structural solution. During the argument with Dean, Sam calls him an "emotional cripple." Dean's eyes "bulged and the cords in his throat were like the knotted roots of a tree." He dies, conveniently, of "a massive coronary occlusion." His lieutenants, realizing that their satrapies will be destroyed when the news of Dean's death is known, place him in a deep-freeze and make plans to liquidate their holdings. This vital and Threatening Force is thus easily dismissed and the issues MacDonald raised are muted by the inappropriate action sequence: Glidden and his beloved Bridget escape by rowing thirty miles to the Grand Bahamas. They marry and go off to Cuernavaca—probably to keep company with the pleasure class for which Sam had such contempt—after another school of corporate barracuda has successfully raided Harrison and fired all the people Glidden wanted to save.

The comment MacDonald wanted to make about business society is still there, but *A Man of Affairs* was about business ethics; he had managed to make us feel that the issues were as important to Glidden and to us as Betty Dawson and Hugh Darren were to us and to each other. To entertain a reader seems to be an easy matter for a man of MacDonald's ability as long as the issues are not close enough to compel us to commit ourselves emotionally to his characters. His very skill as a writer, however, virtually assures that this conflict between his people and his formula will be perpetual in his serious efforts.

This has never been so true as in the major and truly impressive *A Flash of Green* (1962). Grassy Bay, on the western shore of Florida, is being threatened for the second time by developers who want to "reclaim" the land and build a housing project on it. The local conservation group, by gaining the support of the newspaper and the local business community, has previously defeated an outside organization of developers, but the new threat, since it has behind it the same local forces that assured defeat for the outsiders, is much more serious.

Behind the new group is Elmo Bliss, an owner of a large construction business who stands to profit vastly from the defeat of conservationists. He can be crudely typed as a Threatening Force, but his self-awareness and the quality of his perceptions place him firmly in the tradition of the intellectually disarming devil's advocates. As County Commissioner, who has hopes of being Governor one day, Bliss wants his political record unblemished in conservation measures, an important factor in a state that depends for much of its revenues on its climate and facilities for recreation.

A Flash of Green is massive and breathtaking in conception, yet it is in the development of the leading character, a sardonic newspaperman named Jimmy Wing, that it ultimately fails. A maimed hero, Wing is temperamentally and emotionally allied to the conservation group. They are decent people and he is one of them. Their ideas are those of people who respect life and want to save the unspoiled areas, which they believe belong to all the people. Yet Elmo Bliss hires Wing for a hundred dollars a week to spy out the vulnerabilities of the conservationists so that they can be blackmailed and compelled to stop their campaign. That they are liable to pressure because of some past indiscretion or present weakness is not unusual. That Wing, an innately honorable man, would accept the sordid job of spying on people he respects, and one of whom—the widow Katherine Hubble—he loves, taxes the reader's credibility. Yet MacDonald thinks he needs him to spy for the "bonus," the insight into the tactics of "uglifiers, the despoilers, the asphalters, the sign merchants, the tree haters...."

The County Commissioner's strategy is successful: Grassy Bar is turned into a housing project. Jimmy Wing, though, by revealing the extent of Bliss' involvement, has guaranteed that the contractor-politician will have no more than a local importance. Having destroyed his chances with Katherine Hubble, the tormented newspaperman, verging on alcholism now, searches for the technical beatings he periodically receives.

But there is no reason, besides the technical one of providing the "bonus," whose value here is debatable, for Wing to have been placed in the awkward moral position he was in. Like many of MacDonald's heroes, though, Wing and his integrity as a character was sacrificed to the writer's belief that plot considerations demanded a spy in Bliss' camp to fulfill the sense of procedural authenticity that is a major "bonus" of MacDonald's fiction. It is this flaw that so seriously harms *A Flash of Green*.

But assuming it is an artistic failure, why is *A Flash of Green* so impressive? For one thing, it says about the conflict between progress and nature what few other novels have said with so profound a political awareness. For another, it is a deeply pessimistic novel about what MacDonald calls "the plague" that is man, the Threatening Force who cannot accept nature as she is but, in Bliss' words, "wants something going on, like a porpoise coming ten feet out of the water to eat a fish, or pretty girls underwater, sucking air from a hose, and eating bananas."

The significant factor here is that the corrupting forces are the flash of green money and the desire for technological progress (which frequently implies the destruction of nature), both credos of the common man, the audience for whom, presumably, MacDonald is writing. If there is a "villain" here it is man as manipulator, as hater of his given environment, as jailor of himself in the cage of his own technology, as commercial exploiter of the riches of nature. It is clearly not Elmo Bliss who is the evil force in this great warning statement, a statement that might have approached the tragic vision had it not been deeply flawed by MacDonald's relentless need to control and direct, to an excessive point, the destinies of his characters.

A short book MacDonald published in the same year as *A Flash of Green* holds out promise that, after Travis McGee, he might be able to adjust his formula to be an ideal vehicle for his observations of sexual mores and the business ethic.

We find in *A Key to the Suite* (1962) many of the same values as in *Cancel All Our Vows* (1953, 1955) and *The Deceivers* (1958). The latter two are books taken from the same pattern in which MacDonald studies marital tensions and infidelity in a suburban setting, but in *Cancel All Our Vows* the issues are clouded by his introduction of the theme of double-standard morality. Merely by readjusting the formula, by electing to concentrate on the ethics of the business world rather than on infidelity, and by choosing a different kind of leading character, MacDonald has achieved in *A Key to the Suite* his one indisputable masterpiece.[9] Although it contains all the MacDonald staples of heavy plotting, violent conclusion, the hint of illegality and the "bonus" of a sharp insight into mid-century American reality, *A Key to the Suite* succeeds because of the hero's personality and what he represents.

But we must begin with the established pattern. Fletcher Wyant of *Cancel All Our Vows* finds his marriage going sour. His suburban milieu, and the commercialized values and geographical mobility of the executive class to which he belongs, may have something to do with his alienation. He has an affair with Laura, the attractive wife of a subordinate, who is more profoundly than he a rebel against Minidoka conformity. It is her inability to compromise with values she despises and her prodding and planning that result in Wyant's spending a day with her at the red barn, a symbol of the rural past still visible from the picture window of his development home.

The flaw of *Cancel All Our Vows* is that Wyant's world is threatened not by his own affair with Laura but by his wife's seduction, or "willing rape," by a local athlete. If this event had occurred after Wyant's day with Laura at the red barn, the novel's theme would have been more clearly outlined. Jane Wyant would have had an actual grievance, whereas technically her husband is still faithful to her when she is taken by Sam Rice, yet MacDonald uses her seduction as the trigger for the rest of the action.

Because Jane's motivations and reality are suspect, the outline of the plot for which she is such a crucial element is irretrievably harmed; after her guilt has been recognized by her husband and after his affair with Laura, Jane deliberately calls Rice to betray Fletcher again, in full consciousness of her act, for his subsequent betrayal of her. Behavior like this requires us to view her either as a major character, for whom all the events of the novel must be relevant, (which is not the case since *Cancel All Our Vows* is Fletcher's book) or as a complex and living personage who must not be confined to formulaic patterns.

MacDonald does not make this mistake in *The Deceivers,* where Carl Garrett is to Wyant what his next door neighbor, Cindy Cable, is to Laura. The scene is set when Carl's wife, Joan, goes into the hospital for an operation and Cindy's husband, Bucky, whose job demands frequent travel, flies out of town in his company plane.

Carl, an interesting man in his early forties, is aware of his weaknesses and the hypocrisies of suburban life. "Whoever heard of an avant-guard accountant," he asks at one point, and something, some temperamental flaw keeps him from totally identifying with the suburban ethos he sees around him. Through his perspective we see Crescent Ridge in a harsh light, populated by upper middle-class white collar workers who have left Hillton, the nearby city, to evade city problems and are now groping for solutions to civic problems that do not require the hated tax assessments.

About himself in society Carl is very clear-sighted. He is blind, however, to his duties with Ballinger Corporation and to his wife. At work, he is being challenged by Ray Walsh, a subordinate much like Ellis Corban, for not believing in the film, for making "hilarious comments" which reveal his deep alienation from the executive ethos, and for not performing: he has not thought of any cost-saving devices, which is part of his function.

Carl knows he is a maverick. Psychologically estranged from the "smiling rotarian world" of his immediate environment, Carl is ready for a tumultuous affair. This is what Cindy provides, for she is temperamentally incompatible to her stable, uncomplicated husband, and, like Laura Corban, is hostile to the values of intellectual conformity demanded of her by Crescent Ridge.

Their affair begins tempestuously, each looking for something that his mate is unable to provide. Even the ironic Carl allows himself briefly to think he is being animated by something other than pure animal appetite, although he is certain that when Joan returns home he and Cindy will go back to being affectionate neighbors. But granted Cindy's psychological vulnerability and Carl's submerged aimlessness, the affair brings them a self-awareness they might have had at a lesser price.

They are no more compatible with each other than they are with their respective mates, however, and Cindy becomes cold to him when Carl makes it clear that he will not leave his wife for her. Though their affair at the motel loses some of its secrecy, they are not yet discovered. The forces of tension within the novel seem to have exhausted themselves at this point and to have reached a kind of stasis. No rational motive, certainly, beyond an attempt by MacDonald to get the plot off-balance enough to force the action, seems to compel Carl at this juncture to get drunk and go to Cindy. Then the plot mechanism begins: they are discovered by Bucky. Her husband will take the children from her. But first he calls his parents, who never liked his bride, tells them everything, and decides to go to them. Flying through a thunderstorm, he crashes at night and is killed, which makes Cindy, not the most stable person, feel responsible for everything. She undergoes a crisis and is about to be hospitalized, when Carl—realizing she will lose her children—helps her "snap out of it."

For her there is no happy ending. For Carl, who must also confront Ray Walsh's major challenge, there is only an acceptance of his guilt and a channeling of the enormous energies he had previously allowed to lie dormant within him. Carl must confess his infidelity to a convalescent Joan since he might be asked to be a witness for Cindy if her in-laws sue to gain custody of the children. But the reader is kept ignorant of Joan's reaction to his confession in the same way that Fletcher and Jane Wyant's decision as to whether or not they will go through with their planned divorce is not made before the end of *Cancel All Our Vows*.

In both cases, two men for whom we had respect and through whom our distrust of a limited suburban society was authenticated, were taken through an experience that challenged their position in that society and threatened the integrity of their marriages. In *Cancel All Our Vows,* where the material is less tractable and the motivations of the characters flawed, the resolution of Fletcher's and Ellis' promotions is totally unacceptable, while in *The Deceivers* the behavior and attitudes of the characters are creditable, yet the recourse to violent structural solutions, usual with MacDonald, is nevertheless disquieting.

Quite simply, our objections to the novelist's manipulations seem not from his use of formula per se, but from his violation of the characters' freedom of action. We ask why Carl went back to the motel, why Bucky should die in his plane's crash, why it crashed at all. We ask not only how Fletcher and Ellis will be able to get along at Forman Furnace with the red barn in their past, but how Fletcher and Joan were able to get along as well as they had before Sam Rice took her. It is obvious to say that the structural limitations of the formula plot show its rigidity at the conclusion of the novel, but the inflexibility seems to occur before the story began as well.

A Key to the Suite, MacDonald's masterpiece, would seem to have little in common with the two novels of suburban infidelity. Set in the Sultana Hotel during a convention of the heavy machine industry, in an unnamed city in Florida (probably Miami), it tells the story of the initiation into upper-echelon executive power and its consequence, the personal corruption of Floyd Hubbard, a young metallurgist. Hubbard has been sent from Houston to write a report he thinks will determine whether Jesse Mulaney, the Sales Manager of American General Machine, will keep his job. What he does not know is that it is he himself, not Mulaney, who is on trial. John Camplin, Hubbard's immediate superior, has already determined that Mulaney will be sacked the following week with "plaque, citation, tears and full pension," since to have fired him earlier, before or during the industry's national convention, would have resulted in poor public relations.

The crucial question to be answered by Hubbard's behavior at the Sultana is whether he can withstand the pressures on his humanity, deny his sentiments, resist the temptations that will obviously be placed before him, and recommend the firing of Mulaney, a crafty drummer who was effective in another era but who does not belong in modern corporate society. "The world is full of sweet bright young men...with...warm hearts. Group adjusted. Group-oriented," Camplin says, "But if you ask any one of them to fire another, he'll turn ashen and collapse." Does Hubbard have a place in the upper-echelon? Does he have the makings of a Ray Walsh or an Ellis Corban?

MacDonald, merely by rearranging the elements of his formula, has found himself able to fully identify as an artist with a professional like Hubbard who does not demand that he sound maudlin emotion or feign a belief in romantic love. Hubbard has more in common with Corban and Walsh than he has with older executives like Fletcher Wyant or Carl Garrett. Just as Travis McGee has liberated MacDonald from the sentimentality demanded of the escape genre, Hubbard helped him concentrate on the workings of corporate strategy and ignore the less dramatic turmoils of marital infidelity. Since modern businesses, like the masterfully efficient fiction of MacDonald, is as Mulaney complains "cut and dried," Hubbard's frosty presence in *A Key to the Suite* allows the writer full liberty to be as harsh and clinical as he wishes toward business platitudes and convention rituals. The "bonus" here is thus rich and polyphonic, and the maneuver by which a Mulaney associate tries to blackmail Hubbard into giving the Sales Manager a good report comes as a culmination of all MacDonald blackmails.

Corinna Borlund, the lovely and expensive hater of men, is by far the apex of all MacDonald call-girls, and her life story is as specific as case history and as general as mythos. Following her seduction of Hubbard, she says that "after me, your adorable Jan will be like so much oatmeal." And this, like much of what she does, is astute, for Hubbard has just received a letter from his wife in which she reveals her belief that his youthful idealism has been eroded by his administrative position and aspirations. She contemplates divorce because she is repelled by his love for "the manipulation of human beings."

The application of pressure on Hubbard to embarrass him and to tarnish his reputation does not succeed. Hubbard leaves Cory asleep in his room and Dave Daniels, a MacDonald brute of formulaic typicality, who has desired her for days, breaks in, rapes and inadvertently kills her. At this point she has not yet started her campaign to intimidate and embarrass Hubbard, whose drunkenness and withdrawal before the attack on her is made believable by a self-loathing she was skillfully able to motivate in him. Daniels locks the door from the inside and, still not quite sober, attempts to escape by way of the balcony, but he misses his footing and falls. The two deaths are hushed up for a number of reasons: the murderer is dead; his widow would be the only one harmed by adverse publicity; and the newspaper will suffer because of its loss of advertising revenue. The story is muted, finally, by treating the deaths as separate occurrences in different parts of the newspaper.

In effect, Hubbard is saved by the violent plot solution that—unlike the other novels—makes *A Key to the Suite* an aesthetic success because it does not act as a camouflage for the writer's abdication but rescues the protagonist for a deeper understanding of himself and his corruption. Mulaney has no power over Hubbard now and thus Floyd's corruption as a sensitive human being is not related to his infidelity as a husband. When he is pressured by the Sales Manager, Hubbard brutally recommends to Camplin over the phone in Mulaney's presence that he be fired. "The man is too limited for the job," he says. "I wouldn't advise retaining him in any capacity whatsoever."

The novel ends "happily." The man the reader has identified with has passed his test brilliantly. His sexual adventures at the convention may have put a ceiling on his career, but this doubt is not clarified and is no more than a remote possibility. In fact, his ability and luck in evading embarrassment may have proved his great executive potential. Yet, in spite of this apparent fulfilling of the demand for terminal reassurance, *A Key to the Suite* is a story of the corruption of a man who was once idealistic and honorable.

The formula is still there, but it is subdued. It is not obvious to the reader because its components do not gut the characters of their individuality or rob them of their freedom of action. Though they partake of the typicality of similar characters in the MacDonald oeuvre, Hubbard, Mulaney, Corinna, Daniels and Camplin act freely within the confines of the plot. In *A Key to the Suite* MacDonald has shown that formula, if handled with respect for character, can liberate the writer who writes for a mass audience.

Is there any hope of MacDonald's becoming a major serious novelist? Professionalism of such high quality is rare enough at any time and MacDonald, who has comfortably found his lucrative niche, should not be pestered into going after fame that does not seem to interest him. That this niche is not fully satisfying, however, is made evident by the occasional publication of a longer, more serious work. *A Flash of Green* was one such; had it been successful, the achievement would have lifted him out of the category in which his earlier work had placed him.

There are certain elements of serious fiction that tremble on the edge of MacDonald's work, though, but rarely intrude. Too much the professional, MacDonald has never dealt with confessional themes, and those interesting fragments that lie submerged as debris of his characters' past histories are always carefully defused of any emotional power: growing up in a small industrial town; early poverty, perhaps; illness of a father or mother; relations—good or bad—between parents and children; conflicts between family values and the brutal and corrupt society he has written about so brilliantly; early and possibly hopeless love; religious indifference, doubt or certitude. These are the province of serious fiction, perhaps, but there is no reason why MacDonald cannot do as effective a job in it as he has in the other. The use of formula, after all, though hardly ever present in our times in significant fiction, is logically unrelated to the necessity of reaffirming middle class values or reassuring a mass audience, as MacDonald has shown in the education of Floyd Hubbard, and as tragedy has shown in the past.

Notes

[1] I ignore those works that have as their "bonuses" the inner working of prison life, army life, commando missions, etc., which by definition deal with a society fragmented from the conventional or "normal" world.

[2] Terminal reassurance is a more descriptive phrase than the more popular "happy ending" since the latter implies a wholesale righting of all wrongs while the former allows for a relatively flexible quota of innocent corpses.

[3] In MacDonald's potboilers, love is "being good in bed together," a generalization reminiscent of Hemingway, who used phrases like this as ironic thrusts against sentimentalism. MacDonald, though, uses love as a sentimental device his characters fully believe in.

[4] It is astonishing how many MacDonald heroines are widows. Divorcees might offer some disquiet; questions about marital infidelity, incompatibility, possible hatred of men, competitiveness, etc., might not be be easily avoided. Unmarried girls, besides casting doubt on their attractiveness, bring up the issue of virginity and loss thereof due to the bountiful sex they are expected to provide. Widows are ideal in that all the issues are settled, clarified and the death of their mates allows us to credit them with having borne profound suffering.

[5] *The Deep Blue Good-Bye,* Gold Medal Books, Fawcett Publication, Greenwich, Conn., pp. 12-13.

[6] Properly divorced. If he were widowed, he would be much too tame; married, he would be impossibly dull; single, highly suspect.

[7] Op. cit., p. 16.

[8]*A Man of Affairs,* Dell Publishing Co., New York, N.Y. 1957, p. 189.

[9]His other aesthetically successful books, the thriller *Cape Fear* (1957) and the crime masterpiece, *The End of the Night* (1960) do not fit into the interests of this paper. The former is a fine novel with a parable-like plot and serious philosophical resonances, while the latter is powerful enough to invite comparison with Capote's *In Cold Blood* and John Bartlow Martin's *Why Did They Kill?* Although both have formulaic qualities, they are not uniquely of MacDonald's formula, but seem to be inherent in the essentially journalistic nature of the stories.

A Sort of Appendix:
Fiction, Politics and Art

THE FOLLOWING is of course not intended as a model of book-reviewing; far from it. In our diminishing "outlets" it would be wise to leave open the idea of models for academics, for general readers, for those to whom literature is sustenance. The following is rather to illustrate that reviewing can open discussion instead of close it with mere responsiveness, prejudice or impression. Experts in the fields involved are necessary, but they need to be supplemented by others who read and judge for cause. If argument is not to be donkey-like and boring, it must ramify into ideas and literary experiences. Philip Wylie lived a long time and wrote a great deal, a *very* great deal. What remains of his life effort?

PHILIP WYLIE. *By Truman Frederick Keefer.* Boston: Twayne Publishers. UNEQUIVOCAL AMERICANISM: RIGHT-WING NOVELS IN THE COLD WAR ERA. *Macell D. Ezell.* Metuchen, N.J.: The Scarecrow Press.

The Twayne series of American authors is one of the academic phenomena of our time and should at some point be given an overview. There may be few "lit" majors today, but there is a regiment of "lit" Ph.D.s which has dug into individual caches of papers and books and come forth with, as New York restaurants actually tell us, "Your individual can of salmon." What they add up to—the Keefer volume is Number 285—is the issue.

Mr. Keefer thinks Wylie is a great creative writer, and here and there he has been marked as conservative. My argument is that it is possible to look at a writer and not be unwarrantedly swayed by trench warfare psychology. Once there was a Romain Rolland, who held himself above the battle with dignity and effect. Tagore, Gorky, Mann—a cloud of witnesses drew regard from antagonists, and created purposes in life, for critics as well as politics. Keefer's book illustrates what we have lost.

For one thing, there is the lack of quotations. Keefer's original ms. was cut from a thousand pages, he says, but that does not excuse the absence of pointed phrases, sentences, paragraphs which show or show up the author's failure or success. Keefer recounts Wylie's plots, but plots tell us little. Wylie was a fluent, emotional moralist who, by 1942 when he published *Generation of Vipers*, had issued "nearly two score novels and novelettes, at least seventy short stories, and several dozen essays," and he had almost thirty more years of life and writing to go. Keefer sees a number of Wylie's works as masterpieces, and he supports this view with "commentaries about style, character portrayal, and dramatization of themes." How do we receive such method and such claims?

Wylie was a "popular" writer with much to say and little to reveal. Man, to him, was "the magic animal" (this is the title of another book by Wylie) because *he alone knows he is to die*. There have been great popularizers; Will Durant and Paul De Kruif come to mind. But Wylie is not among them. He has no steady vision, and is too vigorous about the accumulations of things he has noticed.

What should concern us is to give him some tangible place in life or letters. There are popular writers on the right and on the left. Wylie despised behaviorists, and admired Freud and Jung, but that tells us little. His "individualism" is sometimes suggestive of Ayn Rand's selfishness-as-virtue syndrome, but though he has a sort of a cause, it is not her cause. Wylie's basic literary "sin" is simplistic thinking, but this does not make him prototypical of *National Review* scribes.

"The just-alive, simplest cell-being...says to itself, always, one of two things: yes and no. *Si et non,* as my friend Rene Spitz has put it." Who is Spitz?—and what does the French add to the message? Wylie is a name and word dropper who is too earnest for the weight he pushes.

Tomorrow (1954) was a scare novel of atomic explosions which, with a small handful of his immense production, is all that remains in memory or in print. His science fiction had movement and vivid detail. But *Tomorrow,* as an example, was based on corny just-folks portrayals not memorable before or after the national catastrophe it described.

Keefer terms *Opus 21* "a great novel and possibly his best book." If our views are not just babble, while students wait for the bell, we need to pause and question. Keefer plays his usual role of retailing the plot: a combination of fact and fiction with Wylie himself at the center. It is presumably a musical arrangement: Scherzo, Tarantella, Andante, Rondo, Coda. The action circles about Wylie's fear of cancer, and attitudes toward family, friends and others. Some of his language is flat, as in life: "Swell," "You're right, Mac." "Lookie," in short, Madison Avenue sentences. Which are preambles to lengthy orations on science, women, religion—after a while their content is predictable, and without depth. "Is a Baptist nobler than a Methodist? Kinder? Wiser? No...Sex follows the same rule—and so does everything else."

So much so, that we know no more than we knew before about Wylie or his characters, or about our own affairs. We learn that Wylie puts his "heart and brain and libido into the composition of gay,mad, happy stories," and that he has to pay for them "in compensatory funk." Fine, and descriptive of compromise lives among more than popular writers. But why need we listen to his generalizations about the evils of American Life? Wylie was author of endless tales of a certain Des and Crunch who ran a fishing boat in Florida waters. *Saturday Evening Post* readers, Keefer says, "found in the stories exactly what they liked: fast moving, clearly presented action; evocative description of locale; a good bit of humor and sentiment; and a suspenseful plot with a happy ending." Keefer thinks these yarns should not be dismissed as "mere escape fiction." Indeed not. The *Post* doted on writers who were experts on every detail except human nature. Des and Crunch tell us about Florida fishing: *Opus 21* about the life of a writer with ready opportunities for sex, introspection, and loose-ended contacts. There is also a message: Love one another. It was also the message of Aldous Huxley's *Point Counter Point,* which probably suggested to Wylie his musical arrangement. But it takes only the briefest comparison to find form and a sense of 1920s society in the one, and a formless ramble of dissatisfaction with personal life in the 1940s in the other.

Generation of Vipers is now a name, and nothing but an out-of-print name, for all the twenty editions it enjoyed, and its absurd rantings say more about the readers who made "momism" a word than about anything else. It can be read as a kind of conservative complement to Roth's liberal *Portnoy's Complaint,* both seeking scapegoats for their own muddlement. There is much more to conservatism than there is to Wylie, and his connection with it can be handled briefly. He hated Russia. He scorned the mob. He struck out, as always without strength, at "handouts and taxpatching." It all added up to bellyaching rather than art informing society.

Ezell's remarks about "Right-Wing Novels in the Cold War Era" no more illuminate our cultural condition. His primary purpose "is to provide bibliographical information and isolate some of the major themes in right-wing novels." So the job of assessing the *fiction* will have to be done elsewhere, by someone else. Right-wing editors and critics liked right-wing story-tellers, though not always. William F. Buckley, Jr. didn't like James Gould Cozzens' *By Love Possessed* because several of his *characters* were cold to Catholics. This says something about Buckley, but not much about *By Love Possessed.* Similarly we could gain by examining some of the tales of Allen Drury, Grace Lumpkin, Ayn Rand, Kenneth Roberts: a varied lot. Ezell might profitably have compared Lumpkin's proletarian novel, *To Make My Bread,* with that fruit of her conversion, *Full Circle*—compared them for style and substance; but of course he doesn't. He does not so much as note J.P. Marquand as a "right wing" novelist.

There are some three pages devoted to John Dos Passos as a conservative and as a novelist.... It is hard to be temperate about such treatment of a life and career which spanned half a century, and which could tell us so much about ourselves. Does Dos Passos's *U.S.A.* still stand up?—better than his later conservative fiction? There is opportunity for exciting, enlightening explication and debate which can answer not only such questions, but give form and significance to such otherwise random and unresolved careers as Wylie's.

Louis Filler

CONTRIBUTORS

Russell Brown is Associate Professor at the University of Toronto, where he teaches courses in fiction and Canadian literature. His most recent fiction has appeared in *Modern Fiction Studies, Mosaic, Journal of Commonwealth Literature,* and *Essays on Canadian Writing.* His critical book, "Kicking Loose: The Trickster Figure in Canadian Fiction," will appear in 1980. He is at work on a second critical study and on a novel.

Lawrence Jay Dessner is Professor of English at the University of Toledo. He has published essays in *PMLA,* the *Journal of Popular Culture, Ariel,* and others, and writes poems for little magazines. His second book, *How to Write a Poem* has been published by New York University Press.

Maurice Duke is Professor of English at Virginia Commonwealth University, and a founding and continuing editor of *Resources for American Literary Study.* He contributes articles on American literature to scholarly journals, and has recently co-edited with M. Thomas Inge and Jackson R. Bryer *Black American Writers: Bibliographical Essays.* He is co-editor with his wife of the *Richmond Times-Dispatch* Book Page. His *James Branch Cabell: A Reference Guide* is published by G.K. Hall and Co., and he is at work on "James Branch Cabell: The Critical Reception," to be published by Burt Franklin and Co.

Thomas Doulis is Professor of English at Portland State University, and has published novels, *Path for Our Valor* and *The Quarries of Sicily.* He is at work on a trilogy of the Americanization of a Greek family. He translates from the Greek and is a critic, most often of Greek literature (*George Theotokas* and *Disaster and Fiction*).

Louis Filler is Distinguished Professor of American Culture and Society at Antioch University. He is author of works in American history and literature, most recently *Progressivism and Muckraking: a Bibliographical Essay, Appointment at Armageddon, Voice of Democracy: A Critical Biography of David Graham Phillips, Journalist, Novelist, Progressive,* and *Vanguards & Followers: Youth in the American Tradition.*

Melvin J. Friedman, Professor of Comparative Literature and English, University of Wisconsin-Milwaukee, is author or editor of a dozen books, most recently, *Samuel Beckett Now* (second ed., 1975), *The Added Dimension: the Art and Mind of Flannery O'Connor* (second ed., 1977), and *The Two Faces of Ionesco* (1978). He is on editorial boards of *Journal of Popular Culture, Journal of American Culture, Studies in the Novel, Renascence,* and *Fer de Lance.*

Barry Gross, Professor of English, Michigan State University, has also taught at the University of Lancaster (England), University of Coimbra (Portugal), Ben Gurion University (Israel). He has articles on F. Scott Fitzgerald, Arthur Miller, James Baldwin, Richard Wright, and Jewish-American literature and culture.

Jerrold Hirsch, Ph.D. candidate, History, at the University of North Carolina, Chapel Hill, is co-editor of *Such as Us: Southern Voices of the Thirties,* and author of several papers dealing with aspects of the New Deal's Federal Writers Project, about which he is preparing an intellectual and cultural history. He is in charge of the "Southern Life Histories Editing and Indexing Project." His *"North Carolina, a Guide to the Old North State* (1939): An Approach to the Vernacular Landscape" is in Doug Swaim, ed., *Carolina Dwelling* (1977).

Andrew Horton, Assistant Professor of Film and Literature, University of New Orleans, has articles in *Cineaste, Film Quarterly, Journal of Popular Film & Culture,* and *Comparative Literature Studies.* He is co-editing "Twice Told Tales: European Filmmakers & the Art of Adaption" for Frederick Ungar.

Victor Howard is chairman of the Program in American Studies and Director of the Committee of Canadian American Studies at Michigan State University. He has written or edited four books on Canadian American Relations, Canadian literature, and Canadian history, with particular respect to the radical movements of the 1930s in that country.